Something Rotten

Irish Banking Scandals

Simon Carswell

Gill & Macmillan

Gill & Macmillan Ltd
Hume Avenue, Park West, Dublin 12
with associated companies throughout the world
www.gillmacmillan.ie
© Simon Carswell 2006

ISBN-13: 978 07171 3972 9
ISBN-10: 0 7171 3972 7

Typography design by Make Communication
Print origination by Carole Lynch
Printed by ColourBooks Ltd, Dublin

This book is typeset in Linotype Minion and Neue Helvetica.

The paper used in this book comes from the wood pulp of
managed forests. For every tree felled, at least one tree is
planted, thereby renewing natural resources.

A CIP catalogue record for this book is available
from the British Library.

5 4 3 2 1

Contents

Acknowledgments

Bankers and people associated with banks prefer to operate far below the parapet of publicity and would shudder at the thought of seeing their names appear in a book, not least one about banking scandals. For all the people quoted in this volume, there are many more whose names do not appear and who assisted with this project. Many interviews were conducted with sources on the basis that they would not be named. They provided invaluable insights into the world of banking and I am indebted to them for their generosity with their time and for their candour.

The material in this book was sourced from those interviews, other books, newspapers, magazines, television and radio reports, and documentaries. A significant number of these scandals would not have come to light if it had not been for the efforts of journalists who broke those important stories, so I am beholden to them for all the hard work they have done before me.

I am grateful to my friends at the *Sunday Business Post* for their assistance with this project and for their helpful suggestions. I must especially thank my colleagues Cliff Taylor, Gavin Daly and Fiona Ness for being so supportive. I would also like to thank Fergal Tobin, Deirdre Rennison Kunz and all at Gill & Macmillan, James and Hollie Engelhardt for their assistance and kindness during my research trip to Baltimore-Washington DC, my family and friends, and especially my partner Vanessa Berman for her endless inspiration and unwavering encouragement.

Simon Carswell
Dublin
July 2006

Introduction

In the mid-1960s Edmond (Mon) O'Driscoll, the Belfast banker and larger-than-life chairman of the Munster & Leinster Bank, was attending the Institute of Bankers annual dinner in the Shelbourne Hotel on St Stephen's Green in Dublin. It was a popular event as the country's most senior bankers gathered to socialise and catch up on developments in the industry.

At one point during the evening O'Driscoll found himself standing at a urinal in the hotel toilet next to John Freeman, his counterpart at the Provincial Bank. A rival of the Munster & Leinster, the Provincial also had branches across the country. Spotting O'Driscoll next to him, Freeman said: 'You know, Mon, we should be getting together.' What he was actually suggesting was a merger of the Munster & Leinster and the Provincial. O'Driscoll later enjoyed recounting the story to colleagues. Freeman's overture eventually led to the union of the Munster & Leinster, the Provincial, and the Royal Bank, and the creation of the country's biggest bank, Allied Irish Banks (AIB), in September 1966. Some might think it odd that the genesis of AIB can be traced to a conversation at a urinal. Others would argue that it was the perfect birthplace for AIB, given the number of scandals that have engulfed it in later decades.

The merger was in response to ground-breaking developments at Bank of Ireland. It had consolidated its position in the industry with its takeover of the Hibernian Bank in 1958 and the Irish branches of the National Bank in 1965. By forming AIB, O'Driscoll and Freeman were responding to changes in Irish banking. The mergers created two major Irish-owned banks, strong enough to fight increased competition from overseas banks at home and unwelcome takeovers from abroad. When AIB was formed it had assets of £255 million and annual profits of £2 million. In 2005 the bank recorded pre-tax profits of €1.7 billion. It had come a long way in 39 years from that conversation in the Shelbourne.

The bank may have grown in size and stature over those four decades, but in early 21st-century Ireland its reputation was not that of a shining corporate star but of an institution plagued by scandals. This book is a potted history of Irish banking scandals since the 1970s, and AIB features in some way or another in more than half the book.

Since 1985 when AIB walked away from a disastrous commercial escapade, its investment in the Insurance Corporation of Ireland (ICI), leaving the state to pick up the tab, it has been beset by scandals. In the 1980s and 90s AIB was an enthusiastic accomplice to the largest fraud ever perpetrated in this state, the bogus non-resident account scam. The bank's justification for its involvement in the affair was: every other bank in the state is doing it, so why shouldn't we. AIB brought it to another level, however. For its sins, it paid the highest tax settlement in the history of the state, despite initially denying that it even had a problem with the accounts. No one went to jail for the crime. Indeed, it was practically unknown for a banker to be brought to book for any banking scandal in Ireland. However, when it came to paying for past mistakes the bank's customers, mostly middle-class people, paid huge sums in taxes and endured financial hardship that forced some to sell properties, to borrow money, and even to take their own lives.

More recently AIB has been caught out by a rogue trading fraud, the fourth largest in the world, at its US bank, costing $691 million in 2002. AIB said some of its staff had 'fallen asleep at the wheel'. It turned out to be a roulette wheel and the rogue trader, John Rusnak, gambled away AIB's money unnoticed for five years.

The bank was only just recovering from that scandal when it was hit by another. In 2004 the bank was caught overcharging customers for not just one or two years, but for eight years, on foreign exchange transactions. Some people remarked that the money involved (€34 million) was small beer. It *was* when you compared it to the amounts involved in previous AIB scandals.

AIB wasn't the only Irish bank to be linked to an overcharging scandal; the Financial Regulator revealed in late July 2006 that 36 Irish banks and financial firms were forced to reimburse €118 million to customers they had overcharged since May 2004. The massive figure shocked customers.

As the overcharging controversy raged at AIB in May 2004, more sensational news emerged from the bank's headquarters. The bank discovered that several former senior executives had tax issues arising from offshore investments, about which most of them knew nothing. Arising from the same investigation the bank discovered dodgy practices in its investment arm, AIB Investment Managers, involving clients' money.

AIB has also played its part in Irish political scandals. Banks know how to pander to the establishment and understand that powerful men can have money troubles from time to time. Showing a rare sensitivity, AIB was more than willing to write off massive bank debts owed by Charles Haughey after he became Taoiseach in 1979, and Garret FitzGerald in 1993, after he had left politics. These were, after all, important men.

Offering an explanation about why AIB suffers from scandals more than most banks, one former senior AIB executive said he believed that the bank was progressive and dynamic, but that its administration struggled to keep up with its continuous growth.

Several other former AIB employees said many bankers did not understand operations involving treasury and information technology, and this may have contributed in part to the Rusnak and overcharging scandals respectively. Another said AIB was such a large company that it was likely to be afflicted by many mistakes and errors causing scandals. But Bank of Ireland is almost as large, so why hasn't it been troubled by the same number of controversies?

Many bankers claim that AIB has a maverick streak that Bank of Ireland has not—or at least did not have in the 1980s and early 90s. Bank of Ireland has traditionally been regarded as a relatively conservative institution. On the other hand, AIB is considered as its aggressive neighbour, taking risks on new ventures and jumping headfirst into fresh challenges. AIB has always pressed hard to grow its profits and market share. However, this sometimes came at a cost.

AIB was also regarded as more of a meritocracy. The better you performed, the more likely you were to rise up the corporate ladder. Staff advanced from lowly positions to the highest ranks within the organisation. This was not the case in the Bank of Ireland, where many of the most senior staff were handpicked from a particular background and standing. AIB's different culture created competition among its staff and may have led to a belief within some lower quarters that it was acceptable to take risks and push the boundaries of acceptable practice. As it transpired, some of those risks turned out to be less measured than others, leaving the bank exposed.

There was another difference between the banks—their structures. Where Bank of Ireland had a centrally controlled structure, AIB was much more decentralised: its decision-making was delegated to operating units and divisions rather than being tightly controlled from the top. This created greater freedom but also greater risk. In AIB's adolescent years, the Munster & Leinster, the Provincial and the Royal all operated separately and were not fully integrated as one bank until 1972. Later on, local managers treated their beats as their own personal fiefdoms where decisions could be made without supervision from above. Localised command structures prevented problems being reported 'up the line'. Since more recent scandals, AIB's structure and culture has moved slightly in the direction that Bank of Ireland has gone. It has become a more centralised entity. However, Bank of Ireland has also recognised the need to decentralise its decision-making processes, especially in response to competition. This is especially so in the commercial and business banking areas, where quick decisions are crucial to winning business.

AIB may be the most scandal-stricken bank in Ireland, but it has certainly not been the only bank affected by controversy. Three Irish banks have collapsed over the last 30 years. Irish Trust was shut down by the Central Bank, the banking regulator, in 1976. The Central Bank was initially concerned about Ken Bates (later owner of Chelsea and Leeds United football clubs) opening his own Irish bank and the fact that he appeared to be treating Irish Trust like his own piggy bank, using the capital generated by the bank to fund risky property deals in faraway lands.

Merchant Banking also failed, going down with the rest of the Gallagher Group in 1982. The bank's owner, the one-time property wunderkind Patrick Gallagher, was later caught with his hands in depositors' pockets in the Republic and in his Northern bank, Merbro Finance. He was jailed in Belfast but not in Dublin, even though the offences in both jurisdictions were similar. Merchant Banking's customers did not get their money back.

PMPA, the country's largest motor insurer, also collapsed, bringing down its own in-house bank, PMPS, leaving thousands of depositors out of pocket.

Although the story of Edmund Farrell's removal from Irish Permanent centres on a building society, it is included in this book. His sweetheart perks and pay, which later cost him his job, came to light as the building society was being transformed into a publicly quoted bank.

And then there are the extraordinary stories of bank-sponsored tax evasion. Ansbacher, the secret Cayman Islands bank set up by Charles Haughey's accountant and confidant, Des Traynor, allowed some of the kingpins of Irish business, political and professional life to dodge their taxes. National Irish Bank ran a scheme similar to Traynor's tax-dodging operation, only for less wealthy people.

The bogus accounts investigation led the taxman to tens of thousands of offshore accounts into which Irish people had deposited large sums of untaxed money to hide it from the taxman. In many cases the customers were enthusiastically assisted by their bankers who were happy to deposit 'hot' money offshore and to make a tidy commission in the process. The banks may have helped customers slip the taxman's net, but the customers were nearly all knowing and willing participants in the fraud committed during a period of stratospheric tax rates and penal economic times.

One of the most striking features in the scandals of the last 30 years is the failure of the banking policeman, the Central Bank and later the Irish Financial Services Regulatory Authority (subsequently abbreviated to Financial Regulator) to patrol the industry adequately. The Central Bank only decided to vet Ken Bates after he had obtained a bank licence for Irish Trust, and even then took ham-fisted and protracted measures to blackball him from Irish banking. It failed to spot the warning signs at Merchant Banking or AIB's exposure to ICI. And when it did find problems—for example, when it stumbled across the suspicious back-to-back deposits in Guinness & Mahon in the 1970s, one of the methods used by customers to hide hot money offshore—it failed to act properly.

Despite the fact that the Financial Regulator was set up in 2003 with a mandate for the strict policing of the financial sector, as of June 2006 it had yet to impose punitive sanctions on any bank, even though the industry had been rocked by major scandals in recent years.

The regulation of financial services in Ireland came in for some unwelcome international publicity in 2005–6 after US prosecutors claimed in one of the world's largest fraud investigations that reinsurance giant General Re, a subsidiary of American billionaire Warren Buffett's Berkshire Hathaway group, routed a $500 million/€387 million) fraud through a Dublin company because Ireland had lax financial reporting and was a country 'without too much regulatory oversight'. Although not connected to an Irish bank, the fraud, which falsely boosted the finances of a General Re client, AIG, the world's biggest reinsurer, through sham reinsurance contracts, prompted the *New York Times* to describe Dublin as the 'Wild West of European finance' in April 2005. The affair was deeply damaging for the entire Irish financial services industry.

There are also patterns running through the scandals. AIB became entangled in the ICI and Rusnak affairs because it failed to rein in a middle manager who was conducting huge volumes of business without proper supervision or control in an outpost of the bank's operations. 'Large volumetric growth is a warning sign that should prompt questions,' said one former AIB executive. In other words, if someone is making unusually large amounts of money, it is important to examine why. In both cases AIB failed to hear alarm bells and got burned.

The controversies at Irish Trust, PMPS-PMPA, Merchant Banking and the Irish Permanent each featured a lack of corporate governance and a dominant personality. In the tax evasion scams at NIB, Guinness & Mahon and practically every other bank involved in the DIRT scandal, bankers turned co-conspirators, helping customers siphon money into bogus and secret accounts.

Despite the hundreds of millions of euro lost during the scandals referred to in this book, only two individuals were ever jailed; neither was prosecuted in the Republic—Merchant Banking's Patrick Gallagher in Belfast and AIB's rogue trader John Rusnak in Baltimore in the US. Punishment more often came in the form of being named and shamed, heavily taxed or rebuked.

Women rarely figure in the top echelons of Irish banking during this period. Mayo TD, formerly of Fianna Fáil and onetime National Irish Bank saleswoman, Beverley Flynn is the only woman to feature in a scandal in this book, showing how the old boys' network continued to dominate the industry right up to the turn of the millennium.

Many commentators argue that the Irish banking sector has been beset by controversies because of the switch in the early 1980s to performance-related pay for bankers. This was introduced by the banks to maximise earnings, bettering each year the profits of the last. To meet expectations, bankers were set impossible targets and put under phenomenal pressure to meet those goals at any cost, while their employers cut costs to boost earnings.

Shortcuts led to problems and later crises. The scandals showed that the customers were the ones who lost out when banks aggressively tried to maximise their profits. There is of course nothing wrong with a bank making plenty of money. A wealthy bank is healthy for the country—it greases the economic machinery of the state and facilitates commerce. However, a bank that prioritises profits over careful, prudent practice can compromise proper checks and balances and find itself swamped in controversy. One former banker said that in the 1980s banks swapped integrity and trust, old cornerstones of Irish banking, for targets and shareholders' interests.

The scandals of recent years have all led to moral outrage among the public and damaged the reputation of the sector. Irish banking was once a respected institution, but endless revelations about tax evasion, overcharging and unscrupulous practices in recent years have knocked bankers from their perch. No longer are they the pillars of the community. No longer can they be trusted. The scandals have forced some customers to question people they once trusted and to scrutinise every statement and document released by them.

The growing level of bank borrowings and personal debt in Ireland has also brought bankers into the spotlight in recent years. Cheaper mortgages and loans, backed by low interest rates, have been aggressively sold by profit-hungry bankers, in most cases to meet the voracious appetite of people who are eager to buy property before they are priced out of the market. In April 2006 the value of private debt stood at a record €268 billion, with households accounting for almost half that figure. This meant that every household in the country owed an average of about €120,000. The massive growth in debt prompted Taoiseach Bertie Ahern to comment in February 2006 on the eagerness of the bankers to sell loans to customers: 'You can go to the bank to cash a cheque and end up being offered a car loan.' As people kept borrowing heavily, concerns grew at the impact of rising interest rates on the pockets of deeply indebted customers.

In this climate politicians criticised the banks for 'excessive profit-taking' and 'milking' customers in order to contribute to 'excessive profits'. However, the Taoiseach became an unlikely public defender of the banks. Concerned at the bad publicity they had suffered, he told the annual lunch of the Federation of International Banks in Ireland in late March 2006 that people should take a less negative view of the enormous profits they make. He said that when businesses in other sectors recorded large profits, they were 'justly' praised. 'But a bank with a similar headline profit is assumed to be doing it at an adverse cost to its customers,' he said. 'This is so even if the bulk of its profits stems from its corporate or international activity, rather than from personal banking. While tax collectors and bankers may never be loved outside their own circles, there is a need to be more balanced and less negative about the essential services they provide.'

Perhaps, though, the biggest scandal in Irish banking in recent years has been the lack of competition in the sector. Ireland has become one of the most profitable countries in the world in which to run a bank. A report by the European Commission published in July 2006 concluded that Irish banks were the most profitable in Europe and had the lowest base costs, making Ireland one of the best places in the EU to operate a bank. The report, which found that Irish customers were paying well above the EU average for credit cards and consumer loans, proved that much more competition was needed in Irish banking. AIB and Bank of Ireland are two of the richest banks in Europe. They had a combined market capitalisation of almost €30 billion in June 2006, employ almost 40,000 people and earned pre-tax profits of €3 billion in 2005. They dominate the Irish banking sector and have a firm control over the current account market, one of the biggest profit generators for a bank and a booming area, given that Ireland is one of the highest users of cash and cheques in the developed world.

This is why foreign banks such as Bank of Scotland (Ireland), the Danish bank Danske and the Dutch giant Rabobank have entered the Irish market. They want a cut of the action and recognise that Irish customers have been getting a raw deal for years. The new members of the Irish banking club have already brought greater competition to the market and better deals for customers.

The new players reflect a positive change in Irish banking. However, the scandals in this book are dominated by the old guard, the long-established players. Behind the complex financial scandals are some of the most intriguing stories to emerge from Irish business life over the last 30 years, and behind the pinstripe suits are some of the country's most colourful characters. These bankers were more accustomed to conducting their affairs behind closed doors, in private boardrooms, until the scandals cast them under the public eye, giving their customers an intriguing glimpse of the inner workings of some of the wealthiest institutions in the country.

Chapter 1

Irish Trust Bank and Ken Bates: Ireland's first major banking collapse

K en Bates may be best known as the man who sold Chelsea Football Club to Russian billionaire Roman Abramovich in 2003, earning millions in the deal, but in 1976 he was at the centre of one of the only banking collapses in Ireland.

Bates's rags-to-riches story has many colourful chapters. Born on 4 December 1931 in Ealing, west London, Kenneth William Bates had an unconventional upbringing. His mother died when he was 18 months old and he was raised in a council flat in London by his step-grandparents. He was 16 years old when he learned that the couple who raised him were not his natural parents. He later admitted that this revelation gave him a good grounding for 'the battles of life ahead'.

His first job was in the ticket office at Paddington Station in London. Bates showed promise early and was quickly promoted to work in the station's administrative office. At 18 he left Paddington to spend two years working as an accountant in the City. In his new job he learned the basics of finance that helped fire his ambition and start his own business. By the age of 22 he was married to Theresa and had bought his first Bentley, showing all the initial signs of his wealthy career ahead. He made his first real money in the quarry and concrete business. After a reconciliation with his estranged father in his late teens, he left the accountancy job in London to work with his father in a quarry business in Manchester. He devoted himself entirely to his new job. He had seen how his step-grandparents scraped by in relative poverty on the London council estate where he grew up, and promised himself that that would never happen to him.

Bates's first business, a quarry near Manchester, flourished and he looked to bigger things, setting up Northmix Ready Concrete, which supplied ready-mix concrete to builders in the growing construction industry. He developed his reputation as an uncompromising businessman, undercutting the established concrete producers by locating his plants near the builders, thereby reducing on transport costs. He ran the firm from 1959 until 1963 when, still in his early 30s, he sold the business for stg£545,500, a massive sum in those days. 'I wasted my 20s like mad,' he said. 'I didn't have time to socialise. I was driven on by ambition.' Northmix set him up for life, leaving him well off. But he did not rest on his laurels—that wasn't his style.

Making money was not Bates's only passion in the 1960s. The other obsession was football. It would later make him a household name in British sport after his purchase of Chelsea FC in 1982. He played the game in his youth, despite the fact that he was born with a club foot and had injured a leg in a motorcycle accident growing up in London. An operation on his foot in 1938 cured him of his limp. He was a tough player and talented enough to win a place in the Arsenal junior side. He played the game as he conducted business: 'I didn't like letting people past or getting the better of me,' he once said. By his mid-30s he had swapped the football pitch for the boardroom. He became chairman of Oldham Athletic in 1965 and quickly established the tough, no-nonsense reputation for which he became notorious as chairman of Chelsea. A year after he joined Oldham, a board member departed saying, 'Bates believes in a committee of two, with one absent.'

Bates's tenacity as a businessman was spotted early in football circles. He featured in the 1968 book *The Football Man* by writer Arthur Hopcraft. The author devoted six pages to the Oldham chairman. Hopcraft wrote that Bates 'chose Oldham Athletic just as he might the takeover of a string of shoe shops and decided it was the only available club with potential to match his ambition . . . and where he has coldly introduced values and methods of the modern business world into a level of football which owes its character to a resolute ignorance of them.'

After selling the concrete business, Bates tried his hand in the world of banking for four years. He was involved in a venture capital business associated with Philip Hill of Hill Samuel, the London merchant bankers. However, his involvement in a construction company, Howarth of Burnley, would cause him major problems in Ireland in the early 1970s. Howarth was launched with much fanfare on the Manchester Stock Exchange in early 1965, but by July 1969 the company had gone to the wall with debts of stg£1.8 million. It had been earning sizeable profits shortly before it went bust and the speed of its collapse shocked many in the industry. A report on Howarth's collapse by its receiver did not reflect positively on Bates. The report said: 'In the absence of further information from Mr Bates, who is believed to have left the country, the failure appears to be due to the building up of the company as a prosperous holding company with a public quotation for its shares, without regard to the continued profitability or otherwise of the companies it acquired.' In other words, the parent company was too busy concentrating on increasing its own profits and not on ensuring that the companies it bought made money. Bates had been chairman of Howarth for several years but had ceased to be a director or shareholder by the time the company ran aground.

Bates later claimed in the High Court in Dublin that he was a director of Howarth for just one day, saying he was appointed to the board and resigned on the day the company was formed. He told the author that Howarth collapsed after he had ceased to be involved in it. One of his friends said Bates had been deeply unhappy with the receiver's conclusions about the collapse of Howarth but had been advised to ignore them and try to get on with his business career. But Howarth reared its ugly head again and caused him problems in Ireland. By the time Howarth collapsed Bates had moved his wife and five children to the British Virgin Islands, where he had big plans for a property venture that would add to his fortune.

After Howarth, Bates did some business with an aircraft manufacturer which introduced him to the British Virgin Islands, a colony of 8,000 people in the Caribbean. He visited the islands on business in 1966 and spotted an opportunity to reclaim land from the sea at a place called Wickham Cay near Road Town, the capital of Tortola, a mountainous island in the colony. Seeing the chance to make more money, he felt he could make a fortune replicating the luxury property developments he had seen in the nearby US Virgin Islands.

The British Virgin Islands' status as a tax haven, its white sandy beaches and warm climate attracted not just Bates and other businessmen but millionaire playboys and film stars. Bates fitted right in. The islands were the perfect destination for a hard-nosed entrepreneur hungry to add to his fortune. Deciding to develop the island of Anegada, he secured an extraordinary deal with the British Foreign Office's representative on the islands. He was granted a 199-year lease over a large tract of land and would not have to pay tax on any money made there for the duration of that lease. The British Foreign Office only found out about the deal in January 1967, four months after it had been agreed.

Even in the late 1960s Bates was hugely ambitious, frequently outspoken and always controversial. Around this time he told the *Financial Times* that he had made his fortune by 'breaking the rules', but that this tactic had not always worked out: 'I over-traded, made a penny . . . and headed straight for disaster—or that's what they said. Let's face it, there are a lot of people who want to see you fail because you don't go by the book.'

Given the way he conducted business, Bates's Anegada project did not go smoothly. His abrasive style rankled with many islanders; they complained about his 'cavalier attitude' and blamed the work being carried out on his project when the island flooded after a storm. Some of his bankers even complained about how the brash Cockney businessman conducted his business. Eventually the project collapsed. He left the islands, however, with a multimillion dollar settlement from the British government over the failure of the project. He left the Caribbean Islands for another island, Ireland, with enough money to fund his next big project, an Irish bank. 'I came back from the British Virgin Islands where the British government behaved disgracefully,' Bates said in an interview with the author in October 2005 in Monte Carlo, where he now lives, 'and I swore I would never live in England again.'

Bates arrived in Ireland in 1970, a year shy of his 40th birthday, with pockets bulging and plans to build a multimillion pound empire in Dublin. He was a dreamer and a fighter with a can-do attitude to boot. On his arrival, he mixed in business circles in Dublin brimming with self-confidence. He was a conservative dresser and was most recognisable for his trademark beard. Although he had plenty of cash when he arrived in Ireland, he wasn't particularly flash with his money, except for his Bentley which he brought with him to Dublin, and the large house he rented on Ailesbury Road in Ballsbridge, one of the most upmarket areas in the city. He later bought Shankill House, a lavish Georgian mansion in south Co. Dublin. The house suited its wealthy new owner. He said he chose Ireland because he and Theresa were looking for a base to raise their five children.

'Ireland struck me,' he says. 'They spoke English which was an advantage. The law was basically English which is an advantage. It was a big enough country to have its own personality and it suited me better than just sitting in Gibraltar or Guernsey waiting for the London papers to arrive. It was a very exciting time in Dublin in the early 1970s. It was a very nice place then.'

One Irish associate who met Bates shortly after he arrived in Ireland said: 'He was a normal, straightforward man. He had penetrating eyes that held your gaze, something that I have found in many entrepreneurs I have met over the years.' The associate said he remembers Bates's strong accent. 'He was a dynamic character,' he said. 'He spoke very quickly and quietly with a strong Cockney accent; you would have to hang on to his every word to understand him.'

He made a lasting impression on the people he met during his early days in the country. He had two important traits needed in business: an unswerving belief that everything he did was right, and buckets of cash to invest. A senior AIB banker of the time described him as 'very arrogant and flamboyant'. Another source who dealt with him in Ireland said: 'There could be no wrong with anything he said. Everything he said was absolutely sacrosanct; he was completely self-assured.' Another source who worked in Irish Trust described him as 'quick-witted with a blustering manner'. Another businessman referring to his entrepreneurial streak said: 'He was unorthodox; he was a very able guy and saw opportunities that others could not see.'

In 1970 Bates—through his connections with a Liverpool merchant business—was introduced to Tom Phelan, a young mover and shaker in Dublin with his own accountancy firm, Phelan Prescott. They met in the five-star Shelbourne Hotel on St Stephen's Green in Dublin and immediately hit it off. Phelan opened doors for Bates. Coming with impeccable business credentials, Phelan had grown to prominence in Irish business as chairman of a textile company based in Drogheda,

Co. Louth, called Greenmount & Boyne Linen, which he had turned around from a poor financial position. He was widely respected and represented heavyweight Irish companies Irish Life and New Ireland Assurance as a nominee director on the board of private companies. 'Bates was a man with great go and energy,' said Phelan. 'He had a vision and we took to each other.' Together they planned how they would set up their new bank. Bates decided to call it Irish Trust Bank because, as he told Phelan, he had travelled considerably and his experience was that a bank with the word 'trust' in its title would have 'a good standing'.

Bates said he decided to open a bank because 'a bank properly run should be very popular and very successful. I was interested in getting involved in venture capital as we had done so before in partnership with Philip Hill in England.' He said he modelled Irish Trust on a South African bank which had taken deposits and acquired stakes in burgeoning businesses. But the bank needed customers, so Bates required well-known and trusted Irish faces to front the operation.

Bates was introduced to Gerry Wheeler, a former partner at the accountancy firm Stokes Kennedy Crowley and a former Irish Exporters' Association president, who agreed to become Irish Trust's chairman. Eamonn Dundon, who had previously worked for the Industrial Development Agency (IDA), the Irish state body responsible for encouraging entrepreneurs, was hired as the bank's general manager. Dundon was invaluable to Bates; having worked in the small and medium-sized industries division of the IDA, his numerous contacts in young and growing Irish businesses was a natural customer base for the new bank. Phelan joined the bank as a director.

Bates headhunted Mayo banker Brian Loughney from AIB to tap his experience in building a deposit base. The Londoner first met him in his AIB branch on Grafton Street. A career banker, Loughney knew how to grow a bank's deposits. He had worked on the development of AIB's branch network in Britain and studied the workings of the North American banking sector during the 1970 bank strike in Ireland. He adopted the personalised approach of US banks at Irish Trust.

Loughney was instrumental in attracting large numbers of American depositors to Irish Trust. He targeted savers in expat Irish communities on the east coast of the US by advertising heavily for depositors in Irish-American newspapers. About 80 per cent of the US depositors were actually known to Loughney personally. By the time the bank went bust in March 1976, about 25 per cent of its 1,200 depositors were based in the US. Another 25 per cent were living in Britain. Most of Irish Trust's US customers were hard-working, Irish-born busmen, barmen and builders who had emigrated to America and saved large nest-eggs. Irish emigrants banked their savings with Irish Trust in the hope that if they put enough money aside they could buy a house or a farm when they returned to Ireland. Their dream would later turn to a nightmare.

In the early 1970s Irish banking regulations were lax. For £5 Bates bought an off-the-shelf bank called Kildare Banking Company in June 1971 and two months later renamed it Irish Trust. He opened at 5 Dawson Street in Dublin, a stone's throw from Trinity College. He fitted out the bank's branch luxuriously. It reflected the type of customer he hoped to attract.

Bates had limited experience of banking, although he knew he could make a lot of money from such a venture. While in the British Virgin Islands he registered the Bank of Anegada, which one source close to Irish Trust said 'could fit in a briefcase'. Irish Trust was ground-breaking in Ireland in that it offered small and medium-sized businesses five-figure loans which they could not get elsewhere. Bates hoped this would lure enough customers.

Loughney said that despite his 'volatile relationship' with Bates, he recognised that the Londoner had an original idea: 'He set out to fund developing businesses, offering loan equity arrangements as low as £25,000. This had never previously been provided by any Irish bank, despite the fact that 85 per cent of all Irish businesses could be described as small and medium sized. The concept was fantastic. I still think there is a void in that market. He was absolutely ahead of his time. It was a failure by the establishment to rein him in and to manage his energy and his ideas.' Mel Kennedy, an accountant hired by Bates to work at Irish Trust, said: 'His idea at the time was to provide banking and related services. Banks have gone down that road since then, but it was a novel approach to take at that time.'

Irish Trust started as a wholly owned subsidiary of an Isle of Man company called International Trust Group, later renamed Irish Trust Group, which was controlled and primarily owned by Bates. Into this company he invested £100,000, a large sum at the time. Eventually the share capital rose to £250,000 and the bank started taking deposits. The large cash injection was Bates's way of flexing his financial

muscles to show the Irish business community that he had the money
to make a difference and that he meant business.

Christmas came two days early for Bates that year. On 23 December
1971 the Londoner and his team of Irish businessmen were granted a
bank licence by the Central Bank, the Irish state body which supervised
the banking sector. As part of the application for the licence, Bates had
to include a short statement detailing his background in business and
listing any companies with which he had been associated. The statement would later lead to a bitter dispute between Bates and the Central
Bank that would last for more than four years and end up in the High
Court on several occasions, all because Bates failed to mention in the
statement Howarth of Burnley, which had collapsed two years earlier.

Irish Trust Bank targeted small savers by offering preferential
deposit rates; its interest rate of 13 per cent compared favourably to
the 11 per cent being offered by most mainstream banks at the time.
Irish Trust offered large introductory fees, well above those of its competitors, to accountants, solicitors and other professionals who acted
as agents for the bank. This helped to generate more business. Irish
Trust Bank also opened a branch in Manchester where Bates maintained various business connections and interests.

The carrots being offered by Irish Trust proved enough of a draw
and Bates's bank was on its way, attracting several million pounds in
deposits. In its first year alone the bank had 1,200 savers. He used his
contacts in the English footballing world to garner some publicity for
his new bank. Manchester United stars George Best and Bobby
Charlton even became depositors. Irish Trust was, however, plagued
by controversy for the five years it was in business.

The Irish Trust Group made its first major play in late 1971. It made
a cash bid of £750,000 for the steel and foundry company Tonge
McGloughlin, which has its name on many manhole covers around
Ireland and owned a number of properties. Irish Trust already owned
25 per cent of the company and was trying to take over the whole
business. The attraction for Bates was that Tonge was publicly quoted
and this would bring Bates and his bank much-needed capital. Tonge
resisted the takeover. The board of the company hired the state-owned
bank, the ICC, to investigate Bates's past to see what information it
could dredge up to stop his attempted takeover.

During the trawl, Bates's involvement in Howarth of Burnley was
discovered. Bates was asked by the ICC if he was the same person who

had been involved in Howarth of Burnley. He was the same man. The information soon found its way to the Central Bank. Acting on the tip-off, the regulator began in early 1972 to investigate Bates's past dealings. They were startled by the findings and acted on them. 'We were hardly a day old when this battle started,' recalled one senior official at Irish Trust. Bates had not told his staff at Irish Trust about Howarth. When they heard about a possible connection, senior management at the bank even carried out their own investigation, unknown to Bates, to try and learn more about his links with the bankrupt English company.

Irish Trust Group's bid for Tonge McGloughlin was eventually defeated, but the Central Bank wasn't happy to let the matter rest. On 5 January 1972 it moved against Bates. It told Irish Trust to decrease Irish Trust Group's (Bates's) stake in the bank to 20 per cent and to increase the bank's paid-up capital, the money funding the bank. Around the same time a Central Bank official wrote to a colleague in the Bank of England to try and find out more about this Bates character.

'It has come to our notice that a Mr K. W. Bates was connected with the firm of Howarth of Burnley, which has been under receivership since July 1969', Central Bank secretary Bernard Breen wrote. 'Assuming he is the same individual I would be very grateful for any information you could let me have in confidence as to Bates's standing and integrity. We have on file the press reports and correspondence on his Virgin Islands project. There is some urgency about the matter at this end.' Ten days later James Kehoe at the Bank of England replied: 'Although we can discover nothing to his discredit, our enquiries suggest that none of those banks with which he has been associated particularly valued his business or would be particularly gladdened if he returned to them. If, therefore, he were to be proposed to me as a banker in present circumstances, I would have no option but to reject his claim and insist upon him working his passage, probably over a period of years. I do not think I need say more.'

The letter raised eyebrows at the Central Bank, where officials were concerned about Bates's failed Caribbean venture and his connections with the Bank of Anegada. Kehoe also spoke to Dr T. K. Whitaker, the governor of the Central Bank, by telephone about Bates and was explicitly more unfavourable about him. Whitaker later told the High Court that he was concerned that Howarth had racked up losses in such a short period and that it was only reasonable for the Central Bank to question the suitability of the man in charge of Irish Trust. On hearing Kehoe's comments, Whitaker and his fellow Central bankers rolled up their sleeves and prepared to take Bates on. But the Londoner was not willing to take the punches.

On 31 January 1972 the Central Bank told Irish Trust Bank that it was deeply unhappy about Bates's involvement as a director and shareholder in an Irish bank which was seeking deposits from Irish customers. It demanded that Bates step down as a director and sell almost all the shares held by his Isle of Man company, Irish Trust Group. The demand incensed Bates.

'The problem with any bank when you open is that the shares, deposits and advances are not widely spread,' said Bates. 'The day you open the bank and take your first deposit, 100 per cent of your money comes from one source, one account, for obvious reasons. And until you do your first capitalisation, the share capital is the same. The Central Bank couldn't see that.'

The Central Bank wrote to the bank on 29 February, again demanding that Bates resign as a director and transfer most of his shares in the bank to an unconnected party. This time, however, it said Bates must resign and sell his shares within a few weeks. The regulator added that if the bank rejected its demands, then it must support its objections with 'an unqualified testimonial of Mr Bates's suitability from a bank director, or chairman or chief executive of one of the London clearing banks'. This infuriated Bates even more. The Central Bank, however, had made a mistake; it failed to say why it was imposing these conditions on the bank, as was required under banking rules. It had to repeat its demand.

On 30 March (Holy Thursday) the Central Bank issued another edict: it ordered Bates to resign as a director of Irish Trust and sell all but 10 per cent of his shares by the following Thursday, 6 April. The order was quite unreasonable, as it was made just before the Easter holidays and gave Bates just one working day to resign from Irish Trust and find an independent person to buy a 90 per cent stake of Irish Trust from him. The ultimatum left Bates fuming. 'I wrote to them saying this was bloody disgraceful and unreasonable,' said Bates. He refused to comply. He resigned as chairman to fight the case, but continued working at the bank's headquarters on Dawson Street and advising the bank. On 5 April Irish Trust Bank slapped a writ on the

Central Bank disputing the legality of what it was doing to Bates and his bank. Bates challenged the regulator to provide evidence showing that he was not a fit or proper person to run a bank.

But taking on the Central Bank was too much for some directors of Irish Trust. It split the bank's board. Wheeler and Dundon thought a High Court case against the banking regulator was a bad idea and resigned. Leslie Calmonson, a partner in Phelan's accountancy practice, and Dublin solicitor Giles Montgomery replaced them. The colourful Manchester scrap metal dealer Freddie Pye, later a director of Manchester City Football Club and one of Bates's closest friends, was appointed to the board of Irish Trust to represent its interests in England. Pye was well known in the Manchester footballing world. Shortly after Pye's appointment to the bank, Irish Trust lent his company more than stg£200,000.

It took the court 19 months to declare a winner in the Irish Trust-Central Bank battle. On 27 November 1973, Bates emerged victorious. The court found that the Central Bank's demands had not been validly imposed and Irish Trust Bank could hold its licence without applying the regulator's conditions. The Central Bank lost on a technicality and was slightly embarrassed by some of the evidence that came up during the case. During cross examination, its governor T. K. Whitaker said his knowledge of banking was limited to his work at the Central Bank and that he had no direct experience of commercial banking.

Whitaker said the Central Bank had interpreted the information it had received about Bates from the Bank of England as, 'don't touch him with a 40-foot barge pole.' He said the judge in the case, the president of the High Court Andreas O'Keeffe, for some reason didn't like the fact that the Central Bank had turned to the Bank of England to obtain information on Bates. 'We tried to blackball Bates under the terms of the Central Bank Act,' said Whitaker. 'We felt that he was an unfit person to conduct a bank business. We knew the bank was heading for disaster because Irish Trust was passing rates of interest on to customers that were way above the average at the time and it could not have been able to do this on the back of the business it was conducting.'

Bates is still proud of his court victory. 'The judge declared the Central Bank's actions unlawful, unreasonable and unconstitutional. You can't ask for a bigger judgment than that,' said Bates. 'I wouldn't have won that case in England because the establishment looks after its own. Good old de Valera! Whether you like him or not, when he set up the Irish state, he put in a written constitution to protect the Irish people from the state apparatus. When we won the case, we were sitting in Sachs Hotel [in Donnybrook, Dublin] drinking champagne, laughing our bollocks off. Everyone was sending drinks over, saying: "Well done! You stuffed the bastards—they needed a lesson." The Central Bank of Ireland wasn't universally popular at the time.'

The Central Bank lost, but that wasn't the end of the affair; the regulator would have the last laugh. Despite its High Court victory, Irish Trust Bank was damaged by the skirmish. Bates had hoped that his resignation as chairman and a director of Irish Trust (Tom Phelan took over the Irish Trust chairmanship after him) would help foster a positive working relationship between the bank and the regulator, but it didn't. 'After the case we went in to the Central Bank hoping to start with a clean sheet, but they were even more unreasonable than before,' said Bates.

By early 1973 Irish Trust Bank was not the only asset of the ever-growing Irish Trust Group. In two years in business Bates's Isle of Man company had amassed a substantial portfolio of business interests. It took over Fred Pye & Son, the English metal company owned and operated by the Irish Trust director of the same name; Kindlon Ryan, a Dublin insurance brokerage; Emerald Isle Holidays, a Manchester tour operator that specialised in package holidays to Ireland; Donegal Securities, a property company in South Africa; and Irish Australia Holdings, which was developing land in Queensland, Australia. The directors of Irish Trust said that most of the time Bates did not inform them about the property deals he was negotiating on the group's behalf.

Irish Trust Bank had more than 1,000 customers at the start of 1973 and had taken in more than £1 million in deposits during the previous year. However, still in the background watching and scrutinising their every move was the Central Bank.

Irish Trust Bank was less active in 1973 because of the controversy arising from its court case with the Central Bank. Towards the end of the year Irish Trust Group spent £250,000 on a 29 per cent stake in Moore Holdings, an Irish public company. Around the same time Bates appointed one of his old friends from the British Virgin Islands, George B. Mitchell, economic adviser to the board of Irish Trust. Mitchell had been one-time financial secretary to the government in the Caribbean Islands, as well as to the government of Tanganyika, which merged with Zanzibar in 1964 to form Tanzania. Mitchell was living in Australia when he joined forces with Irish Trust Bank. Down under, Mitchell was managing director of Irish Trust's property development company, Irish Australia Holdings.

Irish Trust Bank's finances deteriorated in 1974 and 75 as the recession hit. Property prices fell and cash flow dried up, hitting small banks throughout Ireland and Britain. Property had been one of Bates's strengths when investing, but as interest rates rose Irish Trust Bank and the other fringe players in the banking sector were left paying larger interest bills on their short-term borrowings to finance their long-term lending. In other words, the banks were paying more for the money they borrowed than they were receiving from the money they lent to customers. As the rates continued to rise, Irish Trust and other small banks were making substantial losses.

The bank's financial situation became even more precarious when the Irish Trust subsidiary, Moore Holdings, went to the wall in July 1975, forcing the bank to write off its entire investment in the company. Irish Trust Group was also suffering. Its investments in South Africa backfired. Pye Metals, its metal subsidiary in England, was also incurring losses and the group was on the verge of collapse. The future of its banking subsidiary in Dublin and Manchester was also teetering on a knife edge.

Irish Trust Bank prayed for a turnaround in the property market, but it never came. Most small secondary or 'fringe' banks were affected in the same way. Property developers gradually became unable to pay the interest due on the money advanced by the banks. The banks in turn could not sell the developers' properties without incurring a substantial loss. They were locked in. The banks had to sit tight and nervously wait for a recovery in the property market, but there was no let up to the slump. As a consequence, the book value of Irish Trust's properties fell far below the price paid by Bates. Also, much of Irish Trust's own lending was backed by properties which were years away from being developed. This type of land suffered more severely than prime development property in the downturn. The bank was in a sorry state.

The Central Bank made a number of demands on Irish Trust to bolster the bank's reserves in 1974 and 75. However, the regulator was fully aware of the precariousness of Irish Trust's situation; it had been monitoring the bank's monthly returns. Central Bank officials discovered in late 1975 that Irish Trust had too many loans connected to anonymous offshore entities and that the loans were not properly secured or being repaid. This meant that in the event of a run on deposits, the bank would not have been able to repay all its depositors at one time. The Central Bank was also concerned with loans to two companies which had been buying up derelict sites in Dublin as speculative investments. Irish Trust staff were unable to name the owners of the companies. The Central Bank felt there were too many loans to connected parties and directors.

On 9 January 1976 the Central Bank sent in a team of independent investigators—accountancy firm Coopers & Lybrand (later PricewaterhouseCoopers)—to find out what was going on in the bank. It did not like what it found. First, a large proportion of the loan portfolio at Irish Trust Bank was in land, which made the Central Bank deeply apprehensive, given the state of the property market. Second, a loan of more than £1 million—almost a quarter of the bank's total assets—had been granted to Irish Trust Group, Bates's Isle of Man company which owned 20 per cent of the bank at the start of 1976 and accounted for about two-thirds of its income. One source close to the bank said that Bates, through Irish Trust Group, had been using Irish Trust Bank as his 'own little piggy bank' to invest in projects that *he* thought would make money for the bank.

The Central Bank had some success over the course of 1974 and 75 in forcing the bank to reduce its loans to Irish Trust Group. But it was still concerned at the size of its outstanding loan. It was later revealed that the money had been used to fund property deals in Australia and to buy the group's share of Pye Metals and Emerald Isle Holdings. Even though the bank had channelled many loans through Irish Trust Group, the ultimate borrower of the money was often an offshore entity that was shrouded in secrecy with anonymous directors.

Third, the regulator was concerned about personal guarantees given by a director of the bank and a third party on a loan of £41,000, on which the bank said it did not intend to act. The Central Bank was also concerned about the fact that a £61,000 debt had been written off. It found this extraordinary, particularly given that the bank had made a profit of just £78,000 before write-offs were accounted for. At the end of 1975 the bank was in the red. Irish Trust was in dire financial health, and both the bank and the regulator knew it. Now 1,200 depositors and their savings were at risk.

The curtain fell on 18 February 1976. The Central Bank asked the High Court to revoke Irish Trust's licence. Dublin accountant and company undertaker Paddy Shortall of Coopers & Lybrand was appointed provisional liquidator. 'Instead of nursing the bank to a sound basis, the Central Bank lost patience. It didn't have trust in the Irish Trust board,' said a former senior Irish Trust official. The bank's right to take deposits and make payments was suspended. Bates, however, refused to go quietly.

The High Court heard evidence on Tuesday, 23 March—the day the liquidation of the bank was to be made official—that Bates had entered the bank's office on Dawson Street earlier that morning and started filling a sack with documents. At this stage he had not been a director of the bank for almost four years, yet he was still conducting business out of Irish Trust's Dublin office. Shortall had taken control of the bank's premises, documents and other property on 19 February, so the accountant's staff were surprised to see Bates at the bank. When a female member of Shortall's staff told Bates that he had no authority to take documents, he said they were personal papers and that the bank had no authority to keep them. 'See you in court,' he muttered to the woman as he passed her. Bates and his two companions left the building with two sacks of documents. Shortall was concerned that Bates was about to leave the country with files which possibly contained vital information about Irish Trust. The High Court issued a warrant for the Londoner's arrest.

Bates knew he was in trouble. He showed up in court later that Tuesday afternoon, saying nonchalantly, 'I believe you're looking for me.' He explained his actions to a curious judge and apologised. He said the papers were his own and had been taken from a room leased for his personal use and that Irish Trust Bank had been allowed to use the room for board meetings. The court gave Bates 20 minutes to retrieve the documents. Accompanied by a garda, he returned the documents to the court and they were later passed back to the liquidator.

Shortall was confirmed as liquidator of Irish Trust Bank on Friday, 26 March 1976, after some wrangling between depositors of the bank and the regulator about how the bank should be wound up. The collapse of the bank made the front pages of newspapers the following day. Just six years after arriving in Ireland, Bates's burgeoning Irish business empire was in ruins. Irish Trust Bank left about £4 million in debts and

1,200 depositors facing lost savings. Revelations that the bank's money had been used in speculative land deals in Australia shocked customers and the wider Irish business and banking community.

One such customer was Patrick O'Brien, a shopkeeper from the northside of Dublin. He had invested all his life savings, £4,800, in the bank in 1974 and took a loan of £1,700 shortly before the collapse of the bank. After the bank went bust, he assumed the loan could be off-set against his savings, leaving him with £3,100. He was wrong. He was told by the liquidator that he would have to repay the £1,700, a sizeable sum for a small businessman in those days, before any settlement could be made on the money he deposited with the bank. O'Brien set up a picket at the Central Bank's offices in Dublin, claiming that because the regulator had allowed Irish Trust Bank to operate, it should cover its debts. He said the Central Bank had a moral responsibility to com-pensate depositors. O'Brien was not alone. A committee of depositors was formed to lobby the government and the Central Bank to try and compel them to compensate Irish Trust's customers.

Shortall was left with the unenviable task of cleaning up the mess at Irish Trust Bank. There were 1,200 irate depositors demanding blood. When it emerged that they would not be repaid, one depositor picketed Shortall's office with the placard: 'Shortfall for Shortall.' The Dublin accountant spent the following five years travelling to four continents to make sense of the Byzantine structure behind Irish Trust Group and recovering money for out-of-pocket creditors and depositors. He had numerous meetings with Bates. The meetings between the two business veterans were sometimes fractious and always colourful.

Shortall travelled to the Isle of Man, Gibraltar, London, South Africa and remote areas of northern Australia, trying to unravel the complex web of companies behind Irish Trust Bank and Bates. He deciphered intricate transactions and sold the group's assets, which included large tracts of land in the Australian bush. Burying Irish Trust Bank and settling its affairs was a mammoth undertaking which took him 13 years to complete.

The liquidator could only offer depositors a fifth of their money back. Had it not been for a political pledge in the run-up to the June 1977 general election, this is all depositors would have recovered. Recognising that some customers were about to lose their savings, Brian Loughney felt he had to do something. He visited George

Colley, Fianna Fáil's spokesman on finance, at his house in Rathmines, south Dublin, to plead the bank's case. He told Colley that when the secondary banks in Britain collapsed in 1973, the British regulator stepped in to save them and their depositors. He said one bank saved was United Dominions Trust, in which the state-owned Irish Life was a 25 per cent shareholder. Loughney warned Colley that the collapse of Irish Trust could damage the reputation of the larger Irish banks.

In the run-up to the election Colley promised that if his party was returned to power (after four years on opposition benches), it would reimburse Irish Trust's depositors. It was one of the many promises made by Jack Lynch and Fianna Fáil in the election campaign. Fine Gael was livid at the notion of its rival offering public money to reimburse out-of-pocket savers on the collapse of a private bank as political capital in an election campaign. But the promise worked. It helped Fianna Fáil regain power and put its leader Jack Lynch into the Taoiseach's office.

Bates still lays the blame for the failure of Irish Trust at the door of the Central Bank. 'When the bank was shut down, there were assets of £4 million or £5 million, and a quarter of that was in cash. They could have paid out 25p in the pound. The interesting thing is that when Fianna Fáil got back into power and the party had promised to pay back all the depositors, the Central Bank opposed it; it wanted to teach the depositors a lesson. This is the bank that was formed to protect depositors, and the government had to overrule it.' He believes that the Central Bank had always acted vindictively towards him by challenging Irish Trust.

Bates didn't stay long in Dublin; he left for sunnier climes in 1978. He moved to Monaco, the Mediterranean tax haven for Europe's super-rich. From there he concentrated on a travel business in London called Trafalgar Travel, which he had set up some years previously. In March 1978 he took a full-page advertisement in two Irish magazines informing its readers that Trafalgar made a profit of stg£958,000 the previous year. The advert was seen as a two-finger gesture to the Irish banking regulator to show it that he had survived Irish Trust and was doing well.

Shortall eventually pursued Bates for personal guarantees on loans taken from Irish Trust by his Irish Trust Group. Bates initially disputed Shortall's claim, saying the guarantees had not been drawn up properly. Shortall, however, succeeded in obtaining a judgment for

£285,000 against Bates in Irish courts in July 1978. The ever-defiant Londoner responded to news of the judgment with a statement issued to a London investment journal from his home in Monte Carlo. It read: 'The liquidator knows exactly where to meet me as he has my address.'

Bates eventually conceded. At a meeting with Shortall in March 1980 Bates pulled out his chequebook and paid the liquidator stg£285,000 settling the outstanding action against him. 'We are giving him [Bates] a complete pardon,' a barrister for Shortall told the High Court in Dublin when the settlement was announced. The payment marked the end of Bates's involvement with Irish Trust Bank and his four-year battle with its liquidator.

'I was normally obstructive to Shortall,' recalled Bates years later. But Irish Trust's liquidation did not curtail the career of the irrepressible Bates. To him, the liquidation was a badge of honour. He continued investing in other ventures showing his relentless ability to take any knocks on the chin. Irish Trust was nothing more than a minor obstacle on his road to further enrichment. Shortall heard from Bates again in the late 1990s to ask if he would co-operate with a writer who was penning a biography of the Londoner's life. The accountant declined, telling Bates that he would have nothing positive to tell the writer.

Shortall collected more than £3.5 million from the sale of the bank's assets, considerably more than the £2.8 million he initially thought he would recover when the bank went bust in early 1976. He said the liquidation of Irish Trust was without doubt the most complex assignment of his career and definitely the most colourful, given the role played by Bates.

Shortall still files documents for the bank every year in the Companies Registration Office on Parnell Street in Dublin, even though the liquidation was effectively wrapped up in 1989. Records filed in April 2003 showed that Irish Trust's final debts amounted to €5.9 million (£4.6 million); it had assets of €3.5 million (£2.8 million). The affair ultimately cost the Irish taxpayer about £500,000, thanks to Fianna Fáil's pre-election promise of an indemnity for depositors.

Not all Irish Trust's deposits were claimed. Richie Ryan, who was finance minister in the Fine Gael-Labour coalition government at the time of the collapse, claimed in 1977 during a parliamentary row with his successor, Fianna Fáil's George Colley, that some of the depositors were associated with illegal activities and 'the IRA and their allies'. Given the number of Irish Trust Bank deposits coming from the US,

there had been speculation in Dublin that Irish republican fundraising organisations in the US such as Noraid may have set up accounts
using pseudonyms to transfer money to Ireland. Ryan was so convinced of this that the previous year when he was finance minister
he had asked the Gardaí to investigate this matter when Irish Trust
collapsed. Police in the US, Britain and Australia were also involved in
the investigation.

In October 1977, however, Colley went on record in the Dáil to state
categorically that, after some investigation, none of Irish Trust's
deposits had links with republican fundraisers or criminal elements.
One senior official at Irish Trust described Ryan's allegation as 'political
mischief'. Some of the bank's deposit accounts did, however, have fictitious names. The police said some customers opened accounts using
false names to avoid paying tax. Perhaps because of this some of the
bank's deposits were never claimed and their owners never identified.

Bates said the IRA claims arose because Brian Loughney was a guest
at a Noraid dinner when he was working for Irish Trust in the
US. Loughney, however, disputes this. He said he did not attend the
dinner, but that his name may have appeared on a guest list. He said
he knew several Noraid people during his time on the east coast of
America and some of them may have deposited money. 'There was
absolutely no IRA money in the Irish Trust deposits,' said Loughney.
'Those people always represented themselves and no one else when
making deposits.'

Most American investors, however, saved with the bank for a
variety of legitimate reasons. One Irish-American customer told a
newspaper that he invested out of patriotism: 'The purpose for which
we sent our funds to Ireland was to have money invested in our native
homeland. We thought it would be used to aid the economic development of the country. Instead, the bulk of it was invested in risky
foreign situations which none of us would have invested in ourselves.
Investment in speculative ventures in foreign countries was certainly
not what we desired.'

The false allegations about IRA involvement in Irish Trust did not
help the reputations of the Irish managers at Irish Trust. Tom Phelan,
a promising young businessman prior to the collapse of Irish Trust,
said he went from being 'cock of the walk to being cocked'. It was a
tough time for Phelan and his colleagues. The passage of time has,
however, helped to heal some wounds.

In 1978 T. K. Whitaker, then a senator and former governor general of the Central Bank, spoke out against the reimbursement of depositors, saying that Colley's promise went too far. He said any bank which offered exceptionally high rates of interest, as Irish Trust Bank had done, should have been treated with circumspection.

There was a mistaken impression in Ireland at this time that somehow customers' bank deposits were protected and customers would be compensated if a bank went bust. However, the obligation on the state was a moral obligation, not a legal one. It wasn't until 1989, 13 years after Irish Trust's closure, that legislation was passed setting up a scheme to protect customers' deposits. It exists to this day. However, the scheme has never been used because no Irish bank has gone to the wall since the early 1980s. Merchant Banking, which was controlled by property developer Patrick Gallagher, went bust in 1982 owing millions of pounds to depositors. In that case the state did not intervene and depositors were left with their losses (see Chapter 2).

AIB came close to going under in 1985 when it discovered unquantifiable losses in its insurance subsidiary, Insurance Corporation of Ireland. Senior civil servants and government ministers believed at the time that the losses threatened not just the stability of the bank but the Irish economy and the country. In that case the government, fearful of another major knock to the already frail economy, stepped in with a multimillion pound bail-out.

The banking regulator, the Central Bank, didn't exactly emerge unscathed from the whole sorry Irish Trust saga. It failed to protect the interests of depositors, its prime responsibility. The regulator never attempted to save Irish Trust Bank or protect its depositors by facilitating meetings with other banks that might have helped it through its rocky patch in 1974 and 75.

But it was also unreasonable to expect, as some did, that when things went awry the Central Bank would reimburse the depositors of a failed private bank. The Fine Gael-Labour coalition government of the time of the collapse refused to cover the depositors' losses. While the Central Bank exercised wide powers over the banking sector, the act which created those powers stresses that the Central Bank does not guarantee the solvency of a licensed bank, nor is it liable to cover the losses of depositors in the event of a banking collapse. The Central Bank believed it would set a dangerous precedent for the banking sector and the stability of the country if it did. However, if the regulator had concerns about Irish Trust, it should have done its homework properly and investigated Bates's background fully before granting him a banking licence. One senior banker at the time said: 'Bates scared the shit out of the Central Bank.'

The Central Bank failed to vet Bates's credentials in the first place and then clumsily tried to oust him from Irish Trust Bank on a number of occasions without explaining fully why it wanted rid of him. It underestimated the wily entrepreneur and was drawn into a lengthy, acrimonious and very public court battle which it eventually lost.

'Bates did the unmentionable; he took on the establishment and won,' said a prominent Dublin businessman close to the controversy at Irish Trust. But Bates's victory angered the establishment; it bore a grudge and it continued hounding Bates. Tom Phelan and Bates both recall a senior Irish Trust manager warning them against taking a case against the Central Bank. 'Even if you win this, you will lose it,' said the manager. His words were prophetic. Mel Kennedy, an accountant who worked at Irish Trust, said: 'With the benefit of hindsight, it was foolish to take on the Central Bank. I suppose in the business world it was something you didn't do.'

Phelan described Bates as 'an honest buccaneer who would challenge anyone, particularly if Bates thought he was right'. Another person who worked at Irish Trust said: 'The Dublin business environment wasn't ready for a man like Bates. Dublin was a very innocent place then. Our control mechanisms were very innocent and then someone like Bates comes along. He ran rings around our system. Dublin had just never seen anything like that.' Recalling the events at Irish Trust, in October 2005 Bates said: 'We won the battle and lost the war with the Central Bank of Ireland. The only regret I have is that we didn't make Irish Trust Bank into what Anglo Irish Bank [one of the most profitable banks in Ireland] is today. We tried to merge with them at one point and call it the Anglo Irish Trust Bank.'

'I love the Irish and I loved my time in Ireland,' said Bates. 'I was sad to leave, but it became obvious after my battle with the Central Bank that I could never make anything in Ireland. The Central Bank frustrated me at every turn.' He didn't let the matter lie. He wanted to get his own back on the Central Bank. He decided to get even with the bank in the late 1970s by leaking information to Irish newspapers and magazines which showed that the bank's new headquarters on Dame

Street did not meet the requirements of the planning permission granted on the building.

On Saturday, 27 March 1976, the day after Irish Trust closed its doors, a headline in an Irish broadsheet paper read: 'Rise and fall of a money wizard: Mr Kenneth W. Bates.' Bates rose again 27 years later when he sold Chelsea to Roman Abramovich. Pocketing stg£18 million on his original investment of stg£1 in the debt-ridden Chelsea FC in 1982 wasn't bad for a man who in the mid-1970s took on the Irish establishment and lost.

Bates said he never went looking for fights in his career, but that he can look after himself if one starts. His career in British football has proved this. After the Irish Trust-Central Bank scrap, it was the Irish taxpayer, not Ken Bates, who emerged with the bloodiest nose. He lived to fight another day and went on to win many other brawls in his business career.

Chapter 2

Patrick Gallagher and Merchant Banking: the downfall of a property tycoon

Property investor Patrick Gallagher was only 29 years old in 1980, but he was already sitting on land worth almost £70 million. His investments in the heady world of property speculation made him one of Ireland's wealthiest and most audacious businessmen. A mixture of arrogance and youth blurred the risks for Gallagher. Yet when a series of investments turned sour in 1982, to save his skin he used money sitting in his own personal bank that belonged to its customers. If his business had survived, customers would have been none the wiser about the practices at his bank, but when his empire crumbled his depositors lost everything. Financial irregularities were later uncovered landing Gallagher in court and eventually in jail.

Business and property investment was like a game for Gallagher. He did business at a frenetic pace and rarely saw risk. He conducted multimillion pound property deals in an afternoon and netted millions, often by buying land and selling it before the completion of the original purchase. He owned stud farms, racehorses, a classic Rolls

Royce car and fine art. He bragged about his £100,000 wine cellar full of the finest claret and champagne. He rubbed shoulders with some of Ireland's most powerful political and business figures and filled the pages of newspapers and magazines with tales of his daring business deals. He may have pre-dated the entrepreneurs of the Celtic Tiger by 20 years, but in the late 1970s and early 80s Gallagher was an example of what was to come. He was a poster boy for a new and arrogant breed of businessman in late 1970s Ireland.

Ten years later Gallagher had swapped his frantic and opulent lifestyle for the confines of a prison cell in Magilligan Prison near Derry in Northern Ireland. Within eight years he had lost his fortune and was sentenced to two years in prison for theft and providing false information about his bank, Merbro Finance (NI) Limited, the Belfast subsidiary of his group's Merchant Banking based in Dublin. It had been proven that Gallagher had used the bank's deposits to bolster his flagging business empire in the early part of 1982. As his group got deeper and deeper into debt, Gallagher dipped further and further into the deposits to stop his business falling asunder. When the group eventually came crashing down in April 1982, almost 80 per cent of Merchant Banking's assets had been ploughed into the Gallagher Group. Given the fact that the Gallagher Group was effectively bankrupt, the bank and its depositors, mostly elderly and less well-off people, were left with nothing. Gallagher had turned from the golden boy of Irish business to its whipping boy in just two years.

Gallagher's boom-to-bust story is one of the most spectacular in modern Irish financial history. It involved the collapse of one of the country's largest private companies, debts running to tens of millions of pounds and revelations that he had made cash payments to the then Taoiseach, Charles Haughey. It's a story more at home in a Hollywood screenplay. Gallagher is a rare animal in Ireland—a white-collar criminal, a once rich and powerful businessman who was punished for past wrongs. Remarkably, it was not in the Republic but in the Queen's Criminal Court in Belfast that Gallagher got his comeuppance. The establishment in the Republic chose not to take Gallagher on, but the authorities in the North had no such reservations.

The story of Gallagher's steep fall from grace is tangled up in the more complex tale of the failure of the Gallagher Group, of which the two Merchant Banking operations were subsidiaries. Four failed multimillion pound property deals in Dublin in late 1981 and early

1982 forced Gallagher to resort to desperate and ultimately illegal measures to try to save his business. The measures were not enough to save the Gallagher Group from the grave.

It took another eight years before the Dublin businessman faced his greatest ignominy—sitting in a Belfast court facing charges of stealing paintings valued at £110,000, and three counts of false accounting and conspiracy to defraud. He eventually went to jail for the way he ran his Belfast bank. He had treated it as his own personal piggy bank. When he walked through the gates of Crumlin Road Prison in Belfast in October 1990 at the start of a two-year sentence, he was destitute and humiliated. Gone were the Rolls Royce, the racehorses and the dinner parties with powerful friends that Gallagher had once enjoyed. They were replaced by a police van, a prison uniform and criminal companions. It was an astonishing fall for the buccaneer Irish businessman.

Gallagher was not a self-made man. He owed all his wealth and status to the father he idolised, Matt Gallagher. Originally from Tubercurry in Co. Sligo, Gallagher Snr started off his career in England in 1932 as a labourer before setting up his own building business. He would eventually teach Patrick everything about the world of property investment and development.

Patrick was born on 8 May 1951. He started his career earlier than most businessmen, becoming a director of a company at the age of 12 in 1963 when he and his younger brother Paul joined the board of Gallagher Trusts, one of his father's companies. Matt made his fortune in Britain in construction, mining and plant hire during the British building boom of the 1950s. He returned to Ireland as a Paddy-done-good-abroad, a wealthy self-made Irishman coming home to a changing country.

Gallagher Snr was one of a select circle of businessmen who surrounded Seán Lemass, the Fianna Fáil Taoiseach of the early 1960s. Lemass set Ireland on the road to becoming one of the economic powerhouses of Europe. Successful returning emigrants like Matt wanted to help Lemass build an industrial and modern new state. With the arrival of new multinational companies, Lemass needed someone to build homes for their workers and Matt was one of the businessmen charged with the task.

Among the other members of Gallagher Snr's exclusive group of Irish business and political movers and shakers were Charles Haughey, later to become Taoiseach, and politicians Neil Blaney,

Donogh O'Malley and Brian Lenihan. Gallagher showed a particular loyalty to Haughey. The Gallagher patriarch admired the young, arrogant Dublin politician. To Gallagher, Haughey's rise to power was essential if Ireland was to become a great nation, so the millionaire builder became a loyal benefactor. 'Haughey was financed in order to create the environment which the Anglo-Irish had enjoyed and that we as a people could never aspire to,' Patrick Gallagher told journalist Frank Connolly in an interview in the *Sunday Business Post* in 1998. Matt Gallagher was a key figure behind Fianna Fáil's fundraising operation, Taca. 'Fianna Fáil was good for builders and builders were good for Fianna Fáil, and there was nothing wrong with that,' Matt's son Patrick once said.

When Patrick Gallagher became old enough to work in the family business, he had a difficult time living in his father's shadow. Matt had a volatile temperament and sometimes bullied his son. He had once punched Patrick when he found out that his 14-year-old son had over-drawn his bank account. But Patrick put their occasional differences aside; he wanted to be just as successful as his father. The young Gallagher was educated at Clongowes in Co. Kildare, St Gerard's in Bray, Co. Wicklow, and finally Blackrock College on the southside of Dublin. He joined the family business in 1967 at the age of 16. Three years later, at the age of 19, he married Susan Craigie whose family owned the profitable agribusiness, Premier Dairies. The young couple moved into a house on the family's Hollywood Rath estate in Mulhuddart, west Co. Dublin. It was just one of many properties owned by the Gallagher family and their group.

Formed in 1956, the Gallagher Group owned five pubs in Dublin and numerous housing estates throughout Ireland by the early 1970s. Matt Gallagher set up Merchant Banking on 22 February 1961 primarily as a hire-purchase company to complement the Gallagher Group's building operation. The Gallagher Group had a complex corporate structure. The group, including Merchant Banking, was ultimately owned by a company called Bering Estates Company, which was based in the Cayman Islands in the Caribbean. The islands would later become synonymous in Ireland with dodgy banking practices when the Ansbacher deposits, which facilitated tax evasion by prominent Irish figures, were discovered in the late 1990s (see Chapter 6).

By the early 1970s Merchant Banking had wound down its hire-purchase business but continued to operate as a deposit-taking bank, catering for small depositors. At this time Ireland was in poor economic health. An oil crisis had hit world markets in 1973–4 and the Gallagher Group was trading in tough times. The pressure took its toll. Late on the night of 7 January 1974 Patrick received a phone call from his father who was at the family home in Mulhuddart. 'He asked me to call over,' Patrick later recalled. 'When I came in he poured me a whiskey for the first time in his life. Usually I was the gofer. He asked me to look after my sisters. Then he said: "My greatest hero is Napoleon." He lifted his fist and said, "This is my Waterloo" and he died in front of me, sitting in a Queen Anne chair. He went out as strong as he had lived.' That evening, at the age of 22, Patrick inherited a family business of 17 companies worth up to £14 million and was responsible for the livelihoods of 1,600 employees.

Taking over the business, he was faced with an immediate crisis. 'We were so close to going broke in 1974 that I still have a slight shudder when I think about it,' Gallagher recalled in 1990. 'The bottom fell out of the property market and business was taking a nosedive. We were facing serious and almost insurmountable problems. We had an enormous land bank which had been built up over many years. It had been purchased on the basis of a projected interest rate of 7 per cent, but when the oil crisis came the rate more than doubled to 16 per cent and the land bank had become a massive liability. The prospects for the future looked bleak.'

Unknown to ordinary people in the early 1970s, the high interest rates had encouraged the development of the Ansbacher tax dodge, a scheme for wealthy individuals. Only a select few, most of them participants in the scheme, were in the know.

Gallagher saw a way of riding out the economic crisis of the mid-1970s. While many businesses went to the wall at the time, his survived. He sold about 260 acres of land in Mulhuddart, west Dublin, which earned him, at the age of 23, his first million and gave him an appetite for making more money. He laid off hundreds of workers, hiring sub-contractors instead to carry out the group's building work. It was cheaper labour as workers had to be employed only as they were needed. He also changed the focus of the group's activities. Instead of building houses for the masses, he decided to construct more upmarket homes. 'We felt that in every recession there were people who would make it through,' he later said. 'They were the civil servants, the accountants, airline people and so on. So we simply catered for them.'

The change of focus worked and the money flowed in. But, unlike his father, the young Gallagher was a high flier and enjoyed spending money. Matt might have been worth millions, but outside his plush home it never showed; he always bought second-hand cars. Shortly after the death of his father, Patrick splashed out on the ultimate trophy buy—a Rolls Royce. 'He was only a kid but he thought there was some sort of Gallagher magic,' a family friend later said. 'The family told him to take it easy in business, to remember where he came from, but it was like talking to a camel. We and the banks told him to retrench on five occasions. Each time he said he could do it [on his own], that he did not need us.'

Gallagher was unique in Irish business. He was big-headed and aggressive. Buying and selling multimillion pound large tracts of land was the young property tycoon's way of flexing his muscles in the business community. It impressed all around him—his bankers, his friends, his workers. He thought he was unstoppable. No deal was too big. He would buy property, secure planning permission and sell the land to developers, earning a large profit. Sometimes he would split the land and sell it on separately to make even more money. As long as he kept dealing, cash continued to flow through Merchant Banking's coffers.

Prior to the collapse of the Gallagher Group, the business was conservatively worth £20 million on paper, after its liabilities were taken into account. Gallagher's deals astounded the business community. In 1979 he bought Seán Lemass House—later renamed Edmund Farrell House—at 56–59 St Stephen's Green for £5.5 million, paying a deposit of £500,000. Before the purchase was complete, he had sold the building on for £8 million to the Irish Permanent Building Society, making a profit of £2.5 million within weeks (see Chapter 5). These were exhilarating times for the young developer. He thought it would have made his late father proud.

The banks responded to Gallagher's growing deals by throwing more money at him. Using these borrowings he started amassing properties in some of the top city centre locations in Dublin: St Stephen's Green, Mount Street, Clare Street, the former Alexandra College site on Earlsfort Terrace. In addition to these he had the group's properties around Dublin—in Castleknock, Rathfarnham, Coolock and Donaghmede; and around the country—in Boyle, Co. Roscommon; in Co. Limerick and in Greystones, Co. Wicklow, among other properties. It was a vast portfolio. He played the property market like a game of Monopoly. He was undaunted by the size of the deals. But the success of the trades went to his head; he grew cockier, taking more and more risks. He had enjoyed some significant triumphs in the residential market, but the commercial property sector was to prove his undoing. As the recession of the early 1980s began to bite, things did not quite go according to plan.

Gallagher decided to venture into new territory in property. Buoyed by years of profitable dealing in the residential market, he invested in areas he wasn't so familiar with. He bought the Phoenix Park Racecourse in Dublin and tried to acquire the H. Williams supermarket chain. It later became clear that the supermarket deal was a last gasp attempt by Gallagher to acquire a cash generator for his group which was in serious need of some liquid money to keep demanding bankers at bay. Merchant Banking just didn't have enough cash to solve his money problems. By April 1982 the Gallagher Group had assets of more than £60 million but owed almost £30 million to financial institutions. The bankers were nervous about the size of his loans, but Gallagher believed the property market would continue performing well. He was wrong.

First, Gallagher thought the 17-store H. Williams chain, which he tried to buy for £4.5 million, would bring much-needed cash flow into the Gallagher Group. Second, just as the supermarket deal was about to close, he was committed to buying four and a half acres of land at the corner of St Stephen's Green and South King Street (now the site of the St Stephen's Green shopping centre) for £10 million. The site, where rock band U2 played one of their first gigs, had been built up by the Slazenger family, owners of the Powerscourt estate at Enniskerry, Co. Wicklow. The third deal concerned the Phoenix Park racecourse which Gallagher bought for £2.5 million. The deal was not a property play, but a commercial punt. Gallagher ploughed £2 million into the course, thinking he could generate an annual turnover of £3 million from 16 race meetings.

The deals were lined up like dominoes. Gallagher needed one deal to ensure the next. In early 1982 the banks demanded several million pounds from him to reduce his group's borrowings. He desperately needed to close all the deals to raise the cash.

Gallagher's plans for the St Stephen's Green site began to stall. He knew it was worth a fortune but just couldn't close a deal on the property. A London estate agent approached him with a consortium of prospective English buyers who were willing to buy half the site for £11 million. The deal would have allowed Gallagher to make a stage payment to the Slazengers, clear some of the bank debt on the site and earn himself a tidy profit. Soon after, though, Irish Life stepped forward with an offer of £15.75 million for the entire site. Gallagher couldn't refuse it. He felt he could find a similar site in Dublin city centre to sell to the London consortium. He identified some land on Earlsfort Terrace on the other side of St Stephen's Green owned by his uncles, and he agreed to buy it for £9 million and put down a deposit of £475,000, drawn from bank borrowings. With all the deals lined up, he was confident he could close them.

But the banks were still putting pressure on Gallagher to reduce his borrowings from more than £26 million to £10 million. No contracts had been completed and the deals were still up in the air. Money from the H. Williams chain and the all-important Slazenger site would have eliminated all his cash flow problems. But when Irish Life pulled out of the Slazenger deal, Gallagher was left high and dry. 'I found myself on a sticky wicket,' he later recalled. 'But I felt that the thing would resolve itself. I genuinely believed that [Irish Life] would come into the deal again.' Patrick and his brother Paul had to resort to desperate measures. They sold off their own personal assets, including a private art collection and shares in racehorses, to pay back the banks. But it wasn't enough. The bankers called in their chips. He had played all his hands.

Gallagher made some poor personal investments in the run-up to the Gallagher Group's financial difficulties. In the late 1970s the young property tycoon was involved in some extravagant purchases in the horseracing world. In 1978 he bought a quarter share in a two-year-old horse called Try My Best for £750,000. He thought he could make a return of up to £7 million from the animal, but the horse didn't live up to its name. The Vincent O'Brien-trained colt came last in the Newmarket 2,000 Guineas and Gallagher was understandably put out. He offloaded his share at a substantial loss. 'Risks are taken every day,' he said at the time. 'Some come off, some don't. You can't sit around crying when they fail to come off.' It didn't stop him gambling again on another horse. In November 1981 he outbid an Arab oil sheikh for Arkadina, a 12-year-old mare that had had no major racing successes when it was purchased by Gallagher.

Gallagher's lifestyle matched his high-flying business dealings. In the early 1980s he bought Straffan House in Co. Kildare, now home to the K Club, the luxury golf resort. He bought the property for almost £1 million—investing another £500,000 on its refurbishment—against the advice of the wife of a previous owner. She warned him that the house had brought bad luck to its residents. She said her husband had purchased the property from the wife of an Iranian Air Force general who was shot dead during the overthrow of the Shah by the Khomeni regime in Iran in 1979. Gallagher was about to experience some misfortune of his own. D-Day for the Gallagher Group came on Thursday, 29 April 1982.

At 11.30 a.m. that morning, Gallagher received a phone call summoning him to the headquarters of the Northern Bank Finance Co. He was told to bring his solicitor. Gallagher drove the 18 miles from Straffan House to Dublin with his brother Paul. The siblings stopped at Ryan's pub on Parkgate Street, not far from the Phoenix Park and its racecourse, one of the projects that were threatening to destroy his business empire. They arrived at the Northern Bank's boardroom at 2.30 p.m. to meet their fate. It was a tense 30-minute meeting. The bankers told the Gallaghers that the family's business could no longer survive with more than £28 million in debts and collapsing property deals. This was the end, the bankers said. Gallagher reluctantly gave in. As he was leaving the boardroom, he turned to the bankers and quoted Louis xiv: '*Après moi, le déluge* (after me, the flood).' They turned out to be prophetic words.

Not only did the collapse of the Gallagher Group leave the family penniless, creditors out of pocket and Merchant Banking depositors nursing huge losses, but the event led to the exposure of the cash payments made by Gallagher to the then Taoiseach Charles Haughey. The payments were outlined in the records of Merchant Banking and they provided some of the first clues about the secrets behind Haughey's finances. They would later feature prominently in a tribunal.

Based on Clare Street, near Trinity College, Merchant Banking had taken deposits of about £4.5 million from around 600 customers, individuals who were at the other end of the social spectrum from the flamboyant Gallagher. When the group collapsed in 1982, the bank and its subsidiary in Northern Ireland, Merbro Finance, had debts of about £8 million. Paddy Shortall of Coopers & Lybrand, the Dublin accountant who had sorted out the mess at Irish Trust Bank six years previously (see Chapter 1), was called in to act as the liquidator of Merchant Banking.

Shortall was appointed provisional liquidator on 30 April 1982. Another accountant was charged with the task of winding up the bank in the North. Shortall's report—when it was eventually handed to the court in 1984—revealed some astonishing findings. It revealed the cavalier and illegal way that Gallagher managed his bank.

Merchant Banking's depositors were spread throughout the Republic, Northern Ireland, England and the United States. By the time it closed its doors, 90 per cent of its depositors had less than £5,000 in their accounts, while 61 per cent had less than £1,000. These were massive sums of money for depositors when you consider that the average annual industrial salary in Ireland in the mid-1970s was about £1,600. Gallagher took control of Merchant Banking when his father died in 1974. Shortall quickly discovered that the money Merchant Banking had taken from depositors had been used to fund the Gallagher Group and to make loans to people, typically close personal associates of Matt and Patrick Gallagher. Most of the loans had been advanced in the years leading up to and including 1976, when Gallagher decided that he would start winding down the bank. Even though the bank was about to close, few customers left the bank during this period, despite the fact that it was offering a poor deposit rate (9 per cent) for the time.

The bank was not without problems in the mid-1970s. The regulator of the Irish banking sector, the Central Bank, was concerned that the bank was too heavily exposed not just to the Gallagher Group but to the property sector. The Central Bank issued an ultimatum to Merchant Banking on 21 July 1977: it ordered the bank to reduce its borrowings to the Gallagher Group to below £90,000 by 30 June 1978, appoint new solicitors (other than those acting for the bank and the group), and seek the consent of the Central Bank on any loan over £3,000. Patrick had promised to close the bank in an orderly fashion. The bank reduced its activities considerably between 1977 and 1982, but Gallagher did not close down its operations completely. In fact it grew closer to its parent company, the Gallagher Group. Merchant Banking moved from its city centre headquarters on Clare Street to a smaller office within the Gallagher Group's headquarters at the Donaghmede Shopping Centre. Many of the bank's customers came from the surrounding area. Some customers deposited small amounts of money every time they did their shopping at the centre. When the bank closed its doors in April 1982, it had just two employees—a secretary and a rent collector. Most of the bank's work had been carried out by employees of the Gallagher Group. The entities were one and the same.

The Gallagher Group's Northern bank, Merbro Finance (NI), formerly called Merchant Banking (NI), was a wholly owned subsidiary of Merchant Banking until April 1978. Founded in the North on 5 November 1970, Merbro, like its sister bank in the Republic, took deposits from customers. It was granted a deposit-taking licence by the Bank of England in 1979 under the provisions of the UK Banking Act of that year.

In April 1978 Merbro's ownership was transferred from Merchant Banking to another Gallagher Group company called Lerrig. This meant that the Central Bank's 1977 ultimatum no longer applied to Merbro, so the bank in the North could continue making loans to the Gallagher Group. After repeated warnings from the Bank of England, Merbro's deposit-taking licence was revoked on 31 March 1982. The fact that the English banking regulator moved first on the Gallagher Group showed the differences in the standard of regulation between the Republic and the North. On 19 May 1982, William Carson, a partner with Price Waterhouse in Belfast, was confirmed as official liquidator of Merbro Finance. Paul Rowan, a newly appointed insolvency partner in Carson's firm, managed the liquidation on a day-to-day basis. Almost 20 years later, Rowan was to play a major part in investigating the Ansbacher tax evasion conspiracy.

When Merchant Banking collapsed on 30 April 1982, depositors and trade suppliers were owed £4.8 million. The bank supposedly had assets of £5.1 million. However, about 80 per cent of these assets (£4.1 million) was owed by Gallagher Group companies. Given that the Gallagher Group was insolvent, Merchant was effectively bankrupt as a result. The bank could not pay its debts without money from its parent company. Depositors were set to lose all their money. Shortall said in his report: 'The prospects of recovering assets of any substantial value . . . seemed extremely remote.' The depositors were devastated. Many people had ploughed their life savings into Gallagher's bank and his high-risk property deals had cost them their savings.

At the beginning of his no-holds-barred 1984 report on Merchant Banking, Shortall said he believed Gallagher had breached no fewer than 20 provisions of six acts in Irish law, including two Larceny acts and the Prevention of Corruption Act 1906, and had committed bribery and corruption. The liquidator found evidence for a total of

79 possible criminal offences. Shortall was so startled by his discoveries at Merchant Banking that he forwarded his entire report and its damning conclusions to the Director of Public Prosecutions, believing that Gallagher could face criminal charges because of his behaviour at the helm of Merchant Banking.

Shortall found numerous breaches of company law. Merchant Banking had not only submitted false reports and false returns to the Central Bank, it had also not held annual general meetings as was required by law; it had falsified its books; it had obtained assets fraudulently and had made fraudulent statements. After explaining how each breach arose, he stated starkly in his report how he believed Gallagher's bank broke the law.

The findings were sensational. For example, according to the bank's records, Merbro owed its sister bank in Dublin large sums of money. However, according to letters sent by Merchant Banking to Merbro, the Belfast bank owed it no money. In fact, it had deposits in the Dublin bank. Merchant Banking's records were clearly different from those of its sister bank in Belfast. The discrepancies in the figures were never explained. In September 1982, the liquidator of Merbro made a formal claim against Merchant Banking for stg£1.2 million. This claim diluted any money held by the bank that could have been made available to out-of-pocket depositors.

Shortall found it difficult to put an exact figure on the money owed to Merchant Banking by the Gallagher Group because of the highly irregular way the bank's money had been used to fund the group. No proper records were maintained, transactions were not accurately logged, and in some cases not logged at all. This confused the situation as some transactions could not be explained.

Shortall came across cash loans amounting to £258,000 that were advanced by Merchant Banking to 'customers'. However, he learned that these loans were actually gifts because there was no intention to repay the money. He said he expected to recover only about £34,000 of this money. He said the 'advances' were usually given to Gallagher family members and personal acquaintances of Matt and Patrick Gallagher. 'In other cases the "loans" were apparently "forgiven" or otherwise "set off" against liabilities of Patrick Gallagher and/or Gallagher Group companies,' Shortall said in this report. He found that many of the loans were statute-barred, meaning they were so old that he could not take a case to recover them.

Among Merchant Banking's loans Shortall discovered one for £5,234.13 given to a 'C. J. Haughey' with an address at 'Abbeyville [*sic*], Kinsealy, Malahide, Co. Dublin'. This was Matt and Patrick Gallagher's close friend, Charles Haughey, Fianna Fáil leader and Taoiseach during Gallagher's heyday in 1980. Another loan for £11,836 was due to Merchant Banking from Larchfield Securities, Haughey's trust company. Larchfield owned Inishvickillane, Haughey's private island off the coast of Co. Kerry and other properties owned by the Haughey family. The loans were taken out in 1976 and quickly paid back just over a month after Shortall's appointment to the bank, perhaps because Haughey felt that the loans were about to be discovered. The money was repaid by Haughey's money man, Des Traynor, who at one stage was a director of the Gallagher Group. By the time the loans were repaid in 1982, the total amount owing was £23,226. It subsequently emerged that the two loans were repaid with money drawn from one of Haughey's overdrawn current accounts in Guinness & Mahon, the Dublin bank used in the Ansbacher scam.

Gallagher admitted in 1999 in an affidavit to the Moriarty Tribunal, which was set up in 1997 to investigate payments to Haughey and other politicians, that the loans contained 'unusual features'. He acknowledged that 'no demand was ever made' by Merchant Banking for their repayment. Gallagher said he trusted Haughey implicitly and never doubted him, adding that his faith was not misplaced because the loans were repaid in full in June 1982.

Gallagher said his memory of the loans was vague, but from what he could remember Haughey came to him in 1976 and informed him that he needed funds 'to build a house for his daughter Eimear at Kilmuckridge, Co. Wexford'. But no security was ever sought for the loans, lending some credibility to Shortall's argument that the bank never expected them to be repaid.

When journalist Mary Raftery got hold of Shortall's report and tried to broadcast details of the Haughey loans on the RTÉ *Today Tonight* programme in October 1989 and again in the autumn of 1990, the broadcaster's lawyers stopped her. Despite the clear references to Haughey in Shortall's report, the lawyers feared what might lie in store for RTÉ legally if the mysterious loans to the then Taoiseach were revealed publicly.

Among other loans given by Merchant Banking was one in 1975 for £5,795 to Frank Cairns, one-time property editor of the *Irish*

Independent. No attempt was made to collect this loan. Shortall said in his report that on the basis of a conversation he had with the journalist, Cairns said 'the loan was not intended to be a loan, but rather cash advanced to obtain advantageous newspaper coverage for the property developments of the Gallagher Group'. Cairns was apparently shocked that his name had shown up in the loan book of Merchant Banking. He was of the belief that the money had been paid to him and was in no way a loan. This proved that, just as in the Cairns payment, the Haughey money was in all likelihood a gift dressed up as a loan.

Shortall also found during his examination of Merchant Banking that Gallagher had used the bank's funds to bankroll his favourite hobby, horseracing. According to an affidavit sworn by Gallagher and mentioned in Shortall's report, the young property tycoon made a 'loan' of £38,733 to a horse trainer on 24 March 1977 in return for a share in one of the trainer's horses. According to Shortall, the loans in effect contravened five sections of the Companies Act 1963, two provisions of the Larceny acts, one of the Central Bank Act 1971 and one of the Prevention of Corruption Act. He said the Cairns payment constituted bribery, and conspiracy in relation to the Cairns and horse trainer loans. The loans could not be recovered because they had passed their legal sell-by date, leaving Shortall to conclude that there may have been 'intent to defraud creditors by forgiving loans due to the bank'. Again the bank's depositors lost out.

Shortall also uncovered an extraordinary property transaction concerning Donaghmede Shopping Centre in Dublin, in which Merchant Banking and its depositors lost millions of pounds. The shopping centre was purchased by Merchant Banking from a Gallagher Group company for £1.9 million in 1975. Three years later the bank put the centre back on the market with a price tag of £3.75 million, but it didn't sell. In June 1978 a company called Gallagher Group Limited bought the centre from Merchant Banking for £1.9 million, the same price for which the bank bought it three years earlier. In April 1981 Gallagher Group Limited sold the centre to another company within the group for £4.5 million. Merchant Banking effectively lost out on a profit of £2 million because Gallagher structured the deal so that the sale benefited the wider group rather than just the bank. This money could have been used for the benefit of the bank's depositors.

Another bizarre transaction was discovered relating to the Galleria shopping arcade at 6–7 St Stephen's Green in the heart of Dublin city centre. A company called Pescara, a Gallagher Group company of which Patrick and Paul Gallagher were directors, was set up in August 1980 to buy, develop and rent out Galleria. Pescara bought the shopping arcade from Gallagher Group Limited in 1981 for £5.2 million. On 30 March 1982, as the Gallagher Group was falling apart, Merchant Banking bought all the shares in Pescara for £2.3 million through a complex group transaction. But the previous day Patrick and Paul Gallagher gave the deeds to the Galleria to Bank of Ireland to secure a £6.5 million debt the group owed the bank. So when Merchant Banking bought Pescara, it was effectively buying a company that no longer owned the deeds to the shopping arcade.

The deal essentially led to the transfer of £2.3 million from Merchant Banking to another Gallagher Group company. The bank received nothing in return. When Shortall tried to find out if the Galleria could be sold to repay depositors, he was told by Lisney auctioneers that the Galleria was 'in essence both a failed shopping arcade and an unsuccessful property development. Virtually every aspect of the building, its physical fabric, the state of its occupancy, the legal status of its tenants, its trading and income flow is, to be blunt, in a complete mess.' Shortall concluded that there was 'no hope' of Merchant Banking getting its £2.3 million back. It was another dud transaction for the Gallagher bank. Again the bank's money had been used to bolster the group's finances.

In yet another irregular transaction, Shortall discovered that Merchant Banking had paid a £25,000 bill to an auctioneering firm on behalf of the Gallagher Group for relocating a tenant from one of the group's buildings in Dublin city centre to another property across the road. Shortall said the money was never repaid to Merchant Banking. Again the bank's money had been used to the benefit of the Gallagher Group.

Despite the highly critical findings of Shortall's High Court report into Merchant Banking, the first moves taken to reprimand Patrick Gallagher for his management of the group's banking operations occurred in Belfast. The liquidator of Merbro Finance found unsavoury activities within its operations similar to those found by Shortall.

In the North savers had placed stg£3.5 million on deposit with the Belfast offshoot of Merchant Banking. Unlike their counterparts in the Republic, the depositors recovered some money from the collapse of Merbro Finance; they recouped 75 per cent of the value of their deposits, up to a maximum deposit of stg£10,000 from the Bank of England's Deposit Protection Fund, which had been set up by the 1979 Banking Act to safeguard depositors' money. Indeed, the Merbro failure was the first claim made against the fund, and Rowan and his team had to help devise the claims procedure which depositors had to follow. The rest of their money was lost.

The winding up of Merbro followed similar lines to that of Merchant Banking. Shortall and Rowan met regularly to keep each other up to date with developments. While there were many similarities between their cases, there were also significant differences. Merbro operated out of a small ground-floor retail and office building in Lower Donegall Street, not far from the *Belfast News Letter* offices and St Anne's Cathedral in Belfast. Rowan discovered that while there were some basic records in the building, any books, records or documents of importance were kept in the Gallagher Group offices in Dublin and, as it transpired, they were incomplete.

To make progress on the Merbro case, aside from the tedious task of agreeing depositors' claims, Rowan decided to focus on recovering the bank's loans and locating and selling any real assets he could get hold of. He sent one of his colleagues to Dublin to look for some motors cars connected to the business. He located a classic Rolls Royce which he drove back to Belfast. (On his way back he was stopped for speeding, which he talked his way out of.) The Merbro investigating team identified loans which had been used to buy paintings and invest in property in London. After considerable legal pressure, these were turned into cash for depositors.

All this investigative work gradually gave Rowan a gut feeling that some kind of case could be assembled which might, if sold well to the Director of Public Prosecutions (DPP) in Belfast, prompt a criminal investigation. In 1984 Rowan asked a colleague, legal eagle Peter McCloskey, to compile a report which could be used to brief the DPP. McCloskey compiled his report of more than 50 pages in 1986 and delivered it to the DPP in November 1986.

Just as Merchant Banking had done in the Republic, Merbro attracted deposits by offering high rates of interest. Most of its customers were ordinary members of the public, some of whom had invested large sums of money from compensation awards. The money was primarily used to fund Gallagher's property transactions in the Republic, but a property on Ovington Street in Chelsea, London, was also purchased where Gallagher's late sister, Helen, lived. The telephone and electricity bills for the house were paid for by Merbro. Rowan's team eventually served legal papers on Helen Gallagher and later sold the house which had cost about stg£100,000 when it was acquired around 1980. The proceeds were used to repay some of Merbro's depositors.

Again, just as Merchant Banking had provided some 'loans', Merbro had also made loans to individuals, most of whom had never made any repayments to the Belfast bank. The bank failed to make a provision for these bad debts in the accounts or returns made to the Bank of England. Most of these debtors were traced and some money was recovered. One individual who had received a loan from Merbro committed suicide. The loans ranged from a few hundred to several thousand pounds, and there were less than 20 outstanding.

Rowan's team discovered that the Bank of England had been deliberately misled by Merbro for at least two years in returns made to it by the Belfast bank. When the Bank of England demanded that loans to the Gallagher Group be repaid because of its concerns about Merbro's cash flow, the loans were reclassified from being borrowings that would be repaid immediately if so demanded, to loans where a demand for repayment had to be made 12 months in advance. The reason for the reclassification was because Merchant Banking had channelled money to the group and the group didn't have enough cash to repay the loans.

Rowan and McCloskey found a trail of false returns and minutes of meetings taken by Bank of England officials. The minutes set out the regulator's increasing concern with the way Merbro was being run and Gallagher's failure to fulfil promises. Gallagher played along with the Bank of England's demands, fearing that the licence for Merbro, which was pumping cash through his group, would be revoked. By the time Gallagher's Dublin property ventures collapsed, the Bank of England was on the verge of suspending Merbro's banking licence due to its lack of liquidity.

After the collapse of the Gallagher Group in 1982, Gallagher tried to start over again in business. To make ends meet, his wife Susan took a job in a chocolate factory in Naas, Co. Kildare, owned by a niece of Gallagher's friend, the racehorse trainer Vincent O'Brien. In the mid-1980s Gallagher returned to the property market and tried to re-surrect his career. He managed to raise enough funds in London to acquire some properties in the city. He bought a site on Bayswater Road for stg£1 million and resold it for stg£2.5 million. He also flogged off four valuable blocks in Kensington just before the collapse of the building market in England in 1987. His return to the property game and the publicity generated by the deals did him no favours.

'When hundreds of depositors are out looking for your blood it is very, very foolish to show evidence of wealth at all,' one of Gallagher's cousins later told an Irish newspaper. It turned out to be very foolish indeed. In March 1988 police in Belfast were putting the finishing touches to a two-year investigation into Merbro Finance. That month they swooped on the 36-year-old property developer. He was arrested in London and put on a flight from Heathrow to Belfast.

'There was absolutely no warning,' said a family source at the time. 'The police walked into his small office in Knightsbridge where he rents communal secretarial services and asked him to go to the station. Two RUC fraud squad men had flown over from Belfast. It was all gentlemanly and polite.' The arrest may have been gentlemanly, but the gravity of the situation hit the one-time multimillionaire playboy hard when he was placed in a cell reeking of excrement with four prisoners who had 'hardly washed in months', Gallagher later said. At one of the lowest points in his life, Gallagher said he recalled the advice given by his mentor, Charles Haughey. 'I took Mr Haughey's advice when he lost the election in 1981 and said to the few friends that had stayed with him: "No matter what the crisis, you have got to get your sleep."' Arising from the investigation into the collapse of Merbro, Gallagher was charged with stealing two paintings valued at stg£110,000, three counts of false accounting and conspiracy to defraud.

At the end of 1988, Gallagher was remanded on bail. A year later, on the morning of Gallagher's trial, Rowan was asked to come early to meet the lead prosecuting counsel, John Creaney QC, at the court build-ing. Creaney said that Gallagher was going to plead guilty and make an offer to compensate Merbro's depositors. He handed Rowan a bank draft for stg£500,000, telling him it was for the depositors and creditors of Gallagher's Northern bank. Another instalment of stg£400,000 was promised by Gallagher 11 months later. Gallagher pleaded guilty in court to the charges. He received a two-year jail sentence, which was suspended on the condition that he paid the second instalment.

Desmond Boal QC, who defended Gallagher in the case, was a veteran defence counsel who had a well-established reputation for winning cases. By advising Gallagher to plead guilty, Boal tacitly accepted that the case was a strong one, much to the satisfaction of Rowan and his team.

Gallagher tried to raise the remaining stg£400,000 needed to repay Merbro's depositors. He had managed to collect stg£750,000 from friends, but it was not enough to meet the shortfall—legal expenses had eaten away at the rest of the money raised. He didn't have enough to meet the second payment and, in October 1990, he was sentenced to two years in prison.

Mr Justice Robert Carswell, later Lord Chief Justice of Northern Ireland and a law lord, said Gallagher had furnished false information to the Bank of England to obtain a licence to conduct a deposit-taking business and had then used depositors' money to fund his own high-risk development business. 'When these collapsed, so did the savings of the investors,' said Carswell. The judge accepted that Gallagher had not set out to deprive depositors of their money and if Gallagher's deals had worked out, they would not have lost their money. 'But you told lies to the Bank of England to obtain the necessary licence,' said Carswell. 'The law cannot condone this, and it is necessary to mark the gravity of your offence.' The businessman, then 39 years old, was marched off by prison warders using the underground corridor from the court to begin his sentence in Crumlin Road Jail on the other side of the road.

At the time of Gallagher's guilty plea, journalist Mary Raftery and RTÉ were preparing their investigative report into Merchant Banking and had included details of what Shortall described as 'gifts' to Charles Haughey. When the report was eventually broadcast in early 1990, all references to Haughey receiving money from the Gallaghers or the politician's business dealings with the Gallaghers were removed from the final edit of the programme on the advice of RTÉ's lawyers.

However, the Haughey payments from the Gallaghers through Merchant Banking did not go unnoticed. The leader of the Labour Party, Dick Spring, raised the issue in 1990 in a letter he sent Haughey after being tipped off about the revelations in Shortall's report.

Haughey replied to Spring in a note dated March 1990: 'Dear Deputy, I read your letter yesterday with disbelief. I categorically reject your outrageous suggestions and find it deeply offensive that you would write to me in this tone. Yours, Charlie Haughey, Taoiseach.' Details of the payments to Haughey would not fully emerge until 1997 when the Moriarty Tribunal revealed publicly what had already been known in some political and media circles for several years.

In September 1991, while Charles Haughey was still Taoiseach—and almost a year after Gallagher received his jail sentence in the Belfast court—the DPP in the Republic announced that it would not take a prosecution case against Gallagher on the basis of a Garda fraud squad report into the collapse of Merchant Banking. This was despite the fact that two years previously the DPP had asked RTÉ not to broadcast its report on Merchant Banking because it feared it might prejudice a trial against Gallagher. RTÉ delayed the broadcast of its programme for several months, but eventually did so in February 1990.

Shortall was furious with the decision. The day after Gallagher was jailed Shortall said publicly that there were clear parallels between the charges on which the property tycoon was jailed in Belfast and the findings as set out in his High Court report. 'The events in Northern Ireland are extremely interesting and they particularly reflect on the lack of development here [in the Republic],' Shortall said at the time. He said he found that Gallagher had provided false information to the banking regulator—one of the charges for which Gallagher was jailed in Belfast. There were clearly double standards at play in the North and in the Republic. The fact that a similar case was not taken in the Republic infuriated people in the south and baffled people in the North. The issue was raised by TDs; one deputy described the decision as 'puzzling' in light of the Belfast court's finding. Another, Workers' Party TD Pat McCartan, said the Gallagher sentence illustrated 'the clear difference in approach to what is called "white-collar" crime on different sides of the border'.

There was a belief that the DPP in the North took the case because of the public interest at play in the scandal—depositors in the North had lost their money and somebody had to be brought to book over the losses. Gallagher was not really known in the North, and those prosecuting the case would have been unaware of his associations in the Republic. Rowan, following a year of investigating Merbro, recognised that a case against Gallagher could succeed. Initially, Rowan and his team thought they would have to take a civil case against Gallagher, but slowly realised that if they presented the evidence to the DPP in a clear way and make key arguments, a criminal case could proceed. Therefore he persuaded the DPP to take a case and informed the police when Gallagher was in Britain and could be brought back to Belfast to face charges.

No reason has ever been given publicly why no criminal charges were brought against Gallagher in the Republic for his handling of Merchant Banking, despite Shortall's comprehensive report. Shortall went on RTÉ television news to take on the establishment and question why Gallagher was not being pursued on the basis of the findings on Merchant Banking. He suggested that independent accountants were needed to assist the Gardaí in pursuing fraud cases to ensure prosecutions. To Shortall, the evidence against Gallagher was clear and undisputed. On the basis of Shortall's report there were obvious grounds to put Gallagher in the dock in the Four Courts. The DPP's decision was a bitter blow for the depositors.

Gallagher served one year in jail in the North. He kept himself busy in prison, cleaning out the food hall and working in the prison tuck shop. He was later moved to Magilligan Prison in Derry to be near a sick relative. He shared the Belfast and Derry prisons with sex offenders and republican and loyalist paramilitary figures. He moved to Africa in early 1992, his marriage in difficulties and his finances in a sorry state. He was involved in a number of business ventures in Zambia, Zimbabwe and South Africa, and he bought some properties in Kildare, Dublin and Wicklow, but he never became the wealthy deal maker that he once was.

Gallagher died in March 2006 at the age of 54. He pre-deceased Charles Haughey by three months; the former Taoiseach and Fianna Fáil leader died on 13 June 2006 at the age of 80. Shortly after Gallagher's death Paddy Shortall said he was still surprised that no criminal case was ever brought against the property tycoon over the way he ran his Dublin bank. 'I couldn't believe that my report on Merchant Banking was left to gather dust. It detailed the offences that were committed. I did all the donkey work that a barrister would have done in prosecuting the case. It was an outrage that no case was brought on the back of my work. The fraud perpetrated in the Republic was a lot worse than the offences in the North for which Gallagher was prosecuted. They [the prosecutors in the North] had their man in the slammer for much lesser fraudulent activities. It was the first time in my professional life that my professional work was ignored.'

In the summer of 2005, months before his death, Gallagher appeared in a documentary series on Haughey and spoke candidly about how he and his father had supported Haughey financially over the years. The Gallaghers were among Haughey's most generous patrons. Matt Gallagher advised Haughey in 1959 to buy Grangemore and its 40 acres of land in Raheny, north Dublin, for £13,000. In the documentary, Patrick Gallagher described his father's advice to Haughey as 'the same kind of advice as one would give to a friend in a pub'.

At the time of the purchase, Matt Gallagher promised Haughey that he would buy it back from him when his group increased in size. He stood by his promise; the Gallagher Group purchased the property from Haughey for £260,000 in 1969, when Haughey was Minister for Finance, making the politician a profit of £247,000 in a decade. During Haughey's ownership the land had been rezoned with planning permission for almost 400 houses, increasing the value of the property. Haughey's opponent in the 1969 general election, Conor Cruise O'Brien, made an issue of the deal, denouncing the 'Fianna Fáil speculator-oriented oligarchy'.

The Fianna Fáil politician later used this money to buy Abbeville, his stately pile in north Co. Dublin, which Haughey sold in recent years for more than €35 million. The Gallaghers had set Haughey on his way to making a fortune on property deals. The Gallaghers were exceptionally close to Haughey. Patrick Gallagher and Haughey were often seen dining in the Berkeley Court Hotel in Ballsbridge, Dublin. Money wasn't the only support that Haughey received from the Gallaghers. They provided him with cars during the electioneering circuits of Ireland which the politician used to build up his support after his years in the political wilderness in the early 1970s. Patrick revelled in his capital and emotional investment in Haughey. When Haughey beat his long-time political rival George Colley for the leadership of Fianna Fáil in 1979, Gallagher was one of Haughey's only friends from outside politics to turn up at his victory press conference in Leinster House.

That year, Gallagher also helped Haughey out of a massive financial hole. When Haughey was elected Fianna Fáil leader, he had massive debts and needed to pay them off. He owed AIB just over £1 million. He turned to Gallagher and other wealthy friends to help him pay them off.

On the day Haughey was elected Taoiseach in December 1979, he summoned Patrick Gallagher, then only 28 years of age, to his north Dublin home to ask for 'private support'. It was 'panic stations', Gallagher recalled, because Haughey had only 48 hours 'to tidy up his affairs'. 'Tell me the truth. How much do you fucking owe?' Gallagher supposedly asked the newly elected Taoiseach. Gallagher later told the Moriarty Tribunal that he had admired Haughey and had been in 'some awe' of him. Gallagher said they agreed to solve the problem there and then.

Gallagher gave Haughey £300,000—about €1.5 million in today's money—which was used to pay off about a third of AIB's debt. And just like the 'loans' given by Merchant Banking to Haughey and his company, Larchfield Securities, the payment was disguised. The six-figure sum, a massive amount of money in the late 1970s, was described as a 25 per cent non-refundable deposit for an option on the sale of land next to Haughey's home in Kinsealy that he was to pass on to the Gallagher Group within five years. Gallagher never exercised the option and during the intervening years the group collapsed and Haughey kept the money and held on to his land.

Despite the fact that about 590 depositors of Merchant Banking were out of pocket because of irregular practices such as the loans to the likes of Haughey, the property tycoon never expressed remorse for the plight of his customers. In 1996 he undertook in the High Court not to become a director of any Irish company again for five years in order to settle legal proceedings taken against him 16 years previously. But he never apologised for how he ran his bank or how he had ripped off the bank's depositors.

Many observers expected the government to refund Merchant Banking's depositors, just like Irish Trust's customers had been reimbursed by the state five years earlier, but no offer came from the government and the depositors ended up losing everything.

Shortly after the collapse of his high-flying deals and his subsequent fall to earth, Gallagher, the Irish Icarus, was quoted in a lengthy three-part apologia published in the *Irish Independent* saying: 'I have no regrets about what I have done and what I did so far during my business life. I have no ill feelings about what happened. The rules are there and the system is there. You go into business, you understand the system, you make money on the system.'

Gallagher either didn't understand the rules or simply chose to ignore them and pervert the system he referred to. He was eventually punished for breaking everyday rules of business. But his depositors had to live with the pain of losing their life savings and the anger of knowing that the state could not protect them or bring the man responsible for their losses to justice.

Chapter 3

PMPA: the failure of Ireland's biggest insurance company and the lost deposits

Jack Crown thought he had lost his life savings when the Private Motorists Provident Society (PMPS) was ordered to close its doors in October 1983. Crown, a native of Leitrim, emigrated to the United States just after the Second World War. There, he ran a small retail business. He returned to Ireland in the early 1970s and invested his life savings in PMPS on the advice of a relative. PMPS was owned by Ireland's largest motor insurance company, the Private Motorists Protection Association (PMPA). It was essentially a bank—it accepted deposits and gave loans and mortgages. Crown, like nearly all PMPS's customers, had no idea that PMPA was teetering on the brink of bankruptcy in the autumn of 1983 and that his money was at risk.

'I rang him when I heard the news on the radio in October 1983 that the government was appointing an administrator to PMPA,' said his son, John Crown, a consultant oncologist in St Vincent's Hospital in Dublin. 'My father told me: "I haven't lost all of my shirt, although the sleeves and most of the front are gone." He was very bitter about it because he had returned home and invested his money in Ireland.

He felt very let down.' It would take another 22 years before the affairs of PMPS were finally resolved and its depositors would get all their money back.

Jack Crown's case was not unique. About 5,600 PMPS depositors were owed £9.4 million (€12 million) when the company went bust. The average amount owed to each depositor was about £1,500. PMPS continued operating in business until October 1983 when financial difficulties at its parent company, PMPA, brought the bank crashing down.

The insurer had grown too fast in the late 1970s and early 80s, and by 1983 PMPA was suffering under a huge financial strain. In a very short period of time it had amassed a huge slice of the motor insurance market, but the sudden dominance came at a cost. The group had drastically underpriced its rivals but had not set aside enough cash in its reserves to cover the premiums it was writing. Growing a company by offering customers cut-price motor insurance might seem like a clever strategy, but in 1980s Ireland it was a risky business.

In effect, PMPA was growing its business too fast and using the money generated from new business to offer even better deals to other customers. This was a fatal strategy. If the company continued to grow as quickly every year, then each year's insurance premiums could pay for claims on the previous year's business. However, if PMPA's growth slowed or stopped, then it would not be able to afford future claims. The scenario was likened to a man on a bicycle: while he is in motion there is no problem, but once the bike slows down, he falls off. This, coupled with heavy losses in its subsidiary companies, forced PMPA into a corner.

The situation was complicated further by other factors. Not only were there more accidents in Ireland than in other countries, but also damages awarded through the Irish courts over car accidents were considerably higher. There was the added difficulty of the number of uninsured drivers, which amounted to up to a fifth of all Irish motorists. This contributed to PMPA's difficulties.

Matters reached crisis point in the summer of 1983. The Fine Gael-Labour government of the day felt that PMPA's directors seemed to be unaware of the fact that the company would not be able to survive much longer if it kept taking on new business at the rate it was. If the company failed, 400,000 motorists—about 60 per cent of Irish drivers—would have no insurance. This turned the problem into a national crisis, and the government felt obliged to act to stave off a disaster.

The circumstances were made even more problematic by the crippling economic difficulties of the time. The state was borrowing heavily and unemployment was high. A crisis that could bankrupt the country's largest motor insurer was the last thing the government wanted.

Recalling PMPA's precarious situation in the autumn of 1983, Fine Gael's Garret FitzGerald, who was Taoiseach at the time, said: 'The fear was that the company would have collapsed and a very large number of people would be left without car insurance, and we didn't know how that could be remedied. We couldn't prosecute them all because they wouldn't be able to get insurance. We couldn't see how these people could be reinsured. It was hugely dangerous for the ordinary citizens. The feeling all along was that PMPA was a very chancy business.'

FitzGerald was right; rumours had been circulating within official and financial circles about the health of PMPA since the mid-1970s. In 1982 the body which regulated provident societies, the Registrar of Friendly Societies, sent external accountants into PMPS to investigate the business. They discovered that it had only one major asset—a large sum of money owed to it by its parent company, PMPA. They concluded that if PMPA were ever to find itself in trouble, then so too would the bank. Concerned by this potential scenario, the government later sent outside experts into PMPA, and in the autumn of 1983 they concluded that the company was effectively insolvent—it did not have enough money in its reserves to pay claims coming in on its policies.

On 19 October 1983, following months of secret planning by civil servants, the government rushed emergency legislation through all stages of the Dáil in just one day, and the following day an administrator was appointed by the government to take control of the insurance company.

On the news of the appointment, queues of anxious PMPS depositors formed outside PMPA outlets across the country, seeking to withdraw their savings. But it was too late. The government's move had a domino effect—the appointment of an administrator to PMPA meant the bank had to close. Customers were unable to access their money while the mess was being sorted out. Millions of pounds in deposits were at stake.

At the centre of the controversy was PMPA's mercurial chairman, Joe Moore. A strong-minded individual and flamboyant character,

Moore had convinced PMPA's board to cede control of the group's investment decisions to him. Instead of allowing professional managers to administer investments, Moore took an unconventional route—he chose to make those decisions himself. He invested in garages, shops, property, a newspaper and an oil distribution business. In all there were 74 companies within the PMPA Group covering a diverse range of industries and sectors. The late 1970s was not a good period for Irish business generally and the group's subsidiaries did not trade well. As PMPA's premiums increased, its cash reserves started to wane. In 1980, for example, PMPA paid out almost £6.3 million more in claims than it took in.

Moore had fulfilled his goal of creating the country's largest insurance company but then saw it crumble around him. It left tremendous bitterness among PMPA employees who lost their jobs because of Moore's relentless expansion of the group. PMPS depositors—mostly widows, pensioners and elderly customers—were left nursing huge losses and baying for Moore's blood.

The PMPA story began with a letter to a Sunday newspaper in the early 1950s. At the time Moore had been working as a civil servant when he read the letter. The letter-writer complained that the Irish motorist was being ripped off by British insurance companies on high premiums and poor bonuses. For Moore, it touched a nerve. Being intensely nationalistic and a champion of the 'little man', the consumer, he joined a 'protection association' of motorists in 1951 to try and change the Irish insurance industry and offer the Irish motorist a better deal from an *Irish* company. He became the association's paid manager when he left the civil service in 1961. However, he wanted to transform the association into a fully fledged insurance company, protecting Irish motorists from overseas companies and promising lower premiums.

A native of Mountrath in Co. Laois, Moore had qualified as a teacher. However, restless by nature, he joined the civil service in 1935, ending up as a pensions officer working predominantly in the west of Ireland. The state of the insurance market prompted another career change.

Civil servants were alarmed at Moore's plans. His initial application to turn PMPA into an insurance company in 1967 was delayed by the Department of Industry and Commerce, which was responsible for monitoring the insurance industry. Moore had initially put up a lump sum of £100,000—about €1 million in today's money—as a cash reserve to meet the company's insurance claims. However, department officials wanted more, so he added another £70,000 and received the approval he needed. He could now compete with the British companies.

Moore decided to try and shake up the market through innovative changes. He bypassed agents and brokers, dealing with customers directly. The move did not win him any friends in the industry and from the outset he developed an entrenched position against his rivals. An anti-establishment figure and a bit of a maverick, he wasn't fazed by alienating existing players in the industry. After all, he felt he had to if he was to bring in major changes. To help the group on its way, PMPA offered motorists extravagant deals to attract new business. It promised never to refuse insurance to a qualified driver and built up a huge slice of the market.

Moore was an autocratic boss in PMPA and ran the company in an unorthodox way. He certainly was never in danger of winning a management award. One businessman who worked for PMPA said its board comprised just one man—Moore.

Moore quickly became one of the country's best-known business-men and in the 1970s and early 80s became known as 'Mr PMPA'. He did not see a divide between his home and business life, and took it personally when his 'children', his employees, took industrial action. He employed members of his own family—his three sons worked for the company. He also hired several dozen secondary school students, sons and daughters of friends and employees, every summer. Even though most people saw him as a curmudgeon, many spoke of his generosity. He gave staff company cars and loans through PMPS to help them buy their first homes.

As PMPA grew, so too did Moore's standing. PMPA brought him enormous influence in Irish life and he wielded that authority when he felt it necessary. During the 1979 battle for the Fianna Fáil leader-ship, Moore threw his weight behind his friend, Charles Haughey, who was up against George Colley. One evening Moore phoned Fianna Fáil TD David Andrews, a barrister, before the ballot, asking him to vote for the right man. Up to 65 per cent of Andrews' legal practice at the time was personal injury work for the PMPA, but after voting for Colley, Andrews lost all this business and did not regain it for three months. Andrews says he believes Haughey had nothing to do with him losing the business; he felt Moore punished him for backing the wrong candidate.

Moore's office was based in Wolfe Tone House in central Dublin on the northside of the city. The building, on Wolfe Tone Street, is now overshadowed by the Jervis Street Shopping Centre. Inside were complicated security checks because Moore feared attacks by loyalist terrorists from the North. The administrator's staff later dubbed the security checkpoint near Moore's office 'the Berlin Wall' due to the size of the checkpoint and the number of guards manning it. His office had an adjoining bathroom, a lavish perk in penny-pinching 1970s corporate Ireland. The administrator later found a small room in the basement of the PMPA's headquarters that had been used as a wine cellar. Inside they found only cases of Blue Nun, a cheap wine of poor quality. It spoke volumes about Moore and his group; despite being larger than life and in command of a massive business with an equally massive turnover, Moore lived a frugal and modest existence.

Moore's flamboyant manner and madcap takeover bids made him popular with journalists, many of whom realised that a story could be sourced on a quiet news day with a brief phone call to the ever-quotable Moore. They could trust the PMPA founder-chairman to 'shoot his mouth off' on a range of topics and fill their column inches with his comments. One journalist recalled a press photographer being sent out to Moore's bungalow home in Foxrock, south Dublin, to take his photograph. The PMPA boss insisted on moving one of his large armchairs from his living room to the garden, thinking it a much better setting for the portrait.

But the media were not always as co-operative. An investigation by *Business & Finance* magazine in 1975 found that PMPA had been consistently undercharging on its premiums between 1968 and 1973 and had been unable during these years to estimate its claims reserves properly at the end of each year. By continuously underproviding on its reserves, the PMPA was artificially propping up its figures, precipitating a crisis which would not materialise until the growth in premium income declined and the claims started flooding in.

Patrick Honohan, an economic adviser to Garret FitzGerald, said the insurer grabbed a huge slice of the market by underpricing. 'By doing this it meant that they were going to systematically lose money on all of that business,' said Honohan. 'If you watch PMPA's share of the market going up and up, at first their cash flow is very good because it can take a year or so on average before they have to pay out on claims. As long as the insurer continued to grow so rapidly, each year's premiums were sufficient to pay the claims on the previous year's much smaller level of business. But when growth slowed, the fact that they had not charged enough became painfully obvious.'

Despite the flaws in the group's strategy in the mid-1970s, there was no pressure on PMPA from the Fine Gael-Labour coalition government which was in charge of the country between 1973 and 1977, because it was seen as an Irish success story; it was investing in a wide range of industries, and this created the impression that the group was doing very well. The government felt there was no need to fix something that, on the surface, didn't appear to be broken. Besides, it was generating a positive perception for Irish business. But rising income from new insurance premiums was disguising the real picture. Cash flow continued to increase, masking the fact that the group was severely underestimating its potential losses and underproviding for those losses. This would lead to the financial crisis of October 1983.

Moore's investment strategy was seriously flawed. If the company was to have any hope of supporting future claims, it needed to own profitable businesses. However, his colleagues complained that he bought 'anything that moved'. His critics said his obsession with continuous expansion led to his downfall. Among the loss-making businesses he took over were McBirney's Stores, a chain of motor garages called the McCairns Motor Group and several properties. He set up the *Sunday Journal*, even though he knew nothing about the media or publishing. He always wanted to own a newspaper. But this too went out of business not long after it was established.

Moore felt that PMPA was the cash cow that would feed his growing empire, but a change of government in 1977 spelt the beginning of the end for the dogmatic businessman. Despite the fact that he was close to Fianna Fáil (which was elected to power that year) and close to Haughey, he found himself at odds with Des O'Malley, the Fianna Fáil TD who became Minister for Industry and Commerce in 1977. O'Malley started scrutinising the insurance industry, and PMPA more closely. He also introduced new legislation, the Industrial and Provident Societies (Amendment) Act 1978, which had a major impact on a crucial operation within PMPA—the group's treasury operation, PMPS.

The aim of O'Malley's new legislation was to shut down secondary banks which did not fall under the responsibility of the banking regulator, the Central Bank, and to close a loophole that some operators had used to set up back-door banks. He wanted all banking operations brought under the control of the Central Bank. A number of cowboy operations had appeared on the scene and later disappeared. O'Malley did not want any more showing up.

Under the new rules, PMPS, like other provident societies, was ordered to close its doors by 16 November 1978 and give its depositors back their money. But Moore refused. He fought O'Malley's legislation in the High Court and later the Supreme Court, claiming that O'Malley's legislation was unconstitutional. Moore's challenges dragged on for years. Both courts dismissed his claim, however. In 1983 he was awaiting a response to a personal plea made to O'Malley's successor at the department, Labour TD Frank Cluskey, for a stay of execution on the winding up of PMPS when Cluskey asked the High Court to appoint an administrator to PMPA.

Despite the fact that PMPS had been under threat of closure by the government in the late 1970s, the bank continued to take deposits. It also continued to fulfil a vital role in the PMPA operation, selling shares in the insurance company. PMPA was quoted on the Irish Stock Exchange until 1982 when its shares were suspended. This did not stop Moore selling shares in PMPA, however. The shares were heavily promoted in the group's in-house newspaper, *Private Motorist*. PMPS was vital to PMPA's survival. The bank also pushed sales of the group's cars and insurance premiums, which in turn created the cash flow essential for the continuing good health of the overall business. Without PMPS, PMPA would lose an important cash generator.

The beginning of the end for PMPA and PMPS can be traced back to 1978 and the deteriorating relationship between O'Malley and Moore. The two men clashed over how PMPA should be run. Moore was always a controversial figure, but he was at his most outspoken when asked his opinion of O'Malley. He thought O'Malley was out to get his company, and he took it personally. During one bruising exchange Moore described O'Malley in a newspaper article as 'a cantankerous gnat'. There was no love lost between them. Moore felt his attacks were justified because O'Malley questioned publicly the financial health of PMPA. But O'Malley knew something was not right with the group and acted on it in 1982. He was one of the first politicians to question seriously the running of PMPA.

Despite some private misgivings among politicians and civil servants, there were no public moves against PMPA following O'Malley's appointment as minister. However, behind the scenes O'Malley and the officials in his department were getting extremely nervous about PMPA. It was growing its motor insurance business at a furious rate and investing large sums of money in many different industries. In 1978 PMPA had changed its accounting practices—instead of revising estimates of outstanding claims on an individual basis, it published a total estimate of all outstanding claims which was, in the opinion of O'Malley and his officials, not a prudent way to be running an insurance company.

O'Malley bit the bullet in early 1982 when he heard rumours that Moore had put PMPA up for sale. He knew this had been prompted by problems within the group. He sent in independent auditors Coopers & Lybrand to investigate PMPA to try and get a handle on the group's true financial picture. However, the accountants met obstruction and even intimidation when they arrived at PMPA's headquarters on Wolfe Tone Square. Their attempts to investigate PMPA were continually hampered by Moore. Given how he had run the company, Moore was the only person who could help them with their enquiries, and his belligerence made their job all the more difficult. On several occasions they were even thrown out of the PMPA headquarters by Moore. At one point the government threatened legal action against Moore if he did not co-operate.

In May and June 1982 O'Malley took matters into his own hands. Moore may not have been concerned about the financial state of his business, but O'Malley certainly was, given the large number of drivers insured by the company. He felt a contingency plan was needed in case PMPA went bust. To devise a plan, he needed to know how the market would react if PMPA collapsed. In a controversial move, O'Malley invited senior executives from PMPA's competitors in the insurance market to private meetings and asked them if they could cope with the additional business of insuring 400,000 drivers should Moore's company collapse. The details of the meetings were leaked to the media in July.

Moore was furious. The PMPA boss said his business had been seriously damaged by reports of the meetings. He accused O'Malley of being responsible for allowing rumours of the group's financial difficulty to go unchecked and for adopting a 'circumspect posture' towards PMPA when O'Malley's officials had scrutinised the company's returns every year and had seen that the company was profitable.

Asked if there was a political element to the row, given the long-standing divisions between O'Malley and Haughey and Moore's friendship with Haughey, the PMPA chairman said the suggestion was 'complimentary but totally incorrect'. However, Moore added: 'I am not a Haughey man, but I am certainly not a Dessie man either. I have nothing against O'Malley other than that he is a crank and no one could put up with him.'

Moore said O'Malley had been pursuing a campaign against PMPA and that he first attacked the company in the Dáil in March 1976 when the politician asked whether the government would take action to prevent PMPA from bidding for another insurance company, New Ireland Assurance Co. O'Malley responded, saying that Moore's comments constituted 'an unwarranted attack upon the motives underlying my dealings with the PMPA over a long period of time'.

O'Malley's decision to meet PMPA's rival insurance companies sparked chaos in an already difficult market. In July 1982, even though the government reassured the market that PMPA was solid, customers still called in to the company's outlets to see if their premiums were safe. Some PMPA executives did not take O'Malley's behind-the-scenes manoeuvres lying down. They responded to the news of O'Malley's meetings, saying they would consider suing the minister for any losses resulting from his comments. They were right to be worried. About £5 million was wiped off the value of PMPA on the stock exchange following the news of the minister's meetings. Stockbrokers said the market remained nervous about the company, despite O'Malley's assurance that the last accounts showed that the company was in profit.

By the time Coopers & Lybrand completed its report on PMPA in the autumn of 1983, 14 months after starting its investigation, O'Malley was no longer in charge. Cluskey, a member of the Fine Gael-Labour government which had been voted into power in December 1982, had taken over as minister at the renamed Department of Trade, Commerce and Tourism. Cluskey was stunned by the report. PMPA had underprovided for claims by £165 million for 1981 and 1982, according to Coopers and Lybrand, and if this had been accounted for, PMPA would have a deficit of £35 million in 1981 and £75 million in 1982. It was a staggering amount of money. PMPA was clearly insolvent and balancing on a knife edge.

Cluskey commissioned a second report from London financial and insurance consultants Tillinghast Nelson and Warren, which largely confirmed the findings of the first investigation. The government felt it had to act. In the summer of 1983, Cluskey and his civil servants started preparing emergency legislation that would allow the government to appoint an administrator and take control of the company from Moore, enabling it to protect the policy holders.

The legislation was prepared in the utmost secrecy. Cluskey did not want Moore to find out or else he could face a series of legal challenges from the obstinate PMPA boss. He also did not want the public to find out. If they did, PMPS could have seen a run on its deposits and the group would haemorrhage cash. Cluskey and his team were so concerned that 73-year-old Moore might react badly to the government's move that they even considered having an ambulance on standby around the corner from Wolfe Tone House. Cluskey's team didn't even tell the President, Dr Patrick Hillery, that an important bill would be crossing his desk sometime in the autumn and would have to be signed into law by him. They just checked to ensure Hillery was not on holiday on the day they planned to bring the emergency legislation before the Dáil.

To raise the money needed to save PMPA, the government turned to a special fund set up in 1964 to cover defaults in insurance payments. However, by 1983 there was not enough money in the reserve, so the government decided to charge a 2 per cent levy on all non-life insurance premiums. The country's 700,000 motorists would end up paying for PMPA's mistakes.

The bill was eventually introduced in the Dáil on Wednesday, 19 October 1983, the first day of the new Dáil term. No one, least of all Moore, expected it. Such was the level of secrecy that PMPA was not identified in the Dáil when the bill was introduced. The next day the government went to the High Court and identified PMPA, explaining why there were problems at the company.

The court appointed Coopers & Lybrand partner Kevin Kelly administrator. Kelly (who left Coopers & Lybrand in 1991 to become managing director of AIB in Ireland) arrived at PMPA's headquarters later that day to take control of the company from Moore. The two men met for the first time in the PMPA boardroom in Wolfe Tone House. Moore, still refusing to face the reality that he was about to lose control of PMPA, suggested that Kelly use a small room off the boardroom. Kelly responded saying that the boardroom would suit him and his staff just fine. Moore was shocked by the response.

Kelly remembers Moore leaving the building in his chauffeur-driven Jaguar, while he and his staff left in a less salubrious vehicle. Kelly said the contrasting images said a lot about the changes that were to come at the company, and that the picture of Moore's exit stuck in his mind.

One of the first things Kelly did was to bar Moore from Wolfe Tone House. He also started examining why a filing cabinet of important documents had gone missing from the claims department. He recalls that shortly after his appointment he quickly discovered that Moore did not understand how the insurance business worked. 'Moore came at it with only a passion to make insurance more accessible,' said Kelly, 'to take on the British companies. Ironically, with the levy, it ended up costing the Irish motorist more. Moore didn't realise that insurance has a tail of five or six years for claims to come through.'

Kelly's appointment solved the short-term crisis at PMPA, someone who would run it in a prudent fashion and save it from collapse. The levy solved the longer-term problem, the deep financial black hole at PMPA caused by future claims. The levy turned out to be enough to cover the losses and underprovision on the company's reserves. It was initially thought the levy would have to remain in place for 20 years to cover the underprovision. However, this estimate proved to be considerably wide of the mark. The levy was introduced at the start of 1984, reduced to 1 per cent in 1992 and abolished in 1993, by which time it had raised £148 million.

The levy might have imposed a hardship on Irish motorists, but the real pain was felt by PMPS depositors. The provident society was ordered to stop taking deposits on 20 October 1983 and cease trading the day after Kelly's appointment. William Horgan of Arthur Andersen was appointed liquidator of PMPS in the High Court on 19 December 1983.

Among those to lose out in the collapse were Nora Smith and her husband Tom who had returned to Ireland after more than 20 years working in the United States. They had invested £20,000 of their life savings in PMPS. The couple had no choice but to return to the US to work again after the loss of their nest-egg.

The total amount owed to customers was huge. PMPS had £9.4 million in deposits from members of the public. PMPA and other companies within the group owed the bank £4.6 million, and PMPS had given millions more in loans to PMPA employees. It had also given loans of £4 million to members of the public and £2.3 million in loans to allow people to purchase shares in PMPA. Given that PMPA was in administration and its bank in liquidation, it would be difficult to recover this money. Depositors were owed an average of £1,500, and at the time it was thought that PMPS depositors would receive, at most, just under a third of their money back.

A year after his appointment Horgan said: 'There is no doubt that a lot of people lost everything they had saved and there is a very large proportion of these depositors who are elderly people. Some of the hardship cases are quite horrific. I have had very sad letters from people all over the country asking me to treat them as special cases and put them up the priority list. Unfortunately there is little I can do for them.'

PMPS exposed the scale of the problems for Moore. The collapse of the bank left him with some serious questions to answer. Most of the bank's assets were either worthless or difficult to sell. The complex inter-company relationships between PMPS and the other companies in the group made the situation even worse. The entire group was left in a mess.

The sale of shares in PMPA by the bank had also complicated matters. PMPA created a 'market' for its shares after the company was suspended from the stock exchange in 1982 and used PMPS to sell them to customers. Moore's company was effectively naming its own price on the shares and making a tidy profit on the trading. At one point PMPA was selling shares at 46p and then buying them back at 40p. And it wasn't a small-scale practice. In the year to October 1983, PMPS sold more than 10 million shares in PMPA, creating a cash flow of around £400,000 a month for the group. The sales boosted the flagging group by raising more than £4.4 million for its coffers.

Moore had spent the previous five years challenging O'Malley's legislation, which forced the closure of industrial and provident societies, through the courts, but refused to consider the possibility that he might eventually have to close PMPS if his legal action failed. The PMPS bank continued taking deposits and making loans without any concern about its pending closure, and by the autumn of 1983 Moore was relying on a last-minute reprieve from Cluskey to save the business that was helping to bankroll his entire group. Moore's customers seemed to be ignorant of the imminent closure and continued banking with PMPS right up to the end, blissfully unaware of the problems at PMPA that would sink the provident society.

Some blame inevitably lies with successive governments, which were complicit in creating a smoke-screen at PMPA over the previous two years. In July 1982, in response to pressure from PMPA following O'Malley's secret meetings with its rivals, he was forced to issue a statement saying that all was well at the insurance company. PMPA reproduced this endorsement in its newsletter of 16 July 1982, which may well have reassured customers that their money was safe. Throughout that period PMPS was busily selling shares in PMPA and taking deposits from unsuspecting members of the public.

Garret FitzGerald, however, felt that his ministers managed the crisis well. He recalled 22 years later that the government had been fully aware that PMPA was on the verge of collapse because of its two investigations and was ready to act 'in a lightning move'. He said the emergency legislation to protect the company had been prepared 'in total secrecy' because 'any hint that we were engaged in such an operation would lead instantly to the very collapse we feared'.

But the flipside of the secrecy was that the government could not warn PMPS depositors that all was not well at PMPA. Questions were asked about why the law had not been bolstered years earlier and in a more organised manner in an effort to protect PMPS customers. The fact that the government could not even name the company in the Dáil when it introduced the emergency legislation on 19 October led to general confusion that damaged the entire insurance industry.

O'Malley told the Dáil at the time that he had frequently tried to question the running of the company, but was constantly attacked by Moore. He said that when news of his meetings with rival insurers was leaked to the press, he had to sustain a week of abuse from Moore.

'I would have quietened him and put an end to it in ten seconds flat by coming out and telling the truth, but in the interests of the company I could not.' O'Malley said he had to 'not grin and bear it. It was very unsatisfactory that in the short term the public were being given the impression that this company was everything it should be, and that this unreasonable and terrible minister was interfering in a most untoward way with it and trying to damage it.'

O'Malley said that when he advised Moore that he thought PMPA's investments were 'unwise and unsuitable for an insurance company', the PMPA boss told him, department officials and external experts that they did not know anything about the business and that they should mind their own business.

As soon as the administrator was appointed, the PMPA shares, on which many PMPS customers had spent large sums of money, became worthless. Some customers bought shares in PMPA to avail of cheaper insurance, an offer that was promoted by the insurance company. In some instances PMPA was offering customers discounts of up to 25 per cent on their premiums. The lure of cheap premiums was still attracting customers even after rumours of financial turmoil at PMPA surfaced in July 1982. The discounts led to large volumes of PMPA shares being traded, which generated much-needed cash flow. When PMPA was put into administration, thousands of motorists were left with share certificates that were essentially useless pieces of paper.

O'Malley told the Dáil at the time that 'gullible members of the public' had continued to buy shares through PMPS after the company had been delisted from the stock exchange. 'The unfortunate people who invested in them were not institutional investors or others who were in a position to take institutional or professional advice,' he said. 'They were very small people buying a few hundred shares at the time because they were offered gimmicky cut-price offers on their insurance policy. Presumably that is outside the jurisdiction of the stock exchange and presumably it is outside the jurisdiction of the department also, but it is something that should not be allowed to continue. In calmer days when this is all over, the minister should consider introducing legislation to prevent share offers of that kind.'

After the collapse of PMPS, stories about depositors' losses began to appear in the press. At a stormy meeting of depositors on 20 November 1983 in the basement auditorium of Liberty Hall in Dublin, Kevin Phoenix, a father of four, said he had put a pound a month away in accounts for each of his children for years. He said that if big investors had lost money, the government 'would have got off its backside'. Mary Davey from Tallaght cried as she told the meeting that she had intended to use money she had deposited in PMPS to repay a mortgage.

PMPS also lent money to PMPA directors to buy shares in the parent company. Moore had a loan from PMPS but stubbornly chose not to pay it off, firmly believing his group was not in any danger. Asked within days of Kelly's appointment if PMPS depositors would lose their money, Moore said: 'I'll put it this way. PMPS was solvent, just as the insurance company was solvent last week. What is going to happen or what is not going to happen, I don't know. The only thing about the

PMPS would be that quite a lot of its money is in shares in the insurance company and of course if the insurance company shares are valueless as some people say, naturally the PMPS would lose some of its capital. I think it would still be able to meet some of its commitments.'

However, Moore's actions the previous week revealed a different state of mind. On the day the emergency legislation was passed, he sold one million PMPA shares to clear personal loans of £334,000 with PMPS before Kelly's appointment. The sale left Moore with £65,000 on deposit at PMPS. The move saved him a lot of money. Many senior staff who had remained loyal to him felt betrayed by his actions. When the transaction was revealed in public, depositors were furious. However, Moore, just like the other depositors, felt hard done by and saw nothing wrong with the transaction. But he was actually trying to save his own situation. Kelly later successfully sued Moore in the late 1980s over the £400,000 he earned in the transaction. However, Moore's death in June 1989 meant that Kelly would never recover the money.

An action group known as the PMPS protection committee was set up by out-of-pocket depositors to lobby the government to have their deposits reimbursed by the state. Barry Hardy, chairman of the committee, spoke for the depositors when he said in late November 1983: 'We are very upset and very sad. There are many, many hardship cases. But the minister could not give any guarantee whatsoever regarding depositors' funds. He said he will pass on the messages from the committee to the government.'

The messages had no effect. The government refused to reimburse depositors. Hardy said a clear precedent had been set when Irish Trust depositors had been repaid and that they had a strong case to take the government to court. He believed that the government had known in advance that there were problems at PMPA and of their likely impact on PMPS and its customers, and because of this the state should cover their losses. The government refused to budge. It told PMPS customers that the public had been warned repeatedly not to invest in industrial or provident societies as they were unmonitored back-door banks over which it had no control.

After his appointment to PMPA, Kelly closed 17 of its 31 garages with the loss of almost 350 jobs. He also sold other PMPA subsidiaries—the Dublin retailer McBirney's and the oil distribution business—to recoup money for the company. The deficiency at PMPA ended up being £223 million, about 2 per cent of Ireland's GNP. Kelly thought in 1983 that it would take five years to return PMPA to profitability. In that time he cut the workforce from 2,300 to 800. In 1987 PMPA earned premium income of £81.5 million, of which £76.5 million came from motor insurance. Kelly sold PMPA to Guardian Royal Exchange Assurance for £87 million in March 1989. (Guardian Royal was eventually bought by the French company Axa in 1999.) The money brought a small windfall for PMPS depositors.

Kelly said the most unusual aspect of his work at PMPA was the constant publicity. The job was 'a hell of a challenge. Our brief was to rescue and make sound the business that insured the majority of Irish car drivers. I wasn't sure for a long time that we could pull it off.' He said his work was conducted in the public eye and PMPA was the main item on the RTÉ news 'at least once a week' during his time at the company.

In subsequent years Bill Horgan, the liquidator of PMPS, also recovered money for the bank's depositors and creditors. He brought cases against customers who had borrowed money from PMPS to buy shares in the insurance company. The legal action threatened by the PMPS depositors against the state never materialised.

Questions still remain about the handling of PMPA by the successive governments of the late 1970s and early 80s. For years it had been rumoured in certain circles that PMPA was a financial basket case and it was known that its 'back-door bank' would eventually have to close because of O'Malley's 1978 legislation. Yet both continued to trade and deal with customers regardless, without any government action until O'Malley and Cluskey took up the case.

Looking back at the affair, O'Malley says he watched as PMPA built up its market share, knowing that the group was lining itself up for a fall. He said his meetings with other insurance companies were nothing out of the ordinary; executives from these companies had approached him regularly to express their concern about the financial state of Moore's company.

'[The PMPA] did something [grow rapidly] which could not have been done if it had been acting in a prudent fashion,' said the former minister. 'The other companies knew that too and everyone was positioning themselves for when the crash was going to come. The companies—and I had every sympathy with them—didn't want to be there having to pick up all the pieces afterwards and pay for the greed and recklessness of Moore.'

O'Malley said the mistake he made was that he had not done something sooner about the looming mess at the company. 'I had been concerned about it for a number of years because it was run in a most reckless fashion and it was paying claims out of current premiums. It wasn't properly reserved. It didn't make proper provisions. I remember in the department I was constantly told that the accounts were audited by a firm of chartered accountants and that I shouldn't be worrying about them. I remember thinking at the time that it wasn't a question of whether PMPA went under but when it went under. I thought this because of the way the company was run. It was run by a man who was unstable, who did not follow any of the normal prudential rules or the rules of insurance underwriting. I remember making the remark that I hoped I wouldn't be sitting in that seat as Minister for Industry and Commerce when it collapsed. I was lucky in that it didn't go under during my time.'

O'Malley dismissed suggestions that he had taken on Moore and PMPA because of his animosity towards Haughey. His only concern was for the health of the company. 'Whether PMPA was close to Mr Haughey or not, it was run in a reckless fashion and I had a duty to policy holders and to the public to try to get things under control. I got no co-operation from Moore. Moore was a megalomaniac. The press, I am sure, contributed to it. Any old rubbish he came out with, they printed. By implication at least the press held him up as a major Irish entrepreneur who was of great service to the country. Unfortunately, he was able to buy his way into becoming by far the largest single company for issuing private motor policies.'

Moore died in a nursing home in Blackrock, south Dublin, on 20 June 1989 at the age of 80. Right to the end he believed that the government had been wrong about PMPA and should not have taken control of his business from him. Just before his death he had launched a fresh legal challenge against the government, claiming that the administration was illegal.

The case was an attempt to scupper the 1989 sale of PMPA to Guardian Royal Exchange by Kelly. The sale must have left a bitter taste in Moore's mouth. He had grown PMPA with the purpose of challenging the might of the British insurers which he believed were hurting the Irish motorist, and here was his prized possession being sold to one of those British companies. He always maintained that his group was 'smashed' by politicians and civil servants. In the end, Irish motorists were less well off, having to pay a levy on their premiums because of the PMPA mess.

Moore claimed that altruism drove him to set up the PMPA in the first place. 'The funny thing is that I never seek these positions. They are thrust upon me,' he recalled years later. 'I never went into anything with the intention of making money, except when I looked for a job. I always went in as an honorary officer. I made money with the PMPA and, of course, there's no doubt about that. But it wasn't because I wanted to make money. That's what happens to an awful lot of fellas. They go in trying to make money for themselves and end up in liquidation.'

On 26 September 2005, about 100 PMPS depositors gathered in Liberty Hall in Dublin to hear how the liquidation of Moore's bank was progressing. They were mostly elderly people from modest financial backgrounds. Horgan told them that they should each have received all money owed to them in seven payments made over the previous 22 years.

Horgan received claims from depositors totalling £9.4 million (€12 million) and paid them in full. At the meeting Horgan said there was €440,000 left over for depositors, which was 'highly unusual' for a failed company. He said he would distribute this money based on the average interest rate over the intervening 22 years. The depositors supported Horgan's plan.

One depositor in attendance, a nun, told the meeting that she had invested money in PMPS that had been raised at tea parties for overseas charities. Another depositor seemed to sum up the thoughts of all the PMPS customers present when he said: 'I think this should be sorted out quickly; it has been going on long enough.'

Hardy said the fact that the depositors recovered all their money showed that PMPS could have survived. He still believes that the handling of the financial crisis at PMPA had more to do with the personal row between Moore and O'Malley than any real financial crisis. He described the whole affair as 'very, very sad'. He said elderly people lost their life savings and their 'funeral money', and thought the government's solution to the PMPA crisis was 'haphazard, reckless and not properly thought out'. He believes the government should have looked for an alternative solution that could have saved PMPS.

Jane Marshall, a corporate lawyer and restructuring expert who worked on the winding up of PMPS, said the government's decision to appoint an administrator was 'absolutely the wrong thing to do'. She said that by appointing an administrator the state wrote off the PMPS deposits and knocked millions off PMPA's balance sheet. The government's 'gut reaction' at the time was to put Moore out of business, but by doing so PMPA's assets lost 80 per cent of their value. This effectively bankrupted PMPS and left its depositors out in the cold.

Tributes were paid at the September 2005 meeting to those who had spent two decades winding up the company and repaying depositors. It was remarkable that almost 22 years since the collapse of Moore's bank and more than 16 years since his death, PMPS customers were still meeting to find out what had happened to their money. Hardy estimated that at the end of the winding up process, the legal and administrative cost of cleaning up the mess at PMPS amounted to €5 million over the 22 years.

The meeting was proof that the PMPA crisis had indeed been one of Ireland's greatest financial shipwrecks, but with many survivors. It showed that the government had left the PMPS depositors marooned and they remained that way for 22 years.

And during that period, depositors such as Jack Crown died without knowing what became of the savings they had spent most of their working lives building up.

Chapter 4

Insurance Corporation of Ireland: the state's bail-out of Ireland's biggest bank

A IB believed that its investment in the Insurance Corporation of Ireland (ICI) would be a major money-spinner for the bank when it first bought a stake in the company in 1981. But the investment turned into a nightmare for the country's biggest bank. In 1985 the insurance business was on the brink of collapse. It not only threatened to bring down AIB but also jeopardised the entire banking system and the financial stability of the country. ICI was the biggest corporate failure in the history of the state, and AIB tried to run away from it.

1985 was the third year that Taoiseach Garret FitzGerald and his Fine Gael-Labour coalition government were in office. FitzGerald first learned of the crisis brewing at ICI on the evening of Friday, 8 March 1985, when two of his senior government ministers— Minister for Finance Alan Dukes and Minister for Trade, Commerce and Tourism John Bruton—called to his home on Palmerston Road in Rathmines on the southside of Dublin. FitzGerald was sick in bed with the flu at the time. What he heard made him feel considerably worse. His government found itself at the centre of a crisis that, according to the banking regulator, the Central Bank, had the potential to bring down Ireland's biggest bank and possibly the economy. The news stunned FitzGerald. He put the government on red alert and started preparing a rescue plan.

ICI had racked up massive but as yet unknown losses by wildly underwriting high-risk businesses in the insurance market. The scale of the losses was so great that it threatened to bring down its parent company, AIB. The bank had ploughed tens of millions of pounds into the company trying to save it, but it could no longer afford to keep bailing the company out.

On 8 March it dropped a bombshell on the government. It was pulling the plug on ICI because the threat to the bank was too great. It had to walk away. However, by going to the government the bank was playing a clever strategy. It knew the government would not allow ICI to threaten the stability of AIB because the country was so heavily exposed to international institutional investors at that time, and if the country's largest bank failed, then the entire country could well be destabilised. AIB recognised the predicament facing the government and were aware that the government knew this too. The Central Bank and department officials had advised the government that this was the scenario facing the bank and the country.

The manner in which the bank broke the news alarmed FitzGerald and his ministers. By blithely declaring that it could no longer afford to continue funding ICI and was going to allow the company to collapse, the bank was forcing the government into a corner. Terrified at the prospect of the international markets turning on AIB, the government stepped in. It took control of ICI and responsibility for its liabilities. 'Clearly the bank was playing a game of "who blinks first?"' said a former AIB banker. 'And Fitzgerald and his ministers blinked first.'

ICI pre-dated AIB by several decades. Set up in the 1930s, it grew out of an insurance company set up by Irish Shipping, the state-owned merchant shipping business. Initially the insurer sold marine insurance but later moved into general insurance. In 1984 it was the second largest non-life insurer in the Irish market with a turnover of £380 million and a staff of more than 800. The company had offices in Britain, the United States, France, Canada, Australia and the Channel Islands, and on the surface appeared to be thriving. In 1981 the insurance company was enjoying its eighth successive year of profits, earning £8.5 million.

AIB's decision to spend £10.5 million on a 25 per cent stake seemed like a sensible move. The idea of offering customers a 'one-stop shop' for financial services, including insurance, appealed to AIB: draw the customers in and sell them a range of products. Being the second largest non-life insurer in Ireland, it seemed like a good strategic fit for the bank.

AIB chief executive Paddy O'Keeffe drove the investment. 'The thinking at the time was that banks should get into financial services,' said a former senior AIB executive, 'and people felt that banking was similar to insurance.' The bank found out, to its cost, that the sectors were very different.

The bank had not planned to buy the company outright, which it did in September 1983. The market forced its hand. US insurance company Continental Corporation of New York, a shareholder in ICI, put its 7.99 per cent stake in the Irish insurance company on the market in July 1983 and AIB decided to buy. Given that it already owned 25 per cent of the company, Continental's shares brought AIB's stake over the buy-out threshold, and it was forced to take ICI over. It cost £40 million made up of £30 million in shares and £10 million in cash.

To prevent ICI falling into unfriendly hands AIB had been forced to act quickly—perhaps too quickly. The bank was unable to examine the books of the company and carried out a 'superficial' due diligence. Instead it relied on auditors Ernst & Whinney to value the company. It was a risky decision, one that would later cost AIB and the Irish exchequer dearly.

The bank's upbeat assessment of ICI's potential was overshadowed by the fact that in 1983 the bank's profits for the year were revised from £7.9 million down to £2 million.

ICI was a large and important company in Irish business in 1984. It had underwritten about 120,000 insurance policies, of which 30,000 were for motor insurance. The company was the biggest underwriter of employers' and public liability insurance; it had 25 per cent of this market in Ireland. It was the government's sole agent for managing export credit insurance for Irish exporters and it also insured many of the state-owned companies including the national airline Aer Lingus and the transport company CIÉ. AIB felt that by purchasing ICI it could also get a cut of this lucrative action. Such was the scale of its business in the Republic that if ICI were ever to find itself in trouble, so would many Irish motorists and blue chip businesses.

But ICI's problems did not emanate from its operation in Ireland: it was hugely active in 1984 at underwriting high-risk business primarily through its London office, which accounted for about 70 per cent of its business. In the past the office had primarily covered fire, marine and aviation business, but in the early 1980s it started making bigger waves in the market, entering areas where it had little experience of risk assessment and of how to price its risk correctly.

The manager of the London office, John Grace, was a high flyer who aggressively sought out new high-risk business such as insuring satellites, bloodstock and even fairground operators and circuses. These were businesses that other insurers steered well clear of. He even insured telegraph poles in the Australian outback, items that were prone to combustion on a regular basis. Many of these premiums also involved long-term contracts described in the industry as 'long tail' business, meaning that it could be years, perhaps decades, before claims came in.

Grace enjoyed the good life. He was wined and dined in style by brokers who knew he would be more than happy to sign ICI up to high-risk business. He subsequently underwrote all sorts of risks that were regarded as nothing short of wild in the market. The money flowed in, creating the impression that Grace and the ICI were major players in the insurance business.

However, Grace was nothing more than an aggressive sales manager who was not being properly supervised. He was given free rein to attract as much new business as he could bring in. A source close to the bank said that personal pride and self-enrichment was what drove Grace. 'He wanted to be the man,' said the source. And he was. In 1984 the London office was responsible for half of ICI's total gross premiums of £389 million. This was more than 20 times the amount of business written in the previous 12 months.

Grace's office landed with a bump during the downturn in the insurance market in the mid-1980s. ICI had been actively involved in reinsurance, which is effectively the spreading of the financial burden of risk between insurance companies. When the market is performing well, the reinsurance market can be a very profitable business. However, in 1984 the downturn left insurers facing substantial losses. High-risk business was being spread among an ever-decreasing number of companies willing to take a chance on the possibility of large claims years later.

Because of its coverage of high-risk businesses, ICI was affected worst of all. Rumours began circulating in London that ICI's business was in dire financial health. 'The dogs in the street in London knew something was wrong at ICI,' said one AIB insider, 'but the dogs in AIB Bankcentre [the bank's headquarters in Dublin] didn't know a thing.' 'In fact ICI was regarded as something of a joke in the insurance broking community,' said another bank insider. 'It was regarded as the place to offload all the dud risks for premiums that didn't remotely reflect the risks.'

Business was flooding into ICI primarily through Grace and his London office. But as the claims started to flood in, it became clear that the company was paying the price of underwriting the risk far too low. The losses were immense: of the £63 million lost in 1983, £50 million was estimated to be generated by the London office. Grace's aggressive bid to increase the company's market share by taking on risks that had been declined by other insurers was in itself dicey, but with insufficient money to back potential claims, those risks proved to be the business's undoing.

AIB should have spotted the warning signs much earlier. In 1981, four years before ICI imploded, the company had nowhere near the industry average of cash reserves to cover the claims that would be coming in on its insurance policies. That year, general insurance companies had an average ratio of 4.27 times as many reserves as paid claims; ICI had a ratio of just 2.68. Amber lights should have flashed the following year when underwriting losses at the company soared from £422,000 to £7.3 million.

Following an examination of the company's accounts in July 1984, officials from Bruton's Department of Trade, Commerce and Tourism told ICI that it was unhappy with the state of the company. ICI responded, saying that all was fine at the company. But the officials were not satisfied and the government hired actuaries to assess the financial situation at ICI.

By the end of 1984 ICI was in serious trouble. AIB chief executive Paddy O'Keeffe, who made the decision to buy ICI, retired early from the position of chief executive and was succeeded by Gerard Scanlan. Around the same time Tom Mulcahy—Scanlan's eventual successor and an expert on due diligence, investigation and corporate restruc-turing—effectively went on secondment from his post as the head of the bank's corporate and international division to investigate the scale of the losses at ICI.

Press reports about ICI started appearing in November 1984, feeding rumours that all was not well in the insurance company. 'The Can of Worms at ICI', the headline on the cover of *Business & Finance* magazine that month, had tongues wagging. The reports and rumours finally pressed Bruton and his officials into action.

At a meeting in November, AIB and ICI executives informed Bruton and his officials that the bank had decided to invest more money in the company to meet outstanding claims. The actuaries hired by Bruton assured the department that, with the bank's fresh injection of cash into the company, ICI had adequate funds to pay out on its claims. More importantly, at the November meeting ICI and AIB assured Bruton that while there were problems with the insurer's London branch, 'corrective measures were being taken to rectify matters,' the Fine Gael minister later said.

The corrective measures came too late. The bank later admitted that disaster struck at the end of October 1984—before the Bruton meeting—when it was discovered that ICI's forecast profit of £3.2 million for 1984 could actually end up being a loss of about the same amount. Worse still, ICI management estimated that underwriting losses for the year could reach about £23 million. The bank had to invest yet more money, another £5 million, to keep ICI afloat. AIB was pouring money into what seemed like a bottomless pit and was forced to take drastic action.

In a last gasp effort to rescue the situation, the bank seized greater control of ICI. It had initially been told by the Central Bank to keep the business at arm's length after it bought the company. The irony was that while ICI's London office seemed to have *carte blanche* to underwrite hundreds of millions of pounds worth of risk at a time, AIB's own London banking operation was allowed to underwrite no more than £2 million without approval from head office in Dublin.

As the crisis deepened at ICI, AIB sent new managers into the company. A consultancy team was ordered to investigate those parts of the company losing the most money and to quantify the scale of the potential losses. Grace was moved from his executive role in the company to handle some of the lawsuits with which it was faced. He resigned a few months later, citing health problems.

The bank ploughed another £40 million into the company to bolster the floundering business, but the problems facing AIB were spiralling out of control. Other factors complicated the situation further. A strike in Dublin delayed the work of a team of accountants who were sent in to assess the actual financial situation. A large number of records relating to the business conducted in London were held in Dublin, which hindered the accountants' attempts to arrive at an exact figure for ici's trading loss for 1984.

Getting an accurate reading on the loss was essential. Two investigation teams working around the clock and independently of each other came up with a final figure of £60 million on the losses for 1984. The bank then called in actuaries to come up with an estimated upper limit on the company's underwriting losses. The findings shocked the bank. Scanlan asked his deputy Paddy Dowling to investigate. Dowling reported back, saying that the bank could no longer keep pumping money into the company. It had spent £86 million on the company, acquiring it and keeping it afloat. Dowling said enough was enough—aib had to end it immediately.

Because of the number of customers affected the bank was forced, with its tail between its legs, to inform the government. On the evening of Friday, 8 March 1985, the bank broke the bad news to the Central Bank and the government and told them that it had no intention of rescuing its ailing subsidiary. Given the scale of the losses and the unknown and open-ended nature of the liabilities, the bank was forced to cut its losses and its involvement in ici. The politicians were stunned. Only four months previously the bank had said publicly that everything was rosy at ici and that the insurer's depleted resources had been strengthened.

One former senior aib executive said: 'When we started to plumb the depths of the losses at ici and we could not find the bottom, we could not tell the market that we had an undefined loss. If we had said that, we would have been gone.' Instead the bank said it could do nothing with ici; it had to walk away. The alternative was the collapse of aib. The nonchalant manner in which the government was told of the crisis angered department officials and the ministers in charge.

The Central Bank and department officials warned Bruton and Dukes that the potential liabilities and claims from ici's outstanding insurance policies could bankrupt aib, lead to a crisis of international confidence in the wider banking sector and damage the economic fabric of the country. Bruton and Dukes were horrified. Something had to be done before news of the pending disaster leaked out and the financial markets turned on the bank and the fragile economy.

The civil servants explained to the politicians the complex issues facing them. The capitalisation of the country's banks was grounded on loans from other banks which could—in the event of the insolvency of a subsidiary of any of the banks—be withdrawn. There were doubts as to whether the country, which was teetering on the brink of bankruptcy, had the funds to weather the financial storm in such a scenario. The Central Bank's total foreign exchange reserve at the time was only £3 billion, which was about the same as the banking system's liabilities to its lenders.

So the government was faced with two options: let the company go bust and deal with the consequences; or assume ICI's debts and avoid a potential doomsday domino effect.

The politicians were livid at being forced into a corner. Bruton was furious that AIB had left it so late to tell the government about the financial black hole at ICI. He said the bank should have warned them earlier and given them more time to deal with the crisis. He was particularly incensed that the bank had brushed aside his concerns during the crunch November meeting with officials from his department. He told the Dáil on 27 March 1985: 'It is difficult to say how much of the London branch's problems arose while AIB was a minority shareholder and how much actually arose during 1984, at which stage ICI was under the full control and ownership of AIB. It is obvious that a serious lack of management control, particularly in relation to the flow of information between London and Dublin, contributed in no small measure to the present problem. If the problem had been spotted and the position established at an earlier date, then the magnitude of the present difficulties would not be as great. The belated realisation that there were problems in London is, therefore, all the more disappointing.'

Garret FitzGerald now recalls: 'I was absolutely astonished about the way the loan notes could be withdrawn if any part of the bank or any subsidiary of it became insolvent. That could bring down the bank and finish the whole system. This was a mad way to have arranged a banking system as vulnerable as that. The bank put it to us that if we didn't bail them out, they could go under. The advice we got was that could happen.'

Bruton said at the time: 'Ministers had to act in great haste because of the potential situation developing. It was a situation in which possibly no one would have control if we did not act. And it not only affected the insurance sector but also equally importantly the bank sector. We were forced in the circumstances to take the advice of those competent to give it, both here in the department and the Central Bank.'

This was not the first financial crisis to hit FitzGerald's government. It had just recovered from the collapse of the PMPA insurance company 18 months earlier.

During the week following AIB's decision to close ICI down, there were heated discussions between the government and the bank. Sean Dorgan, who later became chief executive of the state development agency, the IDA, represented the Department of Trade, Commerce and Tourism, the government department responsible for overseeing the insurance sector, in the talks. Charlie Smith represented the Department of Finance. Alan Dukes as Minister for Finance held the purse strings. AIB chairman Niall Crowley, a friend of both Dukes and FitzGerald, the bank's chief executive Gerry Scanlan, and deputy chief executive Dermot Egan played hardball on behalf of the bank.

On the evening of Friday, 15 March, the government revealed the ICI crisis to the nation by making an extraordinary announcement: it was buying ICI from AIB for £1 and taking responsibility for its open-ended and unknown liabilities. These debts could potentially run to hundreds of millions of pounds and take years to settle. The announcement had been carefully choreographed so that news would be released late on the Friday after the banks and markets closed. The government decided not to announce it mid-week, fearing for the reputation of AIB and the reaction of the market to the deal. It was also the Friday of St Patrick's weekend, a bank holiday weekend, which gave the bank three days to reassure Irish depositors and investors that the bank was sound, thus helping to avert a run on its deposits. It was reckoned to be enough breathing space to stop the crisis from snowballing.

A source at AIB Bankcentre recalled the day when the bank put out its statement informing the public that it was jettisoning ICI. 'I have never smelt fear and the impending doom as I felt that day waiting for the reaction to that statement,' he said. The public relations management in the bank was superb: PR veteran Jim Milton—who handled many later scandals at AIB—was drafted in on the Irish side, while the bank's PR team in London managed to spin a line to the British media that the 'real' story was about AIB suing Ernst & Whinney over the analysis done by the accountants in 1983 prior to the bank's purchase of the company. This turned the fire on the accountancy firm's involvement and averted any damaging headlines about AIB.

Scanlan went on television to assure depositors that AIB's core operations were safe and that they had now lanced the boil. He went on to assure equity investors that their dividends would be paid as planned. To the bank, it was paramount that it did not flinch in the face of pressure from its international bankers. If those bankers had decided to call in the inter-bank loans that were holding AIB together, then it would have been curtains for the bank.

The strategy worked in the short term. AIB's share price closed the week on a firm note at 155p. News of the crisis had a slight impact on the valuation of the bank—shares dropped to 132p at the close of business on the following Tuesday, the day the markets opened. However, the share price eventually rallied within a short period and returned to its pre-ICI levels.

One senior AIB executive said the public relations exercise within the bank was also excellent. Newsletters and staff circulars kept the bank's employees informed of developments at the time. The executive said one senior English banker advised him at the time: 'The public will forget about this within two years; your staff won't.' The bank heeded this advice.

As the government saw it—and as it was advised by the Central Bank—the prudent way to deal with the crisis was to separate the affairs of ICI from those of AIB and to cope with the crisis at the insurance company as an isolated problem. By taking control of ICI, the government was taking charge of a potential financial time bomb from AIB. Scanlan and his team of bankers had pulled a political masterstroke over the government. The government agreed a deal and no one seemed to question the fact that Scanlan had claimed in late 1984 that all was fine in ICI.

Accountant Billy McCann of Coopers & Lybrand (later PricewaterhouseCoopers) was appointed administrator of ICI on the same evening the government bail-out was announced. His job was to salvage what remained of the struggling company and to ensure that the insurance company kept ticking over so that all its 120,000 policy holders were protected.

The government had felt obliged to step in. 'If the losses [at ICI] could have been accurately quantified,' said Alan Dukes shortly after the deal was announced, 'or their duration clearly limited in time, Allied Irish Banks could, by themselves, have coped with their problem—no doubt at considerable cost to their shareholders and with some disruption. They could not, however, prudently be expected to cope with a situation where both the size of the losses and the duration for which they might run could not be charted with any assurance.' Dukes believed that the Irish taxpayer, not the bank, should pay for AIB's mess, even though there was huge uncertainty over the size of the losses and the length of time that they might last.

This is what made the government's bail-out all the more galling for the public. No one knew how much the collapse would cost the state, yet the government was willing to sign the cheque and then fill in the amount, perhaps several hundred million pounds, at some later date, perhaps decades later. It was a stunning move. Bailing out a private company which had failed to manage its affairs properly was one thing, but agreeing to pick up a massive tab when it didn't even know how much it would be, was something else. The public and opposition politicians reacted with fury.

ICI's losses were estimated to be about £50 million on 15 March—the amount being loaned by the Central Bank to save ICI—but by the following week the figures being bandied about varied wildly from £20 million to £95 million. The estimates did not stop there. About six weeks after the deal a figure of £195 million was cited by an actuary. This heightened fears because the Central Bank had set a limit of £120 million for the cost of ICI's rescue package. Wild rumours circulated that the deal could even cost the state as much as £800 million. AIB had shareholders' funds of £277 million at this time, so ICI's losses, if they proved to be of this magnitude, would undoubtedly have bankrupted the bank. The wild variations in the estimated losses fuelled public concern.

The situation was confused even further by the fact that the government refused to disclose the terms of the secret deal negotiated with AIB over the previous seven days. This fuelled the suspicion that the bank had negotiated a sweetheart deal with the government and led to resentment towards the bank. Bruton, whose department had to deal with the regulatory aspect of the crisis, said the deal was not disclosed in an effort to protect the bank's reputation in the market.

'There was an understanding that if it proved more costly, AIB would give more,' Bruton now recalls. 'The reason it wasn't made public initially was because of a problem of international confidence in the banking system of Ireland generally. Our fear was that if we didn't look after AIB—and we were strongly warned by the Central Bank at that time—it could have huge knock-on effects for the credit worthiness of the state. Therefore we did what you wouldn't normally do. The state was very heavily exposed to international debt . . . and we weren't in a situation to look as coolly and objectively at these sort of warnings as one would like to be able to do. This is how I remember it: once AIB got stabilised—and if the cost of covering the losses at ICI appeared to be greater than we had originally thought—then we expected AIB to pony up more. But we didn't want to put all that in the public domain initially because that advertisement of the ultimate liabilities of AIB might, in the immediate aftermath of the ICI problem, undermine confidence in AIB and thereby defeat the purpose that we were trying to achieve.'

The taxpayer might have been facing huge financial uncertainty, but the bank was off the hook. Its chief executive Gerry Scanlan said the day after the collapse: 'In essence ICI looked like a terrific company at the time . . . I think anybody would say, looking at the company at that time, it was a jewel.' Scanlan was then asked if the bank didn't buy a 'lemon', had AIB turned ICI into one. 'No,' replied Scanlan, 'under AIB's control we identified a lemon.' The bank had deliberately taken an arm's length management approach to running ICI. (It appointed only two non-executive directors to the board of the company up to 1983.) Scanlan said the approach was taken at the request of the insurance regulator, although as FitzGerald's economic adviser at the time, Patrick Honohan, later pointed out, it is hard to believe that the regulator's intention was to limit AIB's ability to protect its investment in the insurance company.

It turned out to be a very expensive lemon for the bank. AIB wrote off its £86 million investment in ICI but, compliments of the government, walked away from hundreds of millions of pounds worth of potential liabilities.

The bank even marked the deal with drinks at AIB Bankcentre the night the government announced it. This angered some ministers. One source close to Bruton said it 'pissed the minister off big time when he heard about that. Instead of accepting this in a grateful way, they had something of a party out at Bankcentre. We had sweat blood and extreme anxiety over the whole thing, and they opened the champagne.' A source close to the bank said officials may have enjoyed a stiff drink after a hard week, but the refreshments were in no way celebratory.

The bank played its hand sweetly. One insider involved in the discussions on the government side said: 'AIB was in the business of protecting AIB and its shareholders, and it played an absolute blinder. They did really well. Every one of us recognised this.' Members of the government at that time still defend the doomsday scenario they painted about the crisis. FitzGerald said: 'It was handled with kid gloves because of the danger that if we didn't, the whole system would have collapsed, we were told. We had no choice in the matter. It wasn't that we were well disposed to AIB. We would have had to deal with the consequences if we didn't get them out of this mess.'

AIB's manoeuvres as the ICI crisis broke in March 1985 have been likened to a Houdini-like escape, but the bank's getaway route had been carefully planned in advance. The bank knew there were difficulties at ICI at the end of 1984. Probing questions about the company's precarious situation from journalists were simply denied at that time. As part of AIB's elaborate public relations exercise, it was decided that when the government rescue was eventually announced the bank's directors would be assigned journalists and analysts to contact to assure them that the bank was stable and would survive the crisis. The bank was ready for the criticism—it had done its homework.

Scanlan and his deputy Egan were the men attributed with having played the government best of all. The pair were 'joined at the hip', said one source. Egan had the people skills that Scanlan lacked, while Scanlan had the demeanour of a hard-nosed negotiator who could stand the bank's ground in heated discussions. 'He [Scanlan] had a very unattractive demeanour to the people on the government side,' said Patrick Honohan, an economic adviser to FitzGerald. 'There was a sense that AIB had put one over on the government and they had come out scot-free.'

A career banker, Belfast-born and Carlow-raised, Scanlan started his career in the bank with the nickname 'Bongo' because of the rhythm he beat on his desk when he stamped cheques. He later became better known among bank workers as the 'Smiling Assassin' after he suspended more than 1,500 AIB staff without pay during the prolonged and acrimonious bank strike of 1992. He was a stereotypical banker. He was a dapper dresser who had a strong interest in horseracing. He was also a shrewd poker player, a skill which benefited him during AIB's negotiations with the government over the ICI mess. He made himself available to speak to the media throughout the crisis. The bank even held a press conference at midnight to ensure it was putting out the right message. However, he did not endear himself to the public when he was photographed with an ear-to-ear smile at one press conference.

Scanlan and Crowley were at the centre of intense talks with Dukes. Scanlan gave the Minister for Finance the impression that AIB could simply walk away from ICI. Dukes had put the two bankers under pressure to force AIB to pay some money towards ICI's debts, but Crowley and Scanlan initially refused to budge. To them, agreeing to pay some unknown quantity at a later date was much too uncertain; this was not within the bank's powers or part of its operation.

Dukes was not sure whether this was just a tactic to get some assistance from the government without having to ask for it, or whether it was a genuine feeling of indifference towards the crisis. 'AIB didn't seem to realise or understand the consequences,' said Dukes. 'They seemed to be under the impression that they could just chop off this limb and walk away, and that there would be no bleeding afterwards. Maybe Scanlan and Crowley were playing an even deeper game than we thought. It was my view—as well as John Bruton's and the Central Bank's—that Scanlan, the main player for the bank, believed he could brazen it out and walk away. And if there was a tab to be picked up, the government would pick it up to save embarrassment to the whole system, but that AIB would not be affected.'

After the initial agreement to bail out the company, the government—not the bank—was on the back foot and trying to force AIB to contribute something towards ICI's liabilities which the state had to pay. Dukes and his Department of Finance officials led the meetings which were often heated and acrimonious. They tried to impress on Crowley and Scanlan that even though they were answerable only to their shareholders, the taxpayers would not tolerate paying a massive bill created in part by the bank's failure to manage one of its subsidiaries.

'They were extremely difficult meetings,' said Dukes. 'I remember saying to Crowley and Scanlan, "Look, this is quite a mess and things are going to get extremely difficult. You may think you are going to win, but there is actually one group of people in this country who are held in lower regard than politicians and that is bankers, and don't you forget it." They were both annoyed at me for saying it, but I felt I had to say something like that to them to put it in a political and decision-making context for them.'

AIB eventually—and reluctantly—agreed to 'pony up' some money, as Bruton put it, to fund the bail-out, but for several weeks in 1985 the stumbling block to an agreement between the government and the bank centred on how much AIB would cough up. 'I remember having a long discussion with them,' said Dukes. 'We weren't getting very far. Eventually they agreed to look at some idea I had. We had a break for half an hour. I went back out to my office and I had a pot of coffee brought into me and I sent a bottle of whiskey into them in the hope that it would soften them up. I don't know whether it did or not, but they consumed some of the whiskey. It was at that point that we were doing those kind of things to help get discussions moving.'

By October 1985 the deficit at ICI was estimated to be £164 million, spread over several years. It was expected that cash of £100 million would be required, £50 million to £70 million of which would be needed in the first year and the rest over later years. Despite the estimated deficit, reports from London still suggested that the overall losses at the insurance company could reach £500 million.

The Central Bank was faced with a difficult task cleaning up the mess; it had to look at ways of raising the £164 million, but could not appear to let AIB off too lightly or penalise the other banks in the Republic over AIB's mistakes at ICI. The final funding plan was released by the Central Bank on 4 October 1985. A new administration company called Icarom was set up to handle the long-term winding up of ICI which would take several decades. It was decided that an advance of £100 million would be made to the company at a low interest rate, initially 2 per cent. This would provide it with enough cash for several years.

AIB got its knuckles rapped by the government in the arrangements. The complex funding plan involved all the Irish banks paying £7 million a year between them to cover the difference between the preferential 2 per cent rate and the market rates. AIB paid £5.5 million a year, far in excess of what others were paying and higher than its proportional share of the banking market. This was because the debacle was regarded as AIB's blunder, so it had to pay extra. 'The ICI mess happened largely because the bank accepted conventional wisdom that banking and insurance were the same business. The bank found that in ICI it had a pig in a poke,' said a former senior AIB executive. The bank was also forced to place a deposit of £70 million with the Central Bank. The £100 million advance given by the state in 1985 was eventually repaid on time, in September 2000.

There was little sympathy in the business community for AIB over the government's deal. According to a survey conducted in September 1985, 78 per cent of 100 business managers said AIB was not paying enough, and 46 per cent felt the bank should bear the full cost.

AIB continued about its business as if nothing had happened. Shortly after ICI's collapse, the bank announced profits of £85.4 million for 1984—almost as much as the bank had lost in the insurer. This prompted debate that the bank should have paid for the ICI clean-up itself. After all, the bank had recorded £83 million in profits in 1983 and £85.4 million in 1984 and would go on to make profits of more than £80 million in 1985; it could well afford to cover the cost of ICI's losses from its own profits.

However, it was the manner in which AIB announced its 1984 profits that bothered the politicians. 'It was very irritating,' said FitzGerald. 'They played the whole affair down once they got the money. Niall Crowley was a friend of mine, but I didn't like the way they behaved subsequently.' Dukes said: 'I thought they were stupid from their own point of view; they created an unnecessary level of aggro against them.' The bank appeared to be only concerned about reassuring its shareholders. This—as FitzGerald wrote in his 1991 autobiography—took 'precedence over any sense of public responsibility on this occasion; and the effect on the credibility of the banking system with the broader public was certainly very negative'.

The bank also announced that it would be paying its shareholders dividends in 1985 despite all that happened. Bruton took this on the chin, again saying this was all for the good of the market. 'While I personally regard this as a somewhat insensitive announcement,' Bruton told the Dáil, 'highlighting the bank's much greater concern for shareholders than for the policy holders at ICI or the general public, I am advised that a cut in dividend would be taken in the stock markets here and abroad as a signal—in this case false—that the underlying strength of AIB was somewhat damaged.'

FitzGerald and Fine Gael suffered for not being able to demand changes at AIB over its handling of ICI for fear of how the stock markets might react. Once again the fear of 'how the market would react' forced Fine Gael politicians into a corner. One economic commentator said the government of the time were 'blinking fearfully at the financial markets like rabbits caught in the headlamps of a truck'. They were terrified of what the markets could do to AIB and the state.

As for AIB, its share price surged by 25 per cent within two days of the Central Bank announcing the rescue package. There were no resignations at the bank. 'AIB had no option but to do what it did,' said a source close to the bank. 'The organisation first had to save itself and bottom out the losses at ICI and then sever its links with the company.'

Another source close to the bank said AIB had to pay dividends after ICI. To the international banks supporting the bank, uncertainty would have led to a withdrawal of cash from AIB. Calling the exact scale of the losses at £86 million and still saying it would pay dividends for the year comforted the international banks and they responded by keeping faith with the bank.

'That essential reassurance saved the bank, but at home it seemed like the height of arrogance,' said one source close to AIB. 'Politicians and the media went wild. Nobody saw that we were fighting for our life and that it could have meant the end of the bank.'

Scanlan did not fare too badly from the whole affair. He bought 50,000 shares in AIB when the share price was depressed on the eve of the Central Bank's announcement. The controversial purchase was raised at the bank's subsequent annual general meeting by a former AIB employee who queried the ethics of the purchase, given that the share price later rose by 165 pence. But Scanlan said his conscience was clear. He said he had spoken about the purchase beforehand with Crowley, who in turn had received the approval of the board. Scanlan said the shares were bought after the company had issued its profit figures for the previous year. He was proud that AIB had got out of ICI 'on the cheap': 'I make no apologies to anyone. The most important thing for us to do was to maintain confidence in the bank. We did what was in the best interests of the bank's stakeholders, its staff, its depositors, its shareholders and the public at large. What do people want?' he said in an interview.

A senior banker who worked with Scanlan said: 'From the bank's point of view Gerry was right to do what he did because there would have been uncertainty. You either find a solution or you walk away. It would have caused difficulty for the bank. The "tail" for the insurance claims was too long, which means the uncertainty was too long.'

The cost of the ICI bail-out resurfaced in 1991 when the leader of the Progressive Democrats Des O'Malley was Minister for Industry and

London businessman Ken Bates photographed in the early 1970s, around the time of his arrival in Dublin and the establishment of Irish Trust Bank. (*The Irish Times*)

Chelsea football club's new owner, Russian billionaire Roman Abramovich, with Ken Bates in the background. Bates sold the club to the Russian in 2003. (Empics)

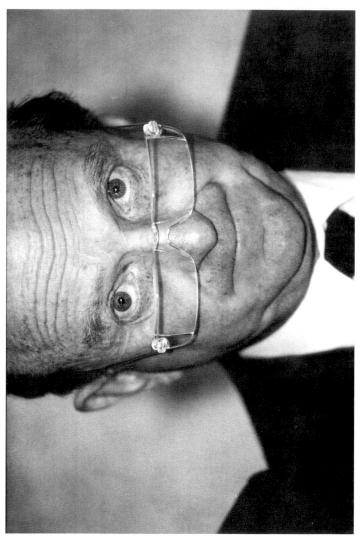

Dublin accountant Paddy Shortall was appointed liquidator of Ken Bates' Irish Trust Bank and Patrick Gallagher's Merchant Banking, to sort out their affairs after the collapse of the banks. (*The Irish Times*)

Property tycoon Patrick Gallagher (right) leaves Belfast Magistrates Court after facing criminal charges over his running of the Northern Irish subsidiary of Merchant Banking. (Pacemaker Press International)

Businessman Joe Moore founded PMPA, one of the country's largest motor insurers. The company's in-house bank, PMPS, went bust when the government appointed an administrator to the insurance company in October 1983. (*The Irish Times*)

Gerry Scanlan, AIB's chief executive at the time of the Insurance Corporation of Ireland scandal, when the state picked up the multimillion pound tab after the failure of the bank's insurance subsidiary. (*The Irish Times*)

Irish Permanent managing director Edmund Farrell arrives at the building society's headquarters in his chauffeur-driven car, for a crunch board meeting to decide his future in the company, in April 1993. (*The Irish Times*)

Businessman Ben Dunne of Dunnes Stores shakes hands with Fianna Fáil leader Charles Haughey in 1986. Dunne's antics in a Florida hotel in 1992 eventually led to the exposure of both massive payments to Haughey, and the secret Irish-managed Ansbacher deposits in the Cayman Islands. (Photocall Ireland)

The late Dublin businessman Des Traynor, Charles Haughey's bagman and the architect of the Ansbacher scheme, concealed his clients' money in the offshore tax dodge. (*The Irish Times*)

Former National Irish Bank chief executive Jim Lacey arrives at the DIRT inquiry in 1999. Lacey was chief executive of the bank when the controversial CMI investment scheme was established. (Photocall Ireland)

Fianna Fáil TD Beverley Flynn leaving Dáil Éireann. Flynn sold CMI products to customers of National Irish Bank before she became a TD. Those customers eventually made large tax settlements. (Empics)

A reluctant whistle blower: former AIB group internal auditor Tony Spollen was one of the first people to question the bank's potential liability to deposit income retention tax (DIRT) on accounts belonging to people who claimed to be living outside Ireland. (Photocall Ireland)

National Irish Bank wrote off £243,000 of a £263,000 loan owed by Fianna Fáil TD John Ellis, after the collapse of his meat business, Stanlow Trading. (Photocall Ireland)

Commerce, in charge of monitoring the insurance sector. O'Malley had been on the opposition benches at the time of the crisis at ICI.

Around 1991, AIB approached him seeking a licence to set up another insurer, this time a life assurance business called Ark Life. O'Malley felt that AIB had already had a shot at the insurance market and failed, and that AIB had secured too sweet a deal from the state seven years previously in the ICI bail-out. He said the taxpayer was unfairly and disproportionately paying for AIB's mistakes of 1985. 'I thought the generosity with which AIB was treated was excessive,' O'Malley said, 'and I couldn't understand why the state had not taken a stake in the bank.'

The PD minister dragged his heels over the Ark Life application, trying to extract more money from AIB. He had been advised by the Attorney General that he could not use the application to leverage more money from the bank, but informally he felt he could put some pressure on the bank to cough up more money. One government source said: 'O'Malley wanted a second bite of the cherry. He was absolutely adamant that there would be no further state bail-out for AIB.'

O'Malley stood firm. In the autumn of 1992, AIB eventually agreed to pay £8.75 million (€11.11 million) every year for 20 years to meet some of the cost in the administration of ICI. It was a controversial decision within the bank, especially given that a cast-iron guarantee had been made in 1985 that it would not have to pay more. Even though some AIB staff objected to the new deal, it was generally felt that, given the bank's growing wealth, it should contribute more.

Peter Sutherland, who was chairman of AIB from 1989 to 1993, said the agreement was in 'the best interests of its shareholders, customers and staff, as well as meeting the concerns of the community at large'. Many politicians and commentators saw it as a much fairer deal for the taxpayer than the agreement negotiated by the Fine Gael-led government in 1985.

'We should have got a lot more,' said O'Malley. 'I would have been anxious that, at an earlier stage, the state should have taken equity in AIB as part of the arrangement because AIB became very profitable very quickly. Its share price wasn't seriously affected. The state would have made a lot of money if equity had been taken in the bank. But it was too late to do this in 1992.'

Many commentators have, like O'Malley, queried why the government did not take a stake in AIB—or at least negotiated an option to acquire shares in the bank at a later date—in return for its extra-ordinarily generous rescue package. A stake could have reaped huge rewards for the exchequer, given the massive rise in AIB's share price in subsequent years.

'I was completely against it,' said Dukes. 'The last thing you need is a state-owned bank because it will end up with every lame duck, politically attractive proposition being brought to it for finance. The more the state owns of it, the less it will be possible to refuse. That's a complete horror story in my book.' FitzGerald agreed. 'The state is better off out of financial institutions,' he said. 'If you don't privatise a bank and it gets in difficulties again, you might not be able to bail it out again. There was a case for taking a stake in the bank, but I was reluctant to do so.'

Honohan said the government was not in a position to demand a stake. 'AIB said they were going to close ICI down. The government wasn't in a negotiating place. Out of politeness, the bank was coming to the government saying: "We are closing this subsidiary." There was nothing for the government to take.'

But the reality was—and none of the politicians knew it—that AIB couldn't walk away from one of its subsidiaries because, according to one experienced banker, in the bonds issued there was what was called in banking circles 'a cross default clause'. This means that if one sub-sidiary defaults on a debt, bond investors are entitled to call a default, which in turn makes all the bank's bonds and inter-bank loans repayable upon demand.

'AIB would have been disgraced in the international capital markets if they had defaulted on the obligations of a major subsidiary,' said the banker. 'Dukes' excuse for not taking equity doesn't hold water. The government could have taken options over 25 per cent of the equity. This would have meant they wouldn't have owned any part of the bank, but over the long term they could have exercised options. Had they done so then, today more than 20 years on, they could have had shares worth over €3 billion.'

As of the end of December 2004, AIB had paid Icarom (the administration company) €134 million with another €89.4 million due over the following eight years. Separately, the state gave Icarom an interest free advance of £32 million (€40.6 million) in 1993. This was due for repayment in 2012, but was repaid ten years early by the company.

Icarom ended up making some money for the state. The administrators sold off ICI's main subsidiaries, Credit Finance Bank and the Insurance Corporation of Ireland (Life), as well as the company's continuing Irish business, raising €173 million for the exchequer. Both subsidiaries traded profitably through the administration and after their sale. The life company and non-life business continue to trade as part of Irish Life & Permanent and the Allianz Group respectively.

More money came from a legal action taken by the bank against Ernst & Whinney when they sued the accountancy firm over the due diligence it carried out on ICI when AIB bought the insurance company in 1983. The case was settled in October 1993—with no admission of liability by Ernst & Whinney—before it went to trial. Ernst & Whinney's settlement ended up contributing roughly £39 million (€49 million) after legal costs. The administrator also managed to recoup about €300 million from ICI's reinsurers.

Patrick Honohan, FitzGerald's economic adviser at the time of the ICI collapse, believes that the pattern of poor management at ICI can be traced back to the days when it was owned by Irish Shipping. According to Honohan, Irish Shipping also failed because, like ICI, it shot too high, gearing itself for rapid expansion but risking it all on the possibility of massive future liabilities.

It is expected that there will be no eventual cost to the taxpayer from the ICI debacle. PricewaterhouseCoopers' managing partner, Donal O'Connor, the current administrator of Icarom, says the only cost to the taxpayer is the interest forgone on the €40.6 million (£32 million) advance between 1993 and 2002. He said current projections show that this cost will be more than offset at the end of the administration. The profit has primarily arisen because of the falling interest rates of the last ten years. Assessing the final financial outcome, Bruton said: 'Our decision to rescue the bank was commercially if not morally vindicated.'

But how much did AIB contribute? A study by the Economic and Social Research Institute (ESRI) revealed that AIB contributed 78.1 per cent to the rescue costs. The Ernst & Whinney settlement provided 17.5 per cent, while the other banks paid a total of 5.5 per cent. The taxpayer's contribution was a negative 1.1 per cent. Honohan found that the cost of the bail-out in 1985 money terms was £185 million. But this figure includes the £85 million that AIB had invested to buy ICI. Leaving this aside, the bail-out cost £99 million in round figures. Of

this, again in terms of 1985 money, Ernst & Whinney's contribution
was £32 million, AIB paid £43 million and the other banks contributed
£6 million. The state's contribution was £18 million.

At what stage the administration of ICI will be complete is anyone's
guess. It is hard to estimate, especially given the precariousness of the
insurance industry. The bail-out of ICI is expected to last until at least
2050 because of outstanding insurance claims. It was reported in 2005
that the company was facing claims totalling €77 million from people
suffering from the effects of exposure to asbestos. Some claims underwritten by ICI in the mid-1980s relate to environmental hazards and
health cover that will lead to claims being processed for another 35–40
years. Given the nature of insurance claims, Icarom is regularly drawn
into litigation dating back several years.

The ICI debacle continues to cost AIB money today, and it will
continue to cost the bank annual multimillion euro payments
until 2012, 27 years after the insurer was put into administration.
Administrators and department officials, as representatives of the
company's owner, the taxpayer, still travel to legal depositions to
testify to being shareholders of the company.

The FitzGerald government is still criticised for being too soft on
AIB back in 1985. It has been suggested that the government should
have played a more neutral role and allowed ICI to collapse without
any intervention by the ruling politicians. However, the government
would have been faced with heavy costs in this scenario with a different and perhaps more costly kind of solution, given the number of
people and businesses with ICI policies.

The country was also still in a deep recession at the time. Allowing
such a large insurer, which had tentacles stretching into businesses and
households across the country, would have sent the wrong message to
the international market and damaged the Republic's credit rating.

The 1985 deal for AIB was also attributed to a lack of business
experience in FitzGerald's government. Others have blamed poor
advice from civil servants. Honohan who was not involved in the
negotiations on the bail-out said: 'The politicians were frightened by
the technical advice they got. They took the only decision that was
presented to them. The technical advice was bad. The people were too
risk adverse for what was facing them as a meltdown situation. That
shows a lack of confidence and real command of the situation. This
was high-wire stuff.'

'It was a sting by the bank,' said another senior civil servant in the Department of Finance at the time. 'The bank knew it was going to lose huge sums of money. It knew it had bought a lemon and it waited until it was at crisis point, and knew that the government could not back off.'

The massive handout of taxpayers' money might well have saved AIB's skin. It is unlikely that the bank would be recording billion euro plus profits now if it had dealt with the clean-up at ICI.

The bail-out was an astounding move by the Fine Gael-Labour coalition government of the day and showed the country's taxpayers that the country's largest bank can always rely on the politicians to bail them out whenever their investments turn sour.

The government said its deal was 'responsible'. In the Dáil debate of 27 March 1985 on the bail-out, Workers' Party TD Tomás MacGiolla said: 'I find when people are being responsible it means they are standing by the big boys in some place or other.'

In the case of AIB in the ICI debacle, the politicians stood by the big boys of Irish banking after they walked away from their mess, leaving the taxpayer to pay for the clean-up.

Chapter 5

Edmund Farrell: his removal from Irish Permanent

The writing was on the wall when Edmund Farrell walked into the boardroom of the Irish Permanent Building Society headquarters on St Stephen's Green in Dublin at 9 a.m. on Friday, 2 April 1993. The board of the building society had gathered to decide on his future as chairman of the Irish Permanent, then the largest building society in the state. Farrell sat at one end of the table, the building society's chief legal adviser Cathal MacCarthy at the other. Between them were the nine members of the board who would decide whether Farrell should remain with the building society, a business with which his family had been connected since 1939.

MacCarthy was charged with the task of leading the investigation into a series of extraordinary payments totalling £1.33 million made to Farrell dating back to 1986. The payments only came to light when stockbrokers, accountants and solicitors trawled through the building society's books while preparing to float the business on the stock exchange making it a public company.

On 2 April, MacCarthy had to explain the payments to the board. The money trail was so complex and the issues so significant for the future of the building society and Farrell that the meeting lasted

12 hours. The extravagant payments ultimately spelt the end of Farrell's 21-year career with the Irish Permanent and the Farrell family's association with the building society that began when Farrell's father joined the society before the Second World War.

The meeting was one of the most dramatic in the history of the Irish Permanent. Everyone in the building society knew it. The newspapers had widely reported that a crunch board meeting concerning Farrell was taking place that morning. At one stage during the marathon meeting the curtains of the first-floor room had to be closed as press photographers had climbed the trees opposite the building in St Stephen's Green, hoping to snap a few pictures of an embattled Farrell facing his interrogators at the boardroom table.

The atmosphere in the boardroom was tense. It was in this room that Mary Aikenhead, founder of the Sisters of Charity, had set up a 14-bed ward in 1834 that later became St Vincent's Hospital, one of the first Catholic hospitals in the country. There was little charity shown on 2 April, however, as financial detail was poured over, detail that would end the career of one of the country's most prominent businessmen.

The board members took careful notes as MacCarthy went through the background to the payments. Few breaks were taken; sandwiches and drinks were brought into the room during the course of the day. Occasionally Farrell left the room to speak in private with his solicitor Stuart Margetson of Matheson Ormsby Prentice, one of Dublin's top law firms. Farrell showed no signs of stress during the proceedings. 'He didn't raise his voice,' said a source who was present at the meeting. 'You never knew what he was thinking. He was grace under pressure.'

When the meeting ended at 9 p.m. about 70 pages of notes had been taken by a secretary who had followed the day's proceedings. The breadth of evidence presented at the meeting and the explosive nature of the revelations was considered at length by the board.

On 19 April the board decided to dismiss Farrell as chairman and as an employee of the building society. The Farrell family's 40-year grip on the Irish Permanent had been loosened. But it would take more than four years of legal wrangling before Edmund Farrell walked away from what many people believed had turned into more of a family heirloom than a financial institution.

Farrell owed his career to his father, also Edmund. Farrell Snr, whose family owned the Capitol and Ambassador cinemas in Dublin, joined the Irish Temperance Permanent Benefit Building Society in 1939. His own father had been Lord Mayor of Dublin. The building society had been established in 1884 to help members build their own homes. When it was expanded to include savers and depositors, the building society was renamed the Irish Permanent Building Society to reflect the change in its status. Farrell Snr became secretary almost a decade before his son Edmund was born. At the time the building society had assets of £3,000. Farrell Snr took charge of the building society when he became managing director in the 1950s.

By the time Farrell Jnr succeeded his father as managing director in 1975, Irish Permanent had outstripped its rivals—it was the country's largest building society with assets of £141 million. It was also one of the biggest lenders in the state. Farrell Snr's drive and strict control of the building society had turned Irish Permanent into one of Ireland's greatest financial success stories.

Speaking publicly for the first time since his removal from Irish Permanent in 1993, Farrell said his father transformed the building society from 'a part-time operation. He was a pioneer and very much based the building society on the English model. He just had a conviction that if people wanted to buy houses, it had to work, so he was prepared to take on the challenge.'

Farrell said his father was a cross between the legendary Dublin hotelier P. V. Doyle and Michael Fingleton who has run the Irish Nationwide Building Society since the 1970s. Those who knew Farrell's father said he was a tough businessman who had strong opinions on business life and how his building society should be run. He was also controversial. At a dinner around 1970, he went around a table of journalists asking each of them who they believed was the greatest person in history. When one journalist turned the question on Farrell, he replied: 'Adolf Hitler.'

Farrell Snr certainly ran Irish Permanent like a dictator. He dismissed any opposition to his plans, believing he knew what was right for Irish Permanent. He was a hugely influential character in Irish life. In the 1960s and early 70s people faced an uphill battle trying to secure a mortgage. People like Farrell provided the money. In the days when people had to queue for mortgages, Farrell opened doors for them. He remained the driving force behind the rapid growth of the Irish Permanent until his premature death in 1975 at the age of 62.

'He didn't get the opportunity to do as much of his hobbies—

golfing, fishing and swimming—as he would have liked,' said Farrell Jnr. 'He was taking over a provident society at the time and his secretary had just died. On his own he was chairman, chief executive and secretary of the building society. It was too much for one person because the growth of the business was explosive.'

The building society sector enjoyed a massive boom in the 1970s and 80s due to economic changes in Ireland. Building societies reacted to growing populations, rising incomes and a tax regime that encouraged people to buy houses, and they enthusiastically developed their branch networks to cope with the demands of savers and borrowers. Three protracted bank strikes between 1966 and 1976 added to the growth of the sector. Building societies grew to such an extent that their deposits accounted for 18 per cent of the total savings in deposit-taking financial institutions in 1985. This compared with 5 per cent in 1965, despite the fact that over those 20 years there had even been a significant reduction in the number of building societies.

Farrell Snr responded to the changing Ireland, transforming Irish Permanent into a major financial institution. By the early 1990s the plan to turn the financial institutions into a publicly quoted bank was conceived. It was no wonder that in the 1970s Farrell Snr was as protective of his building society as he was eager to see his son succeed him at the helm of the business.

The young Farrell initially had no intention of following in his father's footsteps. Instead, Farrell Jnr wanted to become a surgeon. He studied medicine at University College Dublin after attending Blackrock College. He qualified as a doctor, but after a year working as a hospital intern he was diagnosed with an inner ear condition that affected his sense of balance and his ability to treat patients. The condition forced him to drop his plans for a medical career and in 1972 he asked his father for a job in Irish Permanent. It was the only thing he could think of at the time. He worked in several branches getting to know how the business worked.

Farrell Snr's dying wish to the board was that his son would take over from him as managing director of Irish Permanent. The board of the building society was in awe of the man and agreed to his request. In 1975 the 28-year-old Farrell was appointed managing director. That same year, he bought a large new house in Foxrock, one of the more affluent suburbs of Dublin on the southside of the city. The house, Grasmere, would be central to his downfall 18 years later.

After taking control of the building society, Farrell overcame his inexperience and some resentment from the staff, who felt that the company, despite being owned by thousands of shareholders, had become too closely linked to the Farrells.

Farrell took over where his father had left off. He continued to work to grow the business, although he said he was 'more accessible and more of a consensus builder' than his father. However, like his father the young Farrell was more than willing to stand up to shareholders and the state if he felt he was doing the right thing in the building society. Sources who worked with him said his laid-back approach contrasted with his father's management style. Farrell Jnr's independent thinking, though, was quickly recognised. In 1978 and again in 1982 he shunned the Irish Building Societies' Association cartel on interest rates and in 1979 he rejected a government directive to facilitate home loans for low-income families.

In the mid-1980s Farrell became entangled in a row with the Fine Gael-Labour coalition after the Minister for the Environment in that government, John Boland, wanted to dilute the power of the building societies. Farrell's antipathy towards Boland was widely known; he once surprised a financial journalist by offering to have his photograph taken striking the punch-bag in his home gym with a picture of Boland taped to it. Politically, Farrell was very much in Fianna Fáil's corner; he was particularly close to Charles Haughey who led the party between 1979 and 1992.

Farrell also showed he was willing to play big and flash with the building society's chequebook when the need arose. In 1979 he bought the Irish Permanent a new headquarters for £8 million. The building, 56–59 St Stephen's Green, known as Seán Lemass House, was purchased from property developer Patrick Gallagher who, like Farrell, would later see his fortunes fall in Irish financial circles. Gallagher had bought the property for £5.5 million two months earlier. Farrell later named the building Edmund Farrell House after the father he revered. He said he looked at every available office block in the greater Dublin area, but the St Stephen's Green building was the only one that suited Irish Permanent because of its size and central location.

Even though Farrell was managing director of Ireland's largest building society, he was rarely seen in public. In the 1980s he appeared at the ringside whenever Irish boxing champion Barry McGuigan, who was sponsored by Irish Permanent, was fighting. Despite staying largely below the parapet, he did not shy away from standing up to shareholders during the building society's annual general meetings. He spoke out frequently at the meetings, defending the board's decisions during shareholder revolts. He regularly frustrated attempts by ordinary shareholders to be voted on to the board of the building society and to find out exactly how much each Irish Permanent director was being paid.

Under Farrell's control Irish Permanent's assets continued to grow, and Farrell rewarded himself and his fellow directors handsomely. In 1991 the eight directors of Irish Permanent treated themselves to a payout of £716,000 in fees, executive salaries and pensions. This compared to the £404,000 paid to the directors of rival building society EBS during the same year. He used his earnings to live the good life. His interests included jogging, swimming, fishing in Co. Galway and water sports in the Caribbean. A keep-fit fanatic, he trained regularly at the gym in his Foxrock home. The detached house in south Dublin stood on over an acre.

Farrell's own pay and benefits were at this time regarded within the building society as excessive by the standards of the day. He said that in the mid-1980s he was being paid an annual salary of between £150,000 and £200,000, had the use of a chauffeur-driven car and was receiving loans from Irish Permanent at very favourable rates. 'Because I had started as managing director at the age of 28,' said Farrell, 'by 1986 I would have been earning a fairly big whack. It would have been the highest in the society and there was a concern how people would react to it.'

Farrell knew his pay would be viewed as grossly disproportionate and he was concerned that the details would end up in the newspapers, leaving him facing potentially awkward questions from shareholders. For a man who craved privacy, this greatly concerned him.

In 1986 Farrell learned that new legislation was about to be passed which would tighten the rules governing the running of building societies. The new legislation would, among other measures, force the Irish Permanent to disclose how much it was paying each of its directors. Farrell and the building society had to act if they were to keep his salary under wraps.

The new rules were long overdue. It was felt at the time that the Registrar of Friendly Societies, the regulator of building societies, was not providing adequate cover to the sector, especially given that building societies had billions of pounds more on deposit than a decade earlier. In 1986 building societies had to reveal only the lump sum being paid to all its directors in its annual filings to the registrar. They did not have to divulge how much it was paying each director, so any massive salaries paid to individual directors—such as the one to Farrell—could be hidden in the lump sum paid to the entire board. For Farrell there was safety in numbers, but changes were on the way.

In 1986 Farrell and the Irish Permanent tried to devise a way around the pending new rules. He decided to accept a substantial pay cut and in return the building society devised an extraordinary deal as compensation. The negotiations with the board leading up to the deal and the details of his agreement with the building society were revealed to the public when the case between Irish Permanent and Farrell came before the High Court in 1997.

Four years after becoming managing director, Farrell had signed an unusual contract of employment with the building society. On 22 November 1979 the board approved an agreement with Farrell to employ him as managing director until 31 December 2012. Even nowadays a 33-year contract is unheard of in Irish financial circles. At this stage he was being paid an annual salary of £45,000. The 1979 agreement stipulated that the salary was index-linked, meaning that it would increase over time. The agreement also stated that he could be given extra money and top-ups in his salary on a regular basis at the discretion of the board.

It was later claimed in court that from the 1980s up to his dismissal in 1993 Farrell spent long periods of time away from the business, that he could be contacted at home on many occasions, and that he was not actively involved in the day-to-day running of the building society. He said he felt his time was better spent at home planning strategies to develop the building society when he was not needed at the office. During this time Irish Permanent expanded rapidly, earning the largest market share of any Irish building society. The High Court was told in 1997 that the building society was effectively run at this time by senior managers and several directors, and that Farrell played a minimal role in its management.

In June 1986 it was decided that Farrell's salary would have to be reduced to £60,000 a year—in advance of the new legislation—bringing it more in line with the industry norm. However, if Farrell was going to earn less, then he would have to be compensated for the

reduction over the remaining 26 years of his contract. 'If he was getting reduced payments, he wanted his money out,' said a well-placed
source in the society. In addition to the £1.33 million that the society
agreed to pay him in compensation for his reduced salary, Irish
Permanent also offered to pay an additional £1 million as an indemnity if he was forced to pay tax on the lump sum.

A complex structure was set up by Farrell and the society to avoid
the mandatory reporting of the lump sum to the regulator. He would
resign as a director and employee of the society, and a trust company
based in the Isle of Man called Drummond would agree a contract of
service with the building society on his behalf. He would then be re-
employed as managing director. Even though it was later revealed that
Farrell was not one of the beneficiaries of the Drummond trust—
members of his family were—he received substantial payments from
the company.

Transferring the £1.33 million to Farrell created some difficulties for
the building society. The legislation governing the running of building societies meant that they had to seek shareholder approval before
agreeing such transactions with directors. The plan was that he would
resign as a director in order to receive the money. He then would
not have to reveal the payment, as required by law. However, his
resignation was never disclosed to the registrar. He was co-opted back
on to the board again once his new salary arrangements were in place.
He should have stood for election as a director at an annual general
meeting, but this also did not happen.

Discussions took place in the Isle of Man on 30 July 1986 about the
Drummond scheme and Farrell's £1.33 million payment. Farrell and
three others were present at the meeting. A private aircraft was hired
to take the men to the Isle of Man and was paid for by the society. Paul
Gallagher, senior counsel representing the building society in its 1997
case against Farrell, described this meeting as 'farcical'. He said there
was a 'pretence of negotiations' as the service contract had already
been agreed by Farrell and the building society. Even though the
building society was compensating Farrell for 26 years of future earnings, his new contract was only for ten years. 'Apart from the incongruity and absurdity of paying in advance a capital sum for 26 and a
half years' service, they were not even getting that in return . . . all [the
society] was getting in return, on the best view, was a commitment for
ten years,' said Gallagher.

By the end of 1986 Farrell had secured his ten-year contract with the building society and it was agreed that he would be paid £100,000 a year, excluding directors' fees which could increase with the approval of the board. He was also given a company car with a full-time chauffeur-cum-bodyguard as well as travelling and miscellaneous expenses.

However, things did not go according to plan. The Drummond payment of £1.33 million to Farrell eventually collapsed, as the building society needed the Central Bank's permission to make the payment, and Farrell was unwilling to approach the bank for fear it would leak out. According to Gallagher, Farrell and the Irish Permanent were 'paranoid' that if they sought permission from the Central Bank, 'the matter would somehow get into the public domain'. Gallagher said there was also concern about the legitimacy of the tax structure used in the deal.

Some of the £1.33 million was used to buy gilts, a type of security that could be sold outside the state without alerting the financial regulator. But most of the money sat in a bank account waiting to be transferred to Farrell. So a new plan was devised the following year involving a series of transactions to extract large sums of money from the building society.

On 6 August 1987, the board approved the purchase of Grasmere, Farrell's house in Foxrock, for £275,000 and agreed to lease it back to him for £17,500 a year in rent. Three mortgages that had been taken out by Farrell on the property—£43,000 in 1975, £70,000 in 1981 and £95,000 in 1981—were paid off three weeks later. As part of the deal, it was agreed that he could buy the house back at any time at a fixed price of £275,000. The board of the building society justified the purchase saying the house would be used for corporate entertainment. The purchase and lease documents were signed and witnessed by the society's then deputy managing director George Tracey. On the documents Farrell was described as the tenant and the building society as his land-lord. The building society later claimed that the price paid for the house was £35,000 higher than two valuations obtained by the society.

In November 1989 renovations began on Grasmere. The work, which continued until June 1991 when Farrell bought back the house from his employer, cost the Irish Permanent £437,000. Security systems were installed. Gardens were landscaped and the rooms of the house were decorated. Almost £87,000 was spent on 'soft furnishings' such as curtains, bedspreads and rugs. Farrell later repaid only

£34,000 to the building society for these. Among the items bought for the house (by the building society) were black silk sheets for one of the bedrooms. Farrell even deducted some of his rental payments due to the society because of the disruption during the renovations. It was later claimed that Farrell and his wife Zora spent £144,000 of the renovation money in a five-week period without any approval from the board. It was also claimed that information presented to the board regarding the transactions was deliberately misleading.

Farrell said the idea that the building society would buy the house and enter a lease agreement with its managing director was not his. He said the building society had in the 1980s examined the possibility of acquiring or merging with other banks or financial institutions in the United States, Britain and Europe and that it had been proposed to the board that Grasmere could be used to entertain visitors from abroad and as a venue to conduct business. So was any business conducted on the property? 'Not a huge amount as it transpired,' said Farrell, 'but then we had considered extending the property to cater for overseas and overnight guests. That would have meant an extension, but when I saw the cost I said I wouldn't even bring this to the board.' He claimed that the board of the building society approved all the payments on Grasmere.

Irish Permanent later claimed in its legal action against Farrell that in July 1990 Kelvin Smythe, a financial consultant working for the Irish Permanent and a confidant and personal adviser to Farrell, telephoned a director of the building society, Enda Hogan, demanding that £2 million be paid to Farrell. It was not made clear why he was asking for the money, but the full amount was never paid. However, the building society eventually paid £100,000 to a company called Trivo.

This money was eventually used to buy a house called Portcairn Lodge, a fishing lodge on Lough Corrib, which is popular with anglers, near Oughterard, Co. Galway. Farrell became the owner of the property through a complex series of transactions. Farrell said: 'The society claimed that it was their money that was used to buy it on the basis that fees paid to Smythe or his company were used to purchase it. The house was put into my name—or the shares of a company that owned the house—were put into my name. I signed share transfer forms from Mr Smythe to correct the situation, but he kept them until he needed them, until he was accused of conspiring to defraud the society.' Smythe died several years ago.

On 10 February 1988 the building society made a payment of £510,064 to Farrell. The money came in part from the profit on the sale of the gilt that had been purchased by the building society for him. However, £285,000 of the money was described in Irish Permanent's accounts that year as 'sundry advertising'.

In 1991 another novel way of paying Farrell involved a golden hand-cuff payment of £300,000 to compensate him for undertaking not to work for a rival building society for 12 months after his departure. The payment, known technically as a restrictive covenant payment, was bizarre, given that Farrell still had five years left to run on his contract and that Irish Permanent had an option to renew it for another ten years. Again, the payment involved Smythe, but this time he used a company called Quasar Corporation based in Delaware in the United States.

On 18 December 1991 the building society agreed to sell Grasmere back to Farrell for the same amount he received for it in 1987—£275,000—despite the fact that it had spent £437,000 renovating the house and that the house was valued at about £600,000 at the time.

Paul Gallagher told the High Court in 1997 that the golden hand-cuff payment was 'a device probably thought up by Mr Smythe as a means of obtaining from the building society in 1991 a substantial sum of money which would have enabled, and did enable, Dr Farrell to repurchase his home, Grasmere, from the society'. Gallagher said it was 'just part of the devices which Mr Smythe was busily assisting in thinking up and executing to get funds for Dr Farrell'. Farrell said the restrictive covenant payment was not his idea and it had been approved by the board.

Farrell's decision to press ahead with the Irish Permanent's conversion from a mutual society into a demutualised publicly quoted company ultimately exposed the extraordinary payments he received between 1987 and 1991. The men he headhunted to join the board and lead the building society towards a flotation were instrumental in his removal. To float, the building society had to get its house in order, and that involved washing its dirty laundry in public.

Throughout the late 1980s Farrell and the board of the Irish Permanent had been eyeing up a number of possible overseas acquisition and merger targets in advance of a change in the legislation that would allow building societies to compete on a level playing field with the banks. After looking abroad Farrell and the board decided they would try to buy the state bank, icc. In 1990 the London merchant bank Henry Ansbacher advised the building society that the best way to raise the money to buy icc was to convert the building society to a publicly quoted company and apply for a banking licence. (Richard Fenhalls, Ansbacher's then chief executive, even suggested Des Traynor, the Dublin accountant and architect of the offshore Ansbacher scheme, as a possible chief executive of the new bank. Irish Permanent ended up buying Guinness & Mahon, the Dublin merchant bank used by Traynor for his secret Ansbacher scheme.)

To bring about the changes, Farrell needed new blood. Among the directors brought in to spearhead the flotation was Roy Douglas. He was headhunted personally by Farrell from aib in July 1991. Farrell wanted Irish Permanent to be the first building society to float on the Irish Stock Exchange and he believed Douglas was the man to reassure a sceptical Central Bank that this was the right move. Douglas was trusted by the mandarins in Dame Street, having worked in the Central Bank for 17 years. Farrell felt he was the ideal candidate to ensure a smooth transition. Douglas became chief operating officer and deputy managing director.

Other directors who joined the Irish Permanent board at the time included accountant and company doctor Peter Fitzpatrick, who was examiner of beef baron Larry Goodman's meat processing empire, and businessman Peter Ledbetter, a former executive of the gpa aircraft leasing company in Shannon, Co. Clare. Former Labour Party general secretary Brendan Halligan and ex-aib financial director John Keogh joined as non-executive directors. All the new recruits were present at the 2 April board meeting to consider Farrell's dismissal.

The building society underwent a restructuring in January 1993 to prepare for the conversion and stock market listing. Brokers were appointed as advisers; Douglas replaced Farrell who became executive chairman. The reshuffle was seen in the industry as the first sign of the Farrell family's influence beginning to wane over the building society.

Irish Permanent had intended to tell staff at a meeting in the National Concert Hall in Dublin on 14 February 1993, that it would float on the stock market to raise capital to develop the business. However, a boardroom row erupted on 12 February when Farrell and several other directors intervened, saying the new executives were proceeding with undue haste. They claimed that the market conditions were not right for a flotation at that time, but there was also a debate about directors taking share options and the transactions involving Farrell's house. The transactions would have to be brought into the public domain before a flotation.

At this time the building society was preparing its application to convert to a public limited company. This is where problems arose. Irish Permanent's accountants, KPMG Stokes Kennedy Crowley, were asked to prepare a document known as 'the long form' that would be used to convince the building society's shareholders that a flotation was the right way to go. In the form, all relevant information about the finances of the building society and its directors for the two years up to the flotation had to be included. Farrell said that because of delays, a payment for some of the soft furnishings at Grasmere had come within the two-year period covered by the long form and so had to be included in detail on the form.

In January 1993, while Farrell was out on sick leave, a meeting was held in London at which a stockbroker based in the City told the Irish Permanent board that he was concerned about the Grasmere transaction. Farrell said the stockbroker thought it 'was really more of a transaction that you would find in a family-type business and not in a company that was being brought to the stock exchange'. The stockbroker argued that the soft furnishings payment constituted a director's transaction within two years of the planned flotation and so had to be disclosed in the long form. He also argued that if the building society was disclosing this transaction, then all the payments on the Foxrock house must be disclosed. The stockbroker felt the building society could not bring a company to the public without revealing transactions of this nature. He said, however, that he would be happy to proceed with the flotation if the Central Bank was informed about the transactions. After being told, the Central Bank sent a letter to the board in February. 'Apart from raising queries on the property transaction,' said Farrell, 'the letter also stated, in quite unmistakable terms, that the proposed flotation of the building society was on hold until such time as seven queries contained in the letter were answered satisfactorily.'

Farrell said some Irish Permanent board members were apprehensive about the Central Bank's letter for other reasons. The Central Bank had never been keen on an Irish Permanent flotation but wanted the building society to grow organically. This was a major worry for the building society's directors.

'There was an implication that the Central Bank might never consent to a conversion and flotation of the building society in the short term,' said Farrell. 'My fellow directors viewed the Central Bank letter as a showstopper *vis-à-vis* the flotation and some of them said they had never seen such a letter from the Central Bank. Others said that the society would never recover from the impact of the letter and that they could not envisage a flotation occurring for many years, given that we would have to rehabilitate the society with the Central Bank.'

The letter prompted the board to ask its in-house solicitor Cathal MacCarthy to investigate the Grasmere transactions further. At that stage another Dublin legal firm, A&L Goodbody, was already investigating the transactions following the queries raised by the London stockbroker.

'Generally there was despondency among board members about the prospects for a flotation and everybody, apart from myself, viewed the Central Bank letter with a very negative perspective,' said Farrell. 'That letter precipitated the investigation by the in-house solicitor (as opposed to the one A&L Goodbody had been instructed to carry out). The UK solicitors had stated that the entire property transaction fell within the two-year rule for disclosure because of the amount that I paid for soft furnishings, so that amount was material as it related to directors' transactions.'

Farrell said he believed a decision was effectively made by the building society that the best option was to force him out of the building society because the flotation was in jeopardy.

'I believe that the decision of what to do about it and me arose very urgently at that stage,' said Farrell. 'Someone made a decision to get rid of me rather than have an in-depth investigation of what actually had happened two years earlier when the board, excluding me, decided to exercise the option to buy the property back from me. The board agreed the price as well. Everything [relating to the house] had been approved without reservation or reference to me.'

The Foxrock house and the golden handcuff transactions also puzzled KPMG Stokes Kennedy Crowley, and because of the stringent rules to be adhered to, the accountants queried them further, asking why the value of the work carried out on the house was not reflected in the sale price. The Central Bank asked Irish Permanent to seek legal advice on both transactions. The Central Bank was told that the board of the building society intended taking action over both deals as it had doubts over whether they were legitimate.

Some directors who had served on the board for years with Farrell were happy to see the transactions investigated and said as much to the Central Bank, despite the fact that they knew about the transactions and even approved them two years earlier as board members.

Some directors held valuable contracts with Irish Permanent through outside firms and agencies. One senior source in the building society said that because of this the directors may have found it awkward to question Farrell about the Grasmere transactions when they were agreed because he was effectively guaranteeing them lucrative work from the building society.

A legal firm, in which solicitor Paddy Kevans, a director of the society, was a partner, received £166,000 from the Irish Permanent for conveyancing work in 1992. Kevans also received £120,000 for his work as chairman of the society's legal committee set up to examine the legal issues concerning the conversion of the Irish Permanent to a publicly listed company.

Companies connected to Ray O'Keeffe, the one-time chairman of the Irish Permanent, received £160,000 from the society for advertising and public relations work in 1992 and £67,000 the previous year, while legal firms connected to Eamonn Greene, a former director of the building society, received £186,000 for conveyancing work in 1992 and £18,000 in 1991. Greene, Kevans and O'Keeffe resigned from the board in 1992 and 1993.

Farrell defended the fact that these directors had 'business connections' with the building society. 'My feeling was that if they had an interest in the society doing well, then it was likely to do well,' he said. 'You could envisage situations where they wouldn't be independent and the Central Bank pointed that out to me in meetings and most of them resigned. I thought for continuity purposes that we needed some people who were aware of the long-standing history of the building society.' He said he wanted some continuity on the board so both the old and new directors knew about the transactions on Grasmere. He said the new directors found out about the house transaction in the autumn of 1991 when 'the whole property transaction was thrashed out' with some of the directors following fears that a journalist was about to reveal details of the house transaction. He said: 'There were numerous occasions when the house transaction was raised in 1991 and 1992, but a stockbroker and a planned flotation made an issue of it.'

According to Farrell, on Sunday, 7 March 1993, two Irish Permanent directors requested an urgent meeting with him that evening at Grasmere. 'They came out around sixish and over sandwiches and tea told me that the board had come to a conclusion that there was a prima-facie case against me of a conspiracy to defraud the society of money and property. I was incredulous, absolutely incredulous. You can't find words to explain how I felt,' said Farrell.

The following morning Farrell arrived in the office early and two of the longest-serving directors, Ray O'Keeffe and Paddy Kevans, went to his office and advised him to resign.

Two days later, on 10 March, the board met for eight hours to discuss the preliminary findings of its investigation into the Grasmere and golden handcuff transactions. During the meeting Farrell complained that the investigation was 'wholly unnecessary'. He asked that if the current board was claiming he was conspiring to defraud the building society, were they also claiming that the old board were accomplices because they approved the transactions.

The confrontation shocked Farrell, given his years in control of the board at Irish Permanent. However, matters had reached a point of no return. Late on 10 March the board issued a public statement. It suspended Farrell while transactions relating to his Foxrock home were investigated further. The building society assured the public that 'any residual financial impact arising from these transactions is minimal and is fully accounted for in the 1992 results'.

The announcement made the front pages of the following day's newspapers—the scandal had broken. It was the talk of the financial community and stunned Irish Permanent's customers.

Given how matters had escalated, Farrell turned to a lawyer. 'He advised me that the board was effectively trying to overthrow previous board decisions. If they couldn't solve the problem, they could get rid of me. I never had any real doubt that that is what they were trying to do. I tend not to look back at what happened, but at the time I thought it was revolting. I just felt that it was all unnecessary. They did not have to be dealing with these sorts of difficulties this way.'

Farrell said he believed the house transaction was an innocuous matter but that it got in the way of the building society being brought to the market. For the board of the building society, this was the be all and end all. 'I don't think one year more to resolve a relatively minor matter would have been a problem with most people, but I wasn't dealing with most people; I was dealing with financially ambitious people. Nobody can judge fully what happened because nobody knows everything. I have a feeling that the directors were perhaps overly concerned with the property transaction because of the fact that the Central Bank had raised questions. For them, it became a question of whether there was something wrong and whether Dr Farrell would stand aside, but there was no question of them sitting down and having a civil discussion about it in my view,' said Farrell.

A senior source within Irish Permanent familiar with the Farrell affair said that even if some long-standing board members had approved the house transaction, it did not mean it was right. He said the building society later pursued a case against Farrell after he had left the company because it believed the transaction was *ultra vires*. He said the current board could not have been too concerned about a delay in the flotation plans because the conversion was ultimately deferred for a year until 1994—it had been due to take place in early 1993—while the Farrell payments were being investigated, as it had been requested to do by the Central Bank in February 1993.

On 1 April the dispute intensified. Farrell went to the High Court to try and stop the board meeting the following day to decide on his removal. His barrister described the row in court as 'a shabby board-room dispute'. But Farrell failed to stop the meeting. The next day the board gathered for its marathon meeting to hear about the payments made to Farrell over the previous seven years.

One source close to the board said Farrell was 'reserved' through-out the meeting. He described him as a private individual who 'would not tell his right hand what the left hand was doing'. Now all Farrell's secrets were being revealed. At a board meeting on 19 April Farrell was removed as chairman. One director described Farrell's appearance at his last ever Irish Permanent board meeting as 'brave', saying, 'He spoke softly, as he normally does, and without much rancour.'

Over subsequent weeks news leaked out about the payments. It filled the newspapers. Building societies normally offer mortgages to their executives at favourable rates as part of their pay and benefits packages, but few in the financial sector had seen anything like the scale of the transactions emerging at Irish Permanent. At last, after years of trying to find out the salaries of Irish Permanent's directors, the building society's shareholders had a full disclosure of payments made to a top executive. At the April 1991 annual general meeting, for example, shareholders expressed concern that management expenses had increased by £2 million in 1990. In response all Farrell would say was that the only information they were being given was what was required under legislation. It had always been a convenient excuse for him to peddle and one that frustrated the shareholders.

Given the reaction of the media to the emerging scandal, Farrell decided to speak out publicly: 'I say and believe that any persons who heard about my suspension and the alleged investigations taking place must be of the opinion that I have been guilty of serious, dishonest and criminal conduct which justifies the manner in which I have been treated. I say I am not so guilty.'

Further revelations emerged at Irish Permanent following Farrell's dismissal. It was revealed that senior executives at the building society had qualified for tax-free dividends from a subsidiary company. A patent company called Irish Permanent Technologies, which owned the rights to technological products developed for the building society's computer system, had made payments not just to Farrell, but to Roy Douglas too, over and above their salaries. They received a 'performance-related bonus' paid through Irish Permanent Technologies in 1992. Farrell pocketed up to £200,000 and Douglas more than £100,000. The board described the tax-free dividends as important incentives when hiring high-profile executive personnel.

The new guard at Irish Permanent was quick to distance itself from Farrell following the damaging revelations about his house. Speaking to shareholders at the annual general meeting on 29 April, ten days after Farrell's removal, the new chairman, a former Bank of Ireland executive John Bourke (father of Dublin restaurateur and publican Jay Bourke), said: 'The abuse of office and betrayal of trust has disappointed and indeed angered the board, because it has transpired that the board and its committees were misled on certain vital matters and that important information central to these transactions was withheld.'

Record crowds heard Bourke speak at the meeting—almost 800 members attended the five and a half hour meeting in a Dublin hotel. Many attendees complained about the 'money for the boys' culture and were shocked that payments to the ten directors and their pensions had increased by £1 million to £1.9 million in 1992. Bourke accepted at the meeting that the building society had erred by not telling its shareholders about the setting up of the Irish Permanent Technologies patent company controlled by the building society and its tax-free status.

Shareholders could not believe that something like the Grasmere deal could have passed by the board without raising any suspicions. Bourke told a reporter at the time: 'The whole affair is hard to understand. The first thing to remember is that [the payments] took place over a long period of time. The second thing is that the board did approve some of the payments—some but not all, as they didn't see them all. Also the board got legal opinions that said they were okay—at least such transactions as they saw. As well as that it took squadrons of bankers and accountants to eventually bring the affair to light. When they did, the society acted within days, not years. It was the full rigour of the flotation work which examined in detail the five-year history of the society that turned up these events. Mind you, they only turned up at the very end.'

Farrell said: 'They might not have been aware of every purchase or every replacement [on the house], but every receipt was furnished to the society by my wife. When you are dealing with curtains and carpets, it is better to leave it to someone who knows about those things. Those receipts were all furnished and each one was processed before every cheque was withdrawn, so all that information would have been available and pooled in aggregate.'

A stock market flotation would have valued the Irish Permanent at between £180 and £200 million. But in order to realise this value, a full disclosure of the Farrell payments was essential. As a publicly quoted company the building society would have been forced to disclose them publicly before the flotation. This explained the decision to break the news of the investigation before the announcement of the 1992 results on 18 March.

When the results were released—eight days after Farrell's suspension—the building society announced profits of £19.7 million for 1992. When Farrell was suspended the Irish Permanent had 500,000 customers, including 72,000 mortgage holders. It had 90 branches and employed 900 people. Farrell was removed at a time when its top executives were about to become very rich through a flotation. He missed out on a massive windfall at the building society.

The board of the Irish Permanent was not just satisfied with Farrell's dismissal. They wanted the building society's money back, and his home too. In July 1993 Irish Permanent sued him for the recovery of money and property valued at £1.33 million. This included the house in Foxrock which at this stage was valued at £600,000, the £300,000 golden handcuff payment, the £100,000 property on the shores of Lough Corrib and two payments to Smythe, Farrell's personal adviser. About £750,000 was paid to Smythe over the years by the society.

The Irish Permanent claimed that Farrell breached his duties as a director of the company between April 1986 and June 1992 and that because of the payments to Farrell and his wife Zora, it claimed that their home in Foxrock was in effect held in trust for the building society.

Farrell responded by taking his own legal action against the building society, suing it for £4.5 million for unfair dismissal. He claimed that the board members who sat during his tenure as managing director were fully aware of the payments to him. His adviser, Smythe, also issued proceedings against the Irish Permanent seeking the payment of consultancy fees totalling about £30,000 that he claimed were owed to his company, Quasar Corporation.

It took four years for the Farrell case to come to trial and it settled after just one full day of evidence. Wednesday, 19 November 1997, was dominated by an opening statement delivered by Gallagher, the building society's senior counsel. He outlined the Farrell payments and how the former managing director was paranoid that his sweetheart deals would be 'found out'.

As part of the settlement of the case, Farrell retained ownership of the house in Foxrock, and his pension worth £800,000, was released to him. The Irish Permanent, at this stage a publicly quoted bank, received £150,000 from Farrell as well as an apartment in Boston which had been bought with money given to him by the building society. The Boston apartment had been bought in the late 1980s for about $175,000. The money went from the building society to accounts in the Isle of Man, Guernsey and eventually to the British Virgin Islands, before being used to buy the apartment. Farrell agreed to drop his unfair dismissal claim. In 1997 the value of Grasmere and the land around it had soared to £2 million. Both sides agreed to pay their own legal costs, believed to be around £350,000 each. One reason for the settlement was believed to have been the legal costs that each side would have faced, had the case lasted the two months it had been expected to take. Costs could have climbed to £1.5 million for each side.

After the settlement was agreed on 20 November, Farrell left the court with his wife and daughters and refused to answer questions. He referred all queries from the media to his solicitor Kirby Tarrant, who said the former managing director 'wanted to get on with his life'. Tarrant said Farrell was glad the court had agreed that all the transactions had been made known to the board of the Irish Permanent at the time.

Shareholders raised the settlement in April 1998 at the building society's next annual general meeting. Bourke told them that, having set aside a sum to pay potential legal costs and having recovered some money from Farrell, the net effect was a 'small gain' for the bank. It was a far-fetched interpretation of the settlement and it still left shareholders puzzled: why did the Irish Permanent pursue the case so aggressively for so long, only to settle the case one day into the trial without winning the golden prize, the valuable house in Foxrock?

Much was made by the Irish Permanent of how much it had saved in legal costs. But if it had continued with its case, the court might have awarded the bank ownership of the house, which could then have been sold to recoup its legal costs. One source close to the bank said, however, that Farrell's South African wife Zora held a share of what was essentially a family home and that the building society thought it highly unlikely that the court would grant it possession of the property.

The Irish Permanent board was happy with its settlement. It had rid itself of Farrell and his unfair dismissal claim, and had avoided a court battle that could have forced its directors to take the stand and answer awkward questions about procedures at the Irish Permanent. Details could well have emerged during a long-running court case that could have damaged the Irish Permanent, especially given that some directors had served on the board during Farrell's time as managing director. Farrell consistently maintained that the payments made to him were known to the board, so the possibility of embarrassing evidence being revealed loomed ominously for the bank. Besides, in 1997 it had bigger concerns. It was now a publicly quoted bank and its main focus after the Farrell affair was its share price. The settlement of this long-running row brought welcome stability.

The following month shareholders voted for Irish Permanent to be converted into a bank and in October 1994 it was floated on the

Dublin and London stock exchanges. Farrell must have looked with envy as the men he recruited received substantial share options. Within five years those shares made Farrell's £1.33 million payout in 1986 look paltry by comparison. When the company floated in October 1994, its three directors got options to acquire a stake in the company at £1.80 per share. Roy Douglas took options on 366,000 shares, while Peter Fitzpatrick and Peter Ledbetter had options on 256,000 shares each. At the beginning of 1999, each share was worth £8.80, potentially earning each executive a massive windfall. This was on top of their substantial salaries—Douglas was earning £201,000 a year, Fitzpatrick and Ledbetter £140,000 a year each.

Farrell bore no grudge against Irish Permanent or against those who had assisted in the investigation into the payments which led to his downfall. He assisted senior Irish Permanent staff when the bank was called to give evidence at the DIRT inquiry in 1999 into widespread tax evasion by financial institutions and customers, and was conciliatory and courteous with his former colleagues. Likewise, they assisted him when he was asked to give evidence at the Moriarty Tribunal about being solicited for a political donation in 1989 by the then Taoiseach Charlie Haughey. (After the approach Farrell sent Haughey a cheque for £10,000 for his own election campaign and £65,000 from the building society for Fianna Fáil.)

The Farrell episode brought the regulation of building societies under close scrutiny. The Registrar of Friendly Societies had been criticised over its supervision of the sector before the Central Bank took over as regulator with the passing of the Building Society Act 1989. Only a handful of civil servants worked in the registrar's offices, which was hardly enough given the fact that their work involved examining the accounts and practices of building societies that controlled billions of pounds of depositors' money.

The scandal also raised embarrassing questions for the Central Bank: it took over the regulation of building societies in 1989, but why did it take another four years for the details of the Farrell payments to come to light? And even when details of the payments emerged, why were they discovered by advisers to the building society and not by the Central Bank?

The regulator reacted quickly to the emerging scandal, promising closer monitoring of building societies and greater accountability of how they were run. Behind the scenes, the Central Bank put other large building societies under pressure to hire professional advisers such as brokers, accountants and bankers to improve their corporate governance.

Irish Permanent was not the only building society to have difficulties at this time. Shortly after Farrell was suspended by the board, First National Building Society, the second largest after the Irish Permanent, announced unexpectedly on 10 March that its long-serving chief executive Joe Treacy was suddenly retiring. It subsequently emerged that Treacy had left the building society following an allegation that he had sexually harassed a female employee. Treacy too had enjoyed large payments. It subsequently came to light that he received insurance commission payments of about £300,000 over a six-year period, in addition to his annual salary of about £120,000.

The revelations prompted Minister for Finance Bertie Ahern to direct officials at his department to ask the Central Bank whether existing regulations regarding building societies were strong enough to safeguard the public interest. Politicians and officials accepted that the disclosure of the payments had left the public 'uneasy' about how building societies were being managed.

Many top executives at rival building societies, however, argued strongly in the aftermath of the Farrell affair that the 40-year father-to-son regime at the Irish Permanent was unique and that no similar sweetheart payments existed in their building societies. Disturbing concerns had come to light, however. 'There can be no doubt that the Irish Permanent business begs the question as to whether other deals, conflicts of interest or over-generous fee payments to professional advisers remain undisclosed out there,' said one building society expert at the time.

The Farrell affair did raise serious issues about the lack of corporate governance at the Irish Permanent. One source close to the building society at the time of the Farrell controversy said the separation between the roles of the individual and the company director had 'broken down' and led to a collapse of proper guidelines. The munificent payments confirmed that the building society had been run more as a family business than a financial institution accountable to its members.

The scandal turned Irish Permanent on its head and removed any remaining links between the Farrell family and the building society. To herald the transition from a *de facto* family business to a publicly quoted bank in 1994, Irish Permanent changed the name on its St Stephen's Green headquarters from Edmund Farrell House, the name given to it by Farrell in memory of his late father, to the building's basic address, 56–59 St Stephen's Green.

'This was just petty because they said that they were going to retain the name,' said Farrell. 'Life is too short—it doesn't really matter. I don't think my father would have cared either.'

The affair brought the building society sector under real scrutiny for the first time. Previously, building societies were a mystery to their members. Directors could ignore thorny questions at shareholder meetings, comfortable in the knowledge that they had enough votes to dismiss any moves against them at their annual meetings. In the late 1980s building societies wanted to compete with the banks. They got their wish, but the downside was they were brought under the direct authority of the regulator, the Central Bank. This forced them to throw open their books, leading to the disclosure of previously unknown sweetheart deals with their directors.

Farrell eventually sold Grasmere for almost £2 million in 1998. He had sold an option to buy the house several years previously to cover his rising legal fees. Despite his fall from grace, he retained the home and netted a sizeable windfall from the property thanks to his former employer. However, he claimed shortly after his dismissal in 1993 that his reputation had been 'irreversibly damaged'. Overnight he lost his salary of £150,000 and found himself unemployed at the age of 47, his financial career in ruins. He has not worked in the financial sector since 1993. 'You could look back at it and say it was an amazing downfall for a man who was executive chairman of a building society, but then again he should never have been where he was,' said a senior Irish Permanent source familiar with the Farrell affair.

Asked if he should have agreed to the Grasmere and restrictive covenant deals, Farrell said: 'In retrospect I would not have agreed to any of them. I would not have done the property transaction. I didn't request it, seek it or promote it. The restrictive covenant was not my idea either. I should have stuck with my 27-year contract. None of these particular problems would have arisen if I had.' He said he believed the whole saga boiled down to a matter of money—the building society could not deviate from its course towards a flotation to raise much-needed funds, and the best way to solve the problem was to get rid of him. 'It could have been resolved amicably if both sides had been willing to do so, but only one side had been willing,' he said. However, a senior source at the Irish Permanent said Farrell 'went to court first' seeking an injunction to stop his removal, making it impossible for either side to resolve the dispute harmoniously.

Farrell does not look back in anger at his demise; he said he has moved on with his life. 'Somebody said in a film once: "We all get challenges in life, but they do not always come in the form or at the time that you would prefer." That struck a chord with me. I thought my challenge was particularly difficult, but I don't have much time for regret.'

Chapter 6

Ansbacher: a secret bank for Ireland's golden circle

No other banking scandal grabbed the public's attention quite like the Ansbacher affair. It rattled the public and the establishment, not least because it involved a former taoiseach and some of the leading lights in Irish business, the professions and politics in the 1970s and 80s.

At the centre of the scandal was Dublin accountant Des Traynor, a captain of Irish industry in the 1970s and 80s. He knew the international financial environment well and used it to construct a hidden, complex banking system that allowed the *crème de la crème* of the Irish business and professional community to evade tax on tens of millions of pounds deposited with Traynor.

Traynor was responsible for building the secret bank, Guinness Mahon Cayman Trust (GMCT), which catered for the circle of rich and influential people around him. The bank was renamed Ansbacher in 1988 and Ansbacher (Cayman) in 1994. Traynor ran it from 1971 until his death in 1994, assisted by two bankers in the Cayman Islands, his secretary in Dublin and, after 1974, a computer specialist. The bank continued operating after his death until it was publicly exposed in 1997.

Shortly after he became a director of the small Dublin merchant bank Guinness & Mahon in 1969, Traynor helped establish what was in name only a trust business in the Cayman Islands, a tax haven in the Caribbean that is popular with financiers around the word. He then flouted Irish banking rules by running the subsidiary from his base in Dublin serving Irish customers in the utmost secrecy. He was in effect an Irish agent of the Cayman bank and his office the *de facto* Irish branch of the offshore operation. He ran the bank initially from his office in Guinness & Mahon in Dublin and later in the offices of Cement Roadstone Holdings (CRH) at 42 Fitzwilliam Square, also in Dublin, a year after he became its chairman in 1986. Few customers actually knew where their money was going but were happy to trust him. He was after all helping many of them avoid paying large sums of money in tax and to grow their money. Many of his customers thought he was a financial genius, but in fact he was breaking the law.

The Cayman Islands are located 480 miles south of Miami and 180 miles west of Jamaica. They are well known for having some of the most stringent confidentiality laws in the financial world. The islands are not easily accessible from Ireland. Irish visitors must take several flights to reach them. Traynor overcame this inconvenience by opening mirror accounts in Guinness & Mahon. He moved these accounts to Irish Intercontinental Bank (IIB) in 1991.

Traynor operated a clever system. Even though a customer's money was technically thousands of miles away in the Caribbean, Traynor could readily access it for them through the Dublin banks. This was the beauty of the scheme—customers could make withdrawals and lodgements on a regular basis by contacting Traynor in Dublin. The fact that the rate of interest, by which Traynor's customers were growing their deposits in the Cayman Islands, was only one-eighth of one per cent less than they would have obtained had they deposited their money in an Irish bank, showed the real reason why they were using his bank. It had little to do with making a strong return on their money, but more to do with making sure it was hidden offshore.

Confidentiality and anonymity was a key prerequisite of the Ansbacher scheme. Even though there were hundreds of Irish depositors, no complete records were held in Dublin. Names hardly ever appeared on the Irish records; codes were used to identify customers so the identities of the depositors would only be known to Traynor and the few staff he used. This ensured that the accounts would remain hidden, far beyond the reach of the Revenue Commissioners. It was essential that Traynor left no footprints that the taxman could follow back to the customer.

After Traynor's death, the banking service continued under the computer specialist who had begun working for Traynor and Guinness & Mahon in 1974, Padraig Collery. He had administered the customers' deposits for Traynor. Collery continued to take instructions from Traynor after the accountant left Guinness & Mahon in 1989. The scheme would have remained hidden, had Dublin supermarket tycoon Ben Dunne not embarked on a cocaine-fuelled binge with a prostitute in a Florida hotel in February 1992. Dunne's antics set in train a series of events that culminated in the exposure of the Ansbacher deposits and Traynor's clandestine operation.

It is extraordinary that the string of scandals which rocked Irish political and financial life in the late 1990s can be traced back to Dunne's Florida misadventure. The supermarket boss ended up being arrested on drugs charges, and after a well-publicised trial he was ordered to attend a rehabilitation clinic in London. Dunne was later ousted as managing director of the Dunnes Stores supermarket chain, one of the biggest in the country, leading to a family row over the business in the High Court. The dispute was settled in 1994, but not before Dunne stated in an affidavit that he had paid £1.1 million of Dunnes Stores money to the Fianna Fáil politician Charles J. Haughey, who had served as Taoiseach for three terms between 1979 and 1992. Dunne made the statement to prove his allegation that the Dunne's family trust was a sham. The aim of his affidavit was to try to attract as much money as he could from the family in a settlement. He later said he was a mad, suicidal and broken man at the time. (It later emerged that Dunne also handed Haughey another three bank drafts totalling £210,000, bringing the total to £1.3 million.) Sketchy details of the payments to Haughey emerged in 1996 when the media heard whispers about Dunne's sensational claims in his affidavit. On the back of news reports, the government set up the McCracken Tribunal in 1997 to get to the bottom of Dunne's payments to politicians.

The tribunal managed to find some important pieces of the Ansbacher puzzle. It discovered that the money paid to Haughey by Dunne had been routed through Traynor, one of Haughey's most trusted friends. Slowly a picture began to emerge of how Traynor had been a central figure in the story behind Haughey's money. Traynor was essentially Haughey's bagman, running a bill-paying service for Haughey and keeping the politician in the spendthrift lifestyle to which he had grown accustomed over several decades. If Haughey needed money—and he needed it frequently given his flamboyant lifestyle—he turned to Traynor who went looking for funds. Their relationship dated back years. Traynor first met Haughey in 1951 when he joined Haughey Boland, the accountancy firm set up by Charles Haughey and Harry Boland. Traynor and Haughey remained close for the next 43 years. Traynor worked at Haughey Boland until he was appointed managing director of Guinness & Mahon in 1969.

The tribunal subsequently discovered an elaborate money trail from Dunne to Haughey that would eventually expose Traynor's Ansbacher scheme and its other customers. Some time in 1987 Traynor asked Dunne—through Noel Fox, a Haughey supporter and a financial adviser to Ben Dunne and Dunnes Stores—for money for Haughey, then Taoiseach. Traynor said he was looking for several people who could each contribute £150,000 to Haughey. The money needed to be paid in secret. When Dunne heard what Traynor was trying to do, he saw imminent danger. 'I think Haughey is making a huge mistake trying to get six or seven people together. Christ picked 12 apostles and one of them crucified him,' said Dunne at the time.

Dunne agreed to pay Traynor all the money he was looking for. The supermarket multimillionaire said he was someone who helped people out and he paid the money to Haughey so the politician could repay a debt. Traynor initially sought £205,000 in November 1987 and asked for the cheque to be made out to a John Furze. Dunne had no idea who Furze was but made the payment regardless. Furze turned out to be a banker living on the Cayman Islands and a director of Guinness Mahon Cayman Trust, Traynor's secret bank.

Traynor sent the cheque through Guinness & Mahon's London branch and directed that it be sent to a Guinness Mahon Cayman Trust account in Guinness & Mahon in Dublin. The money was eventually lodged to Haughey's Irish bank accounts. The money was used to pay off a loan Haughey had with the state-owned bank, the Agricultural Credit Corporation (ACC), and some of the politician's bills. The tribunal had stumbled upon a curious financial operation within Guinness & Mahon merchant bank in Dublin involving its subsidiary in the Cayman Islands, GMCT.

The tribunal could not penetrate the strict secrecy laws governing banks in the Cayman Islands to get more information, but eventually got hold of documents from Guinness & Mahon in London showing how the Dublin bank managed large deposits for GMCT. The tribunal later discovered that Guinness & Mahon kept in its records details of either a large deposit or a number of deposits held for GMCT (later Ansbacher (Cayman)). However, there was no information in the Dublin bank about who actually owned the money. This is where Traynor came into the equation. He privately kept a secret record of the Irish clients of the Cayman bank whose money had been re-deposited in Guinness & Mahon. This meant that the money had the appearance of being offshore when in fact it remained in Ireland and could be readily accessed by Traynor.

Given that Traynor had died in 1994, the tribunal needed another link to the deposits to find out how the system worked. Through the documents obtained from Guinness & Mahon in London, the tribunal followed the paper trail. It brought them to Collery who was later identified as the man who managed Traynor's system which monitored the Cayman deposits. Collery managed the Irish money through 'memorandum accounts', hidden records or subaccounts within Guinness & Mahon showing who owned what within the Cayman deposits in Guinness & Mahon in Dublin.

McCracken questioned Collery and Traynor's secretary Joan Williams about the operation. It was discovered that Traynor had operated his Cayman Islands bank initially from his office in Guinness & Mahon in Dublin and then from 42 Fitzwilliam Square in Dublin, the offices of Cement Roadstone Holdings (CRH), soon after he became chairman of the company in 1986 until his death in 1994. CRH was a massive entity on the Irish corporate landscape. It continuously ranked among the top five Irish companies at this time. Collery would often let himself into CRH's offices on Saturday mornings to make entries to the memorandum accounts, following up on the work conducted by Traynor and Williams during the previous week.

After Traynor's death the secret Ansbacher financial service moved to offices on Winetavern Street, next to Christchurch in Dublin, belonging to Sam Field Corbett, an associate of Traynor who had worked with him in Haughey Boland. Field Corbett allowed Collery to use the office to store the Ansbacher documents and to record updates on the deposits. Following Traynor's death Collery took his instructions from Furze and continued to maintain the memorandum accounts in secret. He continued his work until the Ansbacher scam was exposed in 1997 and customers started withdrawing their money. Furze died later that year.

McCracken and his team got hold of some important documents from Guinness & Mahon and IIB relating to the Ansbacher accounts. The documents were all coded except for one, a note written by Williams which related to a withdrawal. It stated: 'By hand to CJH.' This was the only reference to Haughey in the documents. Again McCracken's team followed the trail and discovered that it eventually ended up in Haughey's ACC account in Dublin. Although most of the money relating to the Cayman bank was held in pooled accounts in Guinness & Mahon in Dublin, the tribunal also found that some accounts had been identified by codes. Haughey's accounts were identified as S8 and S9.

The tribunal had set out to discover whether Haughey had in fact received over £1 million from Dunne, but it had inadvertently discovered a secret and complex financial service, of which Haughey was only one of potentially hundreds of customers. On 30 June 1997 the tribunal revealed to the nation that it had discovered the Ansbacher deposits and that this did not just involve Haughey but other Irish customers. The tribunal stepped back from investigating any further because the deposits fell outside its remit.

McCracken said: 'It is not the function of this tribunal to examine these deposits in any detail, and it may well be that a number of the Irish depositors may have been people engaged in international business which was greatly facilitated by having a sterling account abroad which did not require exchange control permission to operate. No doubt there were others who deposited the monies in this way from other motives.'

Gerard Ryan, an accountant in the Department of Enterprise, Trade and Employment, continued looking for more pieces of the puzzle in September 1997. On the back of McCracken's report, Tánaiste Mary Harney appointed Ryan an authorised officer to investigate Celtic Helicopters, a company co-owned by Haughey's son Ciaran. The company had taken out loans which had been backed by Ansbacher deposits and loans of £150,000 had been repaid with Ansbacher money. However, Ryan needed further information to progress his investigation, so in June 1998 Harney appointed Ryan to investigate Guinness & Mahon, IIB, Ansbacher (Cayman) (formerly GMCT) and Hamilton Ross, a Cayman trust management company which was part of Ansbacher (Cayman).

In September 1999 the size and scale of the secret Ansbacher bank was revealed publicly. Harney made an application to the High Court seeking the appointment of inspectors to investigate the affair further, which was grounded on an affidavit by Paul Appleby, a civil servant in Harney's department and now the Director of Corporate Enforcement. In his document Appleby said Harney believed that Ansbacher (Cayman) was set up and managed in order to defraud the Revenue and that she was aware that the company destroyed books and documents, in breach of the Companies Act, and had operated a bank in Ireland without a licence for 20 years.

Details of Ryan's report into Ansbacher (Cayman) were also revealed. It named 120 people and companies who were clients of Ansbacher. Ryan believed there were many more who had not been identified. He said £50 million had been placed on deposit by Ansbacher (Cayman) in Guinness & Mahon in Dublin in 1989, but Appleby added that the amount of money in trusts and companies in the Ansbacher deposits could amount to several hundred million pounds. Ryan picked up where the McCracken Tribunal had left off and continued investigating.

Ryan discovered a remarkable document which was headed 'Note to John Furze' and drafted in 1983 by the well-known Dublin businessman Ray McLoughlin. The document was written as a means of marketing the Cayman operation. It outlined how the tax dodge worked. McLoughlin was never a client of Ansbacher himself; he wrote the document after a meeting with John Furze in September 1983, which was arranged by Traynor. The document revealed how false names as well as private companies could be used to give participants extra protection if it was ever discovered by the Revenue. The note said that clients did not like committing instructions to paper, but money could be 'moved, invested or divested from time to time simply through a telephone call to a contact operating on behalf of the trustees'.

The note to John Furze exposed the clear purpose of the GMCT trusts: to conceal customers' money and their identities. It showed the Cayman trust system to be a charade and proved that Traynor's bank had been set up as a vehicle which allowed wealthy customers to evade tax.

The note and Ryan's other findings were enough for Harney to petition the High Court to appoint inspectors to investigate Ansbacher (Cayman) further. The court appointed three inspectors—retired High Court judge Declan Costello, barrister Noreen Mackey, and Paul Rowan, a retired accountant who had worked on the liquidation of Merbro Finance, the Northern Irish division of Merchant Banking (see Chapter 2). For health reasons Costello was later replaced by two individuals—Circuit Court judge Sean O'Leary and Michael Cush SC—given the massive workload. The inspectors were tasked with the job of completing the puzzle. Their report, which was published in July 2002, explained in painstaking detail how Traynor's shady banking operation had been set up and grown.

In 1969 Guinness & Mahon was a small, staid merchant bank run by men from an Anglo-Irish Protestant background. Its directors felt that the bank needed new blood, someone from outside the old boys' club who could attract new business. Des Traynor was that man. He was a formidable financier and someone with connections not just to Haughey and his circle of political movers and shakers but to the wider business community. According to the inspectors, Traynor was 'reserved to the point of taciturnity, a man who could truly be said not to have permitted his left hand to know what his right hand was doing'. Perhaps these were the qualities of a good banker. Also in 1969 Guinness & Mahon decided to set up an operation in the Cayman Islands 'or in some other haven'. The aim was 'to devise an attractive scheme' for the bank's customers. The late solicitor Liam McGonagle established the Cayman companies and John Collins, a Bank of Nova Scotia official working in the Cayman Islands, helped set it all up.

In June 1970 Traynor began taking an active role in growing the Cayman operation. He travelled to the islands to assess Guinness & Mahon's investment there. In January 1971 GMCT was set up to provide trust and other corporate services to Guinness & Mahon's wealthy customers. Collins and another Bank of Nova Scotia official, John Furze, became directors of GMCT and would continue working for Traynor for more than two decades. Later that year GMCT met staff from Kennedy Crowley (which became Stokes Kennedy Crowley and later KPMG), one of Dublin's most prominent accountancy firms, which was interested in the services that Guinness & Mahon's

Cayman bank could offer. This turned out to be 'the genesis of a mutually profitable liaison' between the accountancy firm and Guinness & Mahon, according to the inspectors. Stokes Kennedy Crowley provided a number of links between prominent businessmen and GMCT/ Ansbacher.

Traynor, however, was the pivotal link between many Irish customers and GMCT. As the architect of the Cayman scheme, he created an impenetrable system that allowed the high rollers of Irish society to evade tax. Tax evasion was rife in the 1970s and 80s, a time when personal income tax rates were sky high.

Traynor, with the help of Furze and Collins in the Cayman Islands, set up trusts for Irish customers, but these were only trusts in name. If the trust had been legitimate, then the money would have been transferred to the trust by the Irish client who then would cede control of the money to the trustees. However, in the case of GMCT, the trustees would lodge or withdraw money from the trusts on the instructions of the person who set it up. This proved that the trusts were a total sham.

Interviews conducted by the inspectors revealed that many customers claimed they did not know their money had been invested in Traynor's Cayman bank and only learned of the name 'Ansbacher' when the McCracken Tribunal started investigating the money trail to Haughey.

Traynor used the vast network of contacts he had developed in Dublin to introduce customers to GMCT. When people told him they had money they wanted to set aside, he suggested taking it and investing it for them. Thereafter, if a customer wished to make a lodgment or withdrawal, they would contact Traynor and as a signatory on the GMCT accounts in Dublin, he would issue instructions. The customer might give Traynor a bank draft or cash to lodge in GMCT. For withdrawals, Traynor would send the money to the clients, often in cash but sometimes in the form of a bank draft. After Traynor became chairman of CRH, some customers picked up their money in Traynor's CRH office at 42 Fitzwilliam Square. On other occasions the CRH caretaker and Traynor's driver in CRH would deliver cash to the customers.

Other customers had more specific and regular arrangements. David Doyle, son of the legendary Irish hotelier P. V. Doyle, who were both Ansbacher customers, said he used to meet Traynor before lunch in the lobby of the family's Berkeley Court Hotel in Dublin to collect money he had asked him to withdraw. Another Ansbacher depositor, Dr Colm Killeen, a GP and Traynor's next-door neighbour on the Howth Road in Dublin, told the inspectors that the accountant used to drop 'strips' of paper through his letterbox from time to time. These were statements showing the amount of money he had on deposit with Traynor. There was no letterhead or bank logo on the statements. Killeen told the inspectors that Traynor agreed to set up an account for him in the study of the accountant's house. Killeen gave him cheques and money to lodge to the account.

Statements were, however, rarely sent to Traynor's customers. This was all part of his policy of concealment, the foundation stone of the bank. Any statements handed out were prepared in such a way that they would not reveal the existence of the account or its location. In some cases a handwritten note would be delivered by hand or by post. Traynor tore the GMCT (and later Ansbacher) letterhead off the statements which were prepared and sent by his secretary Joan Williams. Traynor told one client that this was done for security reasons.

In addition to the bank's memorandum accounts, GMCT offered customers back-to-back loans. It was another way of keeping the money offshore and hidden from the Revenue. Guinness & Mahon made loans to GMCT clients which were backed by the money deposited offshore in the Cayman Islands. The bank omitted on the loan document any details about the cash security for the borrowings. The Dublin bank simply wrote in its records that the loans had been 'suitably secured' or 'adequately secured'. In effect the customers were borrowing their own money but it looked like the customer had taken a loan. If a tax inspector came knocking, nothing would appear amiss.

Traynor's range of contacts and networking skills were illustrated in the inspectors' report by the diverse backgrounds of some of the customers of GMCT/Ansbacher (Cayman). He had operated his secret bank for 23 years. He introduced people whom he knew from his days at Haughey Boland and introduced other clients he met from the growing Catholic business classes in 1970s and 80s Ireland. He was a ubiquitous character in the Irish business community. Many people turned to him for advice on financial and investment matters, and they often became customers of his bank as a result. His formidable financial skills brought him into contact with some of Ireland's wealthiest people. A week before the publication of the Ansbacher report in July 2002, businessman John Mulhern, Haughey's son-in-law and a customer of Traynor's bank, told journalist Des Crowley, then writing for the *Sunday Business Post*, that Traynor heard 'confessions' in his home in Dublin every Saturday morning when visitors came to him for financial advice.

Close associates of Haughey appeared in the Ansbacher report as customers of Traynor's bank. Some people who had given money to Haughey or his son's company, Celtic Helicopters, became customers of Ansbacher (Cayman) given the close relationship between Traynor and Haughey. Some depositors would have been financial supporters of Fianna Fáil and had been involved in the party's controversial fundraising group, Taca. It was a golden circle and at its centre was Traynor, a close personal friend of one of the country's most powerful people. Most people, however, didn't even know who else was in the circle, such was the secrecy of his operation.

Haughey's Fianna Fáil colleague Denis Foley, a TD from Kerry, also had an Ansbacher deposit, although he was in denial about its existence for a very long time. He was identified as an Ansbacher customer in November 1999 by the Moriarty Tribunal when he was still a TD. The tribunal discovered Foley's name among documents that the tribunal had not known existed. His account was marked by the code A/A40. Foley organised dances at the Mount Brandon Hotel in Tralee, Co. Kerry. The hotel was owned by property developer John Byrne, another Ansbacher customer. Foley was often paid in cash, so he used the money to buy bank drafts that he kept in a dresser at home. On one occasion when Traynor was down in Kerry doing business in the Mount Brandon, he asked Foley if he had any money to invest. Traynor later opened an Ansbacher account for the Kerryman. Foley subsequently told the tribunal that he collected £10,000 in cash from Traynor at his CRH office on Fitzwilliam Square and on another occasion after Traynor's death he collected £50,000 in cash from Collery in the bar of Jury's Hotel in Ballsbridge, Dublin.

Foley gave extraordinary evidence at the tribunal in February 2000. At this stage it had been known for several years that Traynor and Collery managed the Ansbacher deposits, yet Foley told the tribunal that he was 'shocked' when statements he received from Collery in May 1999 contained the name Ansbacher. His evidence stretched the bounds of credibility. After he received the statements, he thought it was best to ignore them. 'When I looked at them and saw Ansbacher, I left them there and put them in a folder and hoped against hope [that his name wasn't linked to Ansbacher],' he told the tribunal. Foley was later part of the Dáil Public Accounts Committee's DIRT inquiry team that in 1999 investigated widescale tax evasion in the banking sector during public hearings. The irony of his position was only spotted in hindsight. Even though he must have realised that there was some connection between his offshore account and the secret Cayman bank that came to light in late 1996 and early 1997, he still voted for the establishment of the McCracken Tribunal as a member of the Dáil. He resigned as a member of the Public Accounts Committee after he was named as an Ansbacher depositor. Foley later made a settlement of €580,000 with the Revenue as a result of his off-shore account.

Foley's name emerged after Collery's former secretary at Guinness & Mahon, Margaret Keogh, handed a sealed envelope of documents to the Moriarty Tribunal in 1999. Foley's name appeared in the documents. Collery had asked Keogh to keep the sealed envelope in a safe place until he visited her again, but after consulting her solicitor she decided to give it to the tribunal.

Among its contents was a list of names of people associated with Cayman accounts. Collery had compiled the list after a trip to the Cayman Islands in July 1998. He tried to keep Foley's name hidden but Margaret Keogh blew the lid on the Kerry TD's involvement. The purpose of Collery's trip was to bring the balances of the Irish depositors up to date and also to deduct £57,000 from several Irish accounts to pay for legal fees incurred by Furze in connection with proceedings between him and the McCracken Tribunal. Collery spent two and a half days working on the accounts but managed to find some leisure time walking the famous Seven Mile Beach on Grand Cayman. The trip was an audacious move, given that the tribunal was investigating Ansbacher at the time. In March 2006 Collery became the first person to be disqualified from being involved in managing any company as a result of court cases in the Ansbacher scandal. He was disqualified for nine years for his conduct in the management of the Ansbacher scheme.

Fianna Fáil wasn't the only party linked to the Ansbacher deposits. Some customers were Fine Gael supporters and one, Hugh Coveney, was a Fine Gael TD for Cork, minister and Lord Mayor of Cork. Coveney, who died in 1998, had used a Cayman trust for a business deal on a failed property venture in the United States in 1980. He had also deposited the proceeds from the sale of a yacht in an Ansbacher account in the 1970s.

Traynor's skills were clearly recognised at Guinness & Mahon from the very beginning. However, as the deposits grew at GMCT, so too did his influence and his control over the financial affairs of the Dublin bank. According to GMCT's accounts, the Dublin deposits grew from £3.6 million in 1972 to almost £56 million by 1987. By the following year the GMCT (Ansbacher) deposits represented 35 per cent of Guinness & Mahon's deposit base. Traynor's bank had clearly proved popular with his customers. The operation continued to be used by customers in the 1990s. IIB told the inspectors that £96 million passed through accounts belonging to Ansbacher and a related company, Hamilton Ross, between 1991 and 1997. After September 1992, the money that had been held in accounts in IIB in the name of Ansbacher was transferred to new accounts in the same bank in the name of Hamilton Ross.

Traynor also involved some of his associates in his offshore caper. Jack Stakelum, a former accountant at Haughey Boland, sent money offshore for his clients through his friend, Traynor. A company owned and controlled by Sam Field Corbett, another former Haughey Boland employee, was used by Traynor for secretarial services on behalf of many of the companies linked to the Ansbacher deposits.

The inspectors concluded that Ansbacher (Cayman) had not been authorised to operate in the Republic and had been set up with tax evasion in mind. Incredibly, the inspectors found that the Central Bank, the Irish banking regulator, had discovered suspicious practices involving Traynor and GMCT as far back as 1976. That year, the Central Bank went into Guinness & Mahon to inspect its loan book and assess whether loans could be recovered. Central Bank official Adrian Byrne, the lead examiner in the investigation, told the inspectors what they found in the Dublin merchant bank 'just didn't smell right . . . it didn't taste right. There was something wrong.'

The Central Bank officials discovered the back-to-back loans taken by customers of Guinness & Mahon that were secured by cash deposits hidden by those same customers in the Cayman subsidiary. 'We are satisfied from our conversations with Mr J. D. [Des] Traynor that a major part of these companies' activities is in the receipt of funds on which taxation has been avoided,' stated the Central Bank's 1976 report into Guinness & Mahon. 'The bank is in effect offering a special service which assists persons to transfer funds, on which tax has been avoided, to offshore tax havens. The possibility of the bank abusing its position as an authorised dealer in providing this service cannot be ignored.'

Byrne told the inspectors that Guinness & Mahon's concerns to ensure secrecy and to guarantee that information did not find its way into the hands of the Revenue Commissioners were 'completely out of the ordinary'. He said that he had never encountered such a level of concern about a financial institution. The Central Bank said Guinness & Mahon's affairs were 'surrounded by a unique level of secrecy'.

The Central Bank raised concerns about Guinness & Mahon again in 1978, and once again it found that loans at the Dublin bank had been secured with money in its Cayman subsidiary. 'The fact that the bank takes such extreme precautions to keep the existence of the deposits secret from the Revenue Commissioners indicates that the bank might well be a party to a tax evasion scheme,' said Byrne in a note after his 1978 examination.

Incredibly, a Central Bank official crossed out the word 'evasion' (an illegal activity) in Byrne's note and replaced it with 'avoidance' (a legal activity). The change had also been made in Byrne's 1976 report. It was also remarkable that during its 1978 inspection the Central Bank discovered that one of its own directors, Ken O'Reilly-Hyland, had a loan of £416,000 from Guinness & Mahon that was backed by a deposit of £230,000 in Cayman. Byrne recorded the transaction. The Ansbacher inspectors, however, said in the report that there was 'considerable uncertainty as to what, if any, steps were taken upon receipt of this information'.

The inspectors found that there was nothing to show that the Central Bank's management was in any way affected by the fact that O'Reilly-Hyland had dealings with Guinness & Mahon. The Central Bank was eventually persuaded from taking further action on the Dublin bank's back-to-back loans with its Cayman subsidiary, not because it was above board, but because Traynor promised that the volume of loans would decrease. They did not. Traynor provided mis-leading information, falsely showing that the loans were decreasing, when in fact the opposite was the case.

The High Court inspectors were damning in their assessment of the Central Bank's handling of Guinness & Mahon in the 1970s. They said that the bank's failure to 'test, appraise and gather' information that was available to it led to 'the true nature of Ansbacher's activities going undetected for longer than ought to have been the case'. The inspectors said it was 'unwise' and 'regrettable' that the bank accepted Traynor's word on the loans, especially when the Central Bank 'already harboured reservations about his protestations of innocence regarding the back-to-back deposits. Furthermore, there was information available to the bank which on any reasonable analysis demonstrated that Mr Traynor's representations were inaccurate.' The bank should have examined internal audit reports of Guinness & Mahon, in particular one conducted at the Dublin bank in 1989, and if it had, it would have found 'startling' information about an unlicensed Irish bank and Cayman deposits. 'Had the bank probed Traynor's representations further in the early 1980s there is good reason to believe that the bank could have availed of these powers to put an end to the Ansbacher activities in Ireland,' said the inspectors. But it didn't, and Traynor's illegal bank continued operating for another 19 years handling tens of millions of untaxed Irish pounds.

The inspectors praised Byrne for his work on Guinness & Mahon, but they slammed the Central Bank for failing to police the sector adequately. Speaking on radio after the publication of the inspectors' report, Tánaiste Mary Harney said the bank was not the only state agency that failed to do its job. Her comments captured the see no evil, hear no evil culture of the time: 'It seems extraordinary that we lived in a time where the culture, even among state organisations, was one of "let's pretend we don't know" because clearly in some cases where organisations knew or should have known, they seemed to take the view they didn't want to know.'

The inspectors also examined whether CRH as a company knew that Traynor was effectively running an illegal bank from its offices. They concluded that it was a matter for which the company must bear an element of responsibility. Traynor's use of CRH's registered office at 42 Fitzwilliam Square, a Georgian building in Dublin city centre, was central to the smooth running of his illegal bank. He also used other CRH facilities to operate the bank. He used the company's mail system to send out details of lodgements to Ansbacher clients. Williams, his long-time secretary at Guinness & Mahon who helped him administer the bank, became an employee of CRH when her boss moved to the cement company. His driver at CRH delivered bank drafts and cash to Ansbacher clients who had withdrawn money from the bank. Furze

used the CRH office when he visited Ireland and staff knew he was a
banker from the Cayman Islands who was involved in Ansbacher—no
attempt was made to conceal his identity from the staff.

It was clear that Traynor didn't hide the fact that he was conducting
some of his banking business from CRH's offices. Indeed, eight directors
of the company, more than half the board in 1987, were, in a personal
capacity, customers of GMCT/Ansbacher (Cayman). Anthony Barry,
Jim Culliton, Michael Dargan, Gerald Hickey, Diarmuid Quirke, Des
Traynor, Robert Willis and Richard Wood were all customers. The
inspectors said this was 'of some significance when considering the
knowledge of CRH, as a corporate entity, of the activities of Ansbacher
in Ireland'.

In 1979 Traynor had suggested an offshore banking facility to
Culliton, then chief executive of CRH, when Culliton mentioned the
high rate of taxes. (Traynor had been a director of CRH since the
1970s.) Culliton was told that the offshore account would be a secret.
In a tribute to Traynor after his death, Culliton said in an article: 'Des
was the person you went to if you were in trouble, and he took great
pride in helping you resolve your difficulties.' Culliton later served as
chairman of AIB from 1993 to 1996. He also served on the RTÉ
Authority. He resigned from the board of the Hibernian Insurance
Group, the telecom company Nortel, and Jury's Doyle Hotel Group
after he was named as an Ansbacher account holder.

Tony Barry, who succeeded Culliton as chief executive, handed over
to Traynor money (that had been disclosed to the Revenue) to be put
aside for the benefit of his children. He told the Moriarty Tribunal
that he never knew Traynor was operating a secret bank from CRH's
offices on Fitzwilliam Square, but he acknowledged that he had a
banking relationship with Ansbacher and that this had taken place
using CRH's offices. Members of the CRH board clearly knew that
Traynor was up to something at the company's office in Dublin city
centre. However, Traynor never discussed GMCT/Ansbacher (Cayman)
business at board level and directors who were customers of his secret
bank didn't know of any of their colleagues' involvement in the bank.
Traynor had managed the whole unauthorised enterprise under a
heavy blanket of secrecy.

The Ansbacher inspectors found that there was no substantial body
of knowledge within CRH of what Traynor was up to, but rather
'piecemeal knowledge of his activities'. Several CRH directors who gave

evidence to the inspectors spoke of the pride CRH took in its corporate governance. However, the inspectors said: 'Whilst the inspectors have concluded that CRH cannot be said to have knowingly assisted the carrying out of the Ansbacher business in Ireland, they cannot agree that in this matter the CRH systems of corporate governance were deserving of pride.'

The most interesting aspect of the Ansbacher affair was the list of names of people who had in some cases unwittingly become Traynor's customers. Some of the people appearing in the list had connections to Charles Haughey in the past—meat processor Seamus Purcell, property developer John Byrne and hotelier P. V. Doyle. Others found themselves involved in Ansbacher purely by living near Traynor's home on the Howth Road in Raheny on the northside of Dublin and becoming acquainted with him. The Ansbacher report revealed a cluster of depositors in the area. Dr Colm Killeen was not the only Ansbacher customer who was a neighbour of Traynor's— builder Sean McKeon and car dealer Brian Dennis lived on the same road as Traynor and were Ansbacher customers. Traynor also drove the short distance to the Kinsealy, north Co. Dublin home of another Ansbacher client, Charles Haughey, to deal with his financial affairs in the library of his home. John and Eileen Oppermann became clients of Traynor's bank because the accountant ate in his restaurant, Johnny's, in Malahide on a regular basis.

Being named in the Ansbacher report, however, didn't necessarily mean that the individual had evaded tax. Some customers, such as CRH executive Tony Barry, deposited after-tax money in the accounts. However, most claimed they did not know their money had ended up in the Cayman Islands or the nature of Traynor's financial service. 'I am bewildered by the revelations about Des Traynor in the last couple of years,' Ansbacher depositor and former CRH director Jim Culliton told the inspectors, 'because that is not the man I knew as a colleague. I have to say that. I really am bewildered. He just fooled us all.'

Another Ansbacher customer, the late solicitor Gerald Hickey, said: 'People gave him millions, as you know. Everybody had complete confidence in him. He was regarded as a totally honest man and also as a totally able man.' Many of his customers were swayed by Traynor's financial wizardry. 'He was a very ordinary person but in my terms he intimidated me about money and my lack of knowledge about the financial world,' architect Arthur Gibney, another customer of

Traynor's, told the inspectors. 'He was a man of very few words,' Gibney added. 'He never explained anything and I went to him looking for money and he said: "I can get you a loan". I felt he had been extremely generous to me. He had helped me at a time when I was virtually bankrupt and I treated him with great respect.' Another prominent architect, Sam Stephenson who designed the Central Bank building on Dame Street, was also an Ansbacher customer.

Timothy O'Grady Walshe, a former Central Bank general manager, in his evidence to the Moriarty Tribunal, said Traynor was 'very clever, very skilful' and would 'have exploited the limits of the law to the utmost' but that he would not have broken the law. He said that if Traynor was alive today he 'would make a good job of proving that what he was doing was within the law'.

For many people, their investments in Traynor's bank left them with a massive tax problem. As soon as the Ansbacher deposits were revealed by the McCracken Tribunal in 1997, the Revenue started investigating how much tax had been evaded. By March 2006, the Revenue had collected €55.9 million including €23.1 million in interest and penalties from 108 Ansbacher depositors. At that stage the largest settlement received from an individual in the Revenue's Ansbacher investigation related to the late James Murray, a Co. Meath farmer with an address of Hadley, Coast Road, Mornington. Murray had in 1978 given money to his accountant Jack Stakelum, who in turn invested his money in Ansbacher through Guinness & Mahon Bank. His family were forced to pay a tax bill of €3.3 million, including a whopping €2.3 million in interest and penalties on his behalf, all because of his investment in Traynor's offshore bank. Ansbacher made a tax settlement of €7.5 million in 2003 over its business activities in Ireland between the early 1970s and 1997, while Hamilton Ross made a tax settlement of €700,000 in 2005 over its involvement in the scandal.

The average settlement made by individuals in the Ansbacher investigation stands at more than €500,000, reflecting the sizeable investments and wealthy backgrounds of many of the Cayman bank's customers. The Revenue's investigation progressed slowly because of the complex nature of the operation of the scheme. Many depositors have claimed that the monies deposited in Traynor's bank were legitimate trusts.

The multimillionaire property developer John Byrne was still—at the age of 86—in June 2006 challenging the findings of the inspectors about him in their report. Byrne took a High Court case against the inspectors trying to overturn the part of their report which said that he could use a Cayman Islands trust at all times. He argued that this was inconsistent with the finding by the inspectors that he was 'truthful' in his evidence to them. Byrne strongly disputed that he was the beneficial owner of the trust.

It will take many more years for all tax settlements to be completed and finalised, and for the Ansbacher affair to draw eventually to a close.

Ansbacher depositors who found themselves embroiled in this mess must be cursing the fact that Charlie Haughey had ever been involved in GMCT/Ansbacher (Cayman). Had Haughey never held an Ansbacher account, then it is highly likely that the scheme would never have come to light. His ties to Dunne and the subsequent revelations that the supermarket tycoon had paid over £1 million to the Fianna Fáil politician sank the whole Ansbacher ship.

Harney, who initiated the investigations into Ansbacher, described the inspectors' report into the affair as 'a damning insight into a world of conspiracy, fraud and tax evasion over a long number of years'. The scheme had been devised by an astute accountant whose financial skills were so great that it took a tribunal and a team of court-appointed investigators to crack the tax evasion vehicle that he had created and operated for more than two decades. The Ansbacher affair shone a light into a dark corner of Irish banking. The inspectors proved that a golden circle in Irish society, even one that included a one-time taoiseach, could be penetrated and brought to book.

The Ansbacher report marked a watershed because it proved that no one was untouchable in Ireland. It showed that the Central Bank, the banking sector's policeman, had failed to do its job over a long period of time. It was quite unbelievable that the bank discovered serious irregularities at Guinness & Mahon in the mid-1970s and yet did nothing about them after receiving assurances from Traynor. Harney said the report 'demonstrates that we in Ireland now have the capacity and courage to lift the veil of secrecy and the determination to enforce the law'. But no one has gone to jail over the Ansbacher affair. The scandal also showed that the burden of paying for the running of the state in the 1970s and 80s rested firmly with the beleaguered PAYE workers. The rich could simply use a secret bank to avoid paying their share.

Chapter 7

National Irish Bank: encouraging tax evasion and ripping off customers

The 1997 Ansbacher scandal had focused the nation's attention on a tax evasion scam by an elite group of business people and politicians in Irish society, but soon afterwards a new scandal surfaced which revealed that people lower down the social echelons were at the same game. The controversy began in early 1998 and this time the bank at the centre of the scandal was the country's fourth largest, National Irish Bank (NIB), formerly known as Northern Bank.

The bank had been selling a range of offshore investments from a life assurance and investment company based in the Isle of Man called Clerical Medical International (CMI) since the early 1990s. To the bank, it was a prudent and attractive investment proposition by which it could make money. To the customer, it was a way to evade tax. After the scandal broke, the NIB-CMI investment scheme became known popularly as the poor man's Ansbacher. However, many of the customers were not exactly poor. A large number owned cash businesses. They were farmers, publicans, shopkeepers and garage owners who had large sums of 'hot' money—income that had not been declared for tax. Their money was hidden in fictitious accounts and bogus non-resident accounts. Sitting in these accounts, the money appeared to belong to people living outside of Ireland but it was in fact owned and controlled by people living in the Republic. Not all the customers had their own businesses, however. Some had lump sums from a redundancy or work-related illness, while other clients simply had invested money they had inherited or saved and set aside for their retirement. A small number of customers might have innocently invested their money with the bank after being convinced by NIB that the investment in a CMI product was above board. However, most of the customers who bought a CMI product clearly recognised that it was a way of keeping their money off the radar of the Revenue Commissioners. The CMI scheme provided them with an easy way of doing just that.

The general public knew nothing about the CMI scheme until RTÉ journalists Charlie Bird and George Lee cracked the story and revealed the secret tax dodge in mid-January 1998. However, as they continued their investigations into NIB, they found even more rotten practices at the bank, practices that would have its customers, politicians and the general public up in arms.

Bird first caught scent of the story in mid-January 1998 when a trade union source contacted the RTÉ correspondent to tell him that he had come across information about an offshore investment scheme that NIB had been selling to customers through an Isle of Man company called Clerical Medical International. The purported aim of the scheme was to put an investment offshore, allowing it to grow for the depositor. However, the customer's money did not stay offshore. The money initially went offshore to CMI but was soon afterwards sent back to NIB in Ireland. The money was then held in an account that was identified only by a number, not by a name. This prevented the Revenue finding the name of the individual who owned the account, while the customer could easily gain access to their money on a daily basis, if necessary, through their local NIB branch. It was a simple scheme dressed up as a legitimate investment but designed to help customers keep their hot money hidden.

Bird and Lee set about trying to find an NIB insider who might provide more information to help prove what the trade union activist had told Bird. After secretly making a number of calls to bank officials,

Bird eventually found an NIB banker and cajoled him into assisting the reporters with their investigation. The banker handed over internal NIB documents that revealed dodgy practices at the bank relating to the CMI scheme. NIB introduced customers to the CMI scheme by approaching individuals who had large sums of money, predominantly amounts of more than £50,000 deposited in NIB accounts. The bank encouraged these people to invest their money in CMI products. Once they agreed to join, their money was sent offshore to CMI and then sent back to NIB in a numbered account after CMI's set-up charges and the bank's commission had been deducted. Under the new arrangement, the customers would earn the same amount of interest as if the money had never been sent offshore in the first place. For the service, NIB charged a large fee, 9 per cent of the money deposited. One customer was charged £45,000 for investing about £500,000 in a CMI product for just five months. It seemed odd for the bank to be charging such a large fee for a scheme that offered little more reward than if the money had been deposited as normal in an Irish account.

It soon became clear to Bird and Lee why the bank was charging so much for the CMI investment—anonymity came at a cost. The bank was focusing on specific customers—those with hot money in bogus non-resident accounts or accounts with fictitious names. NIB officials recognised that customers with hidden deposits wanted to keep their nest-eggs hidden from the Revenue, but the bank officials also realised that the customers still wanted to earn interest on their money by placing it in a deposit account. The CMI scheme provided a straightforward means of doing this. For 9 per cent of their money, the customers got a numbered account and anonymity. It was an expensive but necessary cost for tax dodgers who did not want to be hit with a massive bill from the Revenue.

The journalists had stumbled across a clear and blatant case of institutional tax evasion at a national bank. Several hundred NIB customers had invested in the CMI scheme, and the fees and charges earned on the scheme had helped boost the bank's income. Since NIB started selling the CMI scheme in the early 1990s, the bank had enjoyed double digit annual growth. By 1993, when the bank posted annual pre-tax profits of £14.6 million, it was in control of roughly 5 per cent of the banking market and was growing its branch network aggressively—it had 57 branches across the country and employed about 800 people.

What surprised the journalists most, however, was the amount of money passing through the CMI scheme. Documents leaked by their NIB insider showed that in the mid-1990s the bank had £30 million worth of investments with CMI and 173 numbered accounts. The CMI scheme was proving very attractive to some customers.

NIB had initially begun marketing the offshore CMI investment products in 1991. The following year the bank's Financial Advice and Services Division (FASD) started a road show of the CMI products, visiting branches with an official from CMI in the Isle of Man to explain to branch staff how the company's products worked. Customers signed up to the CMI products through their branches; branch managers or officials referred them to the small team working with FASD who were signing up customers. One member of the team was Beverley Flynn, the daughter of erstwhile Fianna Fáil minister Padraig Flynn and later a Mayo TD herself. She worked as a financial services manager at FASD from September 1989 until June 1997 when she was elected to the Dáil.

On Friday, 23 January 1998, RTÉ ran a news report by Bird and Lee on the *Six-One News* which outlined the findings of their investigation into NIB. The report revealed how the scheme worked and the money involved, and how the Revenue was now investigating it. Within hours of the broadcast, the bank responded, saying it was carrying out an internal investigation, that it did not condone tax evasion and that it would co-operate with the Revenue.

The following week politicians reacted to the RTÉ report. Labour's finance spokesman Derek McDowell told the Dáil that the NIB-CMI scheme was not like Ansbacher—it did not involve super-rich people, but a different class of tax evader. 'We are talking about the local businessman, the local hotelier, the local garage owner: people involved in cash businesses who ultimately couldn't resist the temptation to hide their earnings from the Revenue. These are not just a few people living in exclusive mansions; they are the middle classes, the respectable businessmen from all over the country,' said McDowell. 'I believe this is profoundly important and has the capacity to provoke a public reaction, public resentment way beyond Ansbacher.'

However, the Fianna Fáil Minister for Finance Charlie McCreevy played down the report in an interview with Lee. 'These things must be borne in context,' he said. 'The total amount of revenue collected every year from all tax sources is of the order of £14 billion or thereabouts.

The vast majority of taxpayers are compliant and pay their taxes on time—including business people—and the sums which you are talking about, they are a small proportion of the overall total sums of money involved in banks.' McCreevy said that 'things should be borne in context' because some people had been making 'some ridiculous and outlandish allegations both against the Revenue Commissioners and against other people as well'. He also peddled a line that in part defended the bank's role in the whole affair: 'National Irish Bank have pointed out themselves that the sums of money involved represent 0.5 per cent of their own total resources.' Lee asked if McCreevy was 'trivialising the story'. McCreevy replied: 'I'm not, but I'm trying to bring some reality to the situation with some of the outlandish accusations that have been made all round.'

By this stage the bank's cage had been well and truly rattled and it resorted to legal means to muzzle RTÉ from broadcasting further reports about NIB and its customers. The bank knew the journalists had more information and it felt they needed to be gagged. NIB obtained a High Court injunction stopping RTÉ from broadcasting any further reports about the bank or its customers. Playing the confidentiality card, the bank claimed it had to protect its customers.

Sunday newspapers carried follow-up reports on the emerging scandal at NIB. The *Sunday Tribune* got its hands on a letter sent by NIB to a potential CMI customer promoting the benefits of the scheme. The newspaper said the letter 'spelt out in no uncertain terms that if a person wanted to hide their funds for whatever reason, it would be easy to do so'. The *Sunday Times* reported that 'authoritative bank sources' had told the newspaper that NIB knew CMI customers were tax evaders and that NIB managers 'openly discussed how the scheme could be used to dodge tax'.

While RTÉ was waiting to challenge NIB's High Court gagging order in the Supreme Court, Bird and Lee continued their investigation into NIB. Bird met his NIB insider again, and the source handed over more internal bank documents that provided further information about how the scheme was operated by the bank. In one letter dated 5 April 1993 from the NIB branch in Church Square, Monaghan, to another manager, the branch recommended to the manager that it 'may be worth your while contacting [the customer] below named'. Written in the letter after the name of a customer, a farmer from Munster, was, 'Milks 259 cows; hot money potential.'

The NIB insider told Bird he had another story, an even bigger one concerning NIB. The CMI scheme was 'small beer compared to some of the other stuff that went on', the source said. He handed documents to Bird which showed that the bank had been loading customer accounts with interest and adding on fees to boost profits and ultimately bankers' earnings. NIB had effectively been stealing from its customers. Incredibly, when this was discovered by the bank's internal auditors, the bank stopped the practice but did not reimburse unsuspecting customers.

An internal audit report into the NIB branch in Carrick-on-Shannon, Co. Leitrim, showed what had been going on. 'It was noted that interest charges were increased without legitimate reason or customers' knowledge on 20 accounts in November 1989 and 33 accounts in February 1990. The above practice could lead to loss to the bank through customer dispute, litigation or adverse publicity.' The memo continued under the heading 'remedial action required': 'Interest amendments may only be made to correct branch errors. The practice of "loading" interest in this manner must be discontinued.' And under the heading 'response by branch management', the memo read: 'We note that as and from now only branch errors can be corrected using interest amendment sheets. While we only loaded interest rates for customers who were very demanding, we were certain that we were safe in applying the additional interest charges. No queries ever came back from customers who [*sic*] interest was loaded.'

Further documents proved that senior NIB managers, including the bank's chief executive Jim Lacey and general manager Frank Brennan, knew about the interest-loading because, according to the audit report, the Carrick-on-Shannon records had been circulated to them. Another audit report—detailing more interest-loading, this time at NIB's branch in Carndonagh, Co. Donegal, in 1990—had also been circulated to senior management at the bank.

Bird persuaded the NIB insider to do an interview with RTÉ and to reveal to the general public the crooked practices that had taken place at the bank. In the interview, broadcast in late March, the banker's face and voice were disguised so he could not be identified. The banker said that the customers with hot money had been specifically targeted by the bank.

The RTÉ reporters got their hands on more documents which showed that senior NIB management were made well aware of the practice of interest-loading and fee-adding at some of the bank's branches. In response to the Carrick-on-Shannon internal audit report, Brennan told Kevin Curran, the manager for the area: 'Given that the auditors found 33 cases of loading it would appear that that branch have used the "soft option principle" widely and this is unacceptable.' The 'soft option principle' was NIB speak for taking extra money from customers' accounts. In another memo, Lacey responded to the internal audit report for Carrick-on-Shannon, saying that interest-loading on customers' accounts must be stopped. Lacey said nothing about paying the customers back their money.

The reporters convinced the NIB insider to give a second interview about the loading of interest and extra charges on to customers' accounts. The NIB banker admitted that he himself had loaded customer accounts with interest and that his bosses had encouraged him to cover up the practice by replacing computer bank statements with false, manually typed statements. He also confessed to loading fees on to customer accounts. He said this occurred in the vast majority of NIB branches and that the bank earned millions from the practice from the early 1980s until at least the mid-1990s.

'There was extreme pressure on branch managers to increase their fee income and their interest income,' the NIB insider said in the RTÉ interview. 'League tables were prepared by senior management in the bank, highlighting the top achievers in this area. People at the bottom of the ladder felt pressurised . . . there was no legitimate reason [for the loading] other than that pressure was on the branch manager to achieve a certain level of fee income.'

The banker's comments were shocking. For the first time, the journalists had tied a bank official on television to the dodgy practices at the bank. They corroborated their story using other NIB sources— the practice of fee and interest-loading through the filing of false debit slips had been widespread within the bank and had gone on for many years. A former internal auditor at the bank confirmed their findings, adding that this had gone on in part because the audit division had been starved of resources and had frequently been unable to do its job properly. A Dublin-based manager also agreed to be interviewed. He too confirmed that the practices had taken place.

RTÉ was unable to broadcast the findings of its latest investigation into NIB because the High Court's gagging order was still in place. NIB had argued that RTÉ's reports could damage the confidence of its

customers in the bank, while RTÉ believed that it had a right to publish details because, as the High Court judge said in summing up the
case: 'There is no reason whatsoever for a customer to invest in such
a scheme other than to avail of the anonymity and therefore the tax
evasion potential of the scheme.' The High Court judge eventually
sided with RTÉ in his judgment, preferring the 'public interest in the
disclosure of such information as against the interest in preserving
[the bank's] confidence'. However, an appeal by the bank sent the
matter up to the Supreme Court. On the morning of Friday, 20 March
1998, the Supreme Court found in RTÉ's favour. Mr Justice Lynch said:
'The allegation which they [RTÉ] make is of serious tax evasion
and this is a matter of genuine interest and importance to the general
public and especially to the vast majority who are law-abiding
taxpayers, and I am satisfied that it is in the public interest that the
general public should be given this information.'

On the day the court judgment was delivered, Noel Treacy, the
Fianna Fáil junior minister at the Department of Science, Technology
and Commerce which was responsible for monitoring life assurance
companies like CMI, was preparing to send an officer from his department into NIB to investigate the Isle of Man-based scheme. On Monday,
23 March, civil servant Martin Cosgrove was named authorised officer
to investigate NIB's insurance business. More critical information
about the dubious practices at NIB would later emerge.

On Wednesday, 25 March, RTÉ broadcast the news report by Bird
and Lee about the interest and fee-loading at the bank. The report
which began on that evening's *Six One News*, 'Revealed: how National
Irish Bank secretly overcharged some of its customers', was devastating
for NIB.

'The pressure to make profits for the bank created a culture where
at certain NIB branches money was taken without any legitimate
reason from customer accounts and kept for the bank's own profits,'
said the report. 'When the bank became aware of this from its own
internal audit reports, RTÉ's investigations indicate that the vast
majority of customers who had this money taken from their accounts
were neither told of what had happened nor paid back.'

The RTÉ report outlined how interest had been increased or loaded
on to customer overdrafts and how extra fees had been charged on
accounts without the agreement or knowledge of customers. A short
time after the report was broadcast, NIB issued a statement attacking

RTÉ, saying that the incidents dated back many years and did not reflect 'the current practices of the bank'. However, the bank did admit that customers affected by the 'unauthorised practice' did not know about it and were not reimbursed. NIB said it would seek to identify the accounts and undertake to reimburse the affected customers. This was a black and white admission by NIB—RTÉ's story was right.

Reaction to the report was overwhelming. One hour after the RTÉ report, the cabinet met for two hours to discuss the revelations. A government statement was released later that evening. It announced that the Garda Fraud Squad, the Central Bank, the Director of Consumer Affairs and the Attorney General would start an investigation into NIB. The government mentioned in the statement its 'grave concern' and 'determination' to see that the money taken from customers would be 'made good by the bank'. NIB held a crisis meeting to deal with the fall-out.

The following day NIB's owner, National Australia Bank, feared a run on the bank's deposits and issued a statement to reassure customers that 'all deposits in National Irish Bank are safe and no depositor need have any cause to be concerned'. But the damage had been done.

That day normal Dáil business was suspended to allow time for a special emergency debate about the NIB scandal. Taoiseach Bertie Ahern told the Dáil that 'the bank must be made accountable. Its customers must be properly compensated and steps must be taken to ensure that the banking system is not tainted by this activity.' Tánaiste Mary Harney attacked the bank over the revelations in the RTÉ report. News of the irregular practices at NIB was, she said, 'disturbing in the extreme' and 'those responsible for such wrongdoing will be named and treated with the severity which their actions justify'. She announced that she would be seeking the appointment of an inspector in the High Court to investigate NIB.

The inspectors, she said, would find out all about the shady practices at NIB, whether staff were disciplined, why misappropriated funds were not repaid to customers and who was responsible for the decision not to repay the customers. She added that the inspector would find out whether the directors of NIB and senior management at the bank had encouraged, condoned or ignored these practices. The managing director of National Australia Bank in Europe had earlier apologised for the overcharging at the bank. Harney said the apology was 'too little, too late'.

NIB's reputation was in tatters. But worse was to come for its CMI customers. The scheme was based in the Isle of Man, but NIB sold life assurance policies to its customers. This created a paper trail in the Republic which the Revenue could use to trace each and every one of the investors involved in the NIB-CMI scheme. The Revenue could use Irish law to gain access through the courts to the depositors' names.

Within days of the scandal breaking on RTÉ, the affair had its first major victim. Lacey had stepped down as chief executive of NIB in 1994, but as a result of the high-profile job he became one of the public faces of Irish banking. This profile brought him to the attention of kidnappers in late 1993. After leaving the bank he was appointed chairman of the Irish Aviation Authority and to the board of the Dublin Docklands Development Authority. On 27 March, two days after RTÉ's report, Lacey resigned both positions. As Lacey was stepping down from these posts, Mary Harney was granted her wish. The High Court appointed former Supreme Court judge John Blayney and PricewaterhouseCoopers accountant Tom Grace inspectors to investigate NIB.

Prior to their appointment, the High Court heard that Cosgrove, the civil servant who had been appointed to investigate NIB's insurance business the previous week, found that the money passing through the bank's offshore tax scheme was huge—£50 million had been invested in roughly 500 offshore insurance policies sold by NIB since 1991. He found that the money had been invested in unauthorised insurance-linked investment policies, most of which had been sold to Irish residents. In about half of the 77 investment policies examined by Cosgrove, the money had been invested 'offshore' but had ended up back in NIB branches. Eighty per cent of those policies 'gave cause for regulatory concern,' he said. On 8 June 1998 Harney sent Cosgrove's interim report to the Director of Public Prosecutions.

Later that month RTÉ ran a news report by Charlie Bird claiming that Beverley Flynn (then Cooper-Flynn and a TD for Mayo) had—while working for NIB—told retired farmer James Howard that he did not have to avail of the tax amnesty of 1993 and that if he invested his savings in a CMI product the taxman would never find his money. The amnesty had been devised by the Fianna Fáil-Labour coalition government as an olive branch to tax defaulters, allowing them to settle their tax affairs by paying just 15 per cent of the tax due to the Revenue.

Flynn sued RTÉ, Bird and Howard over the report, claiming that she had been defamed. The case, which was heard in the High Court in early 2001, became the longest libel case in the history of the state. Flynn claimed that she had never told customers that investing in a CMI product was a good way to hide money from the Revenue or that she had encouraged tax evasion. During the evidence, three NIB customers who had invested in CMI came forward to give evidence against Flynn. One customer, Joy Hawe, a retired boutique owner, said Flynn had told her that her name would not be attached to her CMI investment and that the Revenue would not be able to identify the owner of her money. Another customer, coach business operator Sean Roe, said Flynn had told him that the taxman would never get his hands on his money if he invested it in a CMI product. He claimed that she told him he would be giving away 15 per cent of his money if he availed of the tax amnesty. Flynn denied these claims and said she had not even met Howard. She said the CMI investment was a 'perfectly legitimate product'. She said she was not a tax adviser but an investment adviser, and that it had never occurred to her to ask clients where their money had been invested or whether they had paid tax on it. In summing up the case, Flynn's barrister Garret Cooney SC claimed that RTÉ had built up a 'house of lies'. He demanded 'swingeing compensation' for his client.

The jury, however, didn't entirely believe her but they didn't think that RTÉ had proven its case fully either. The jury found that there had not been enough evidence shown by RTÉ to prove the claims made by Howard. However, they found that Flynn's reputation had not been affected because RTÉ had shown, by hearing evidence from other CMI customers, that Flynn had in fact encouraged NIB customers to evade tax while working with the bank. The jury found that Flynn's reputation had not been damaged because she was in fact someone who had advised customers to evade tax. The case lasted 28 days in the High Court. Flynn left with no damages and a legal bill of more than €2 million.

Flynn, however, refused to accept the jury's decision. She lodged an appeal to the Supreme Court. In April 2004 the state's highest court unanimously rejected her appeal. She was later thrown out of Fianna Fáil. Her disastrous court case had cost her her place in the party and millions of euro in legal fees. She was one of the biggest casualties of the NIB scandal.

It emerged in the High Court during the Flynn libel case that NIB had referred in an internal letter to potential CMI customers as 'people who have money invested offshore already or whose money is "hot"'. A senior investment NIB adviser told the court in evidence that he believed 'hot' to mean 'a hot prospect for investment' rather than undeclared money. His evidence stretched the bounds of credibility.

The inspectors' investigation continued throughout 1998 and 99, but the going was tough. In July 1998 a group of NIB managers and senior executives appealed a court decision that they must answer questions put to them by the inspectors about the practices at NIB. The bank's staff were concerned that they might incriminate themselves by making statements to the inspectors. The Supreme Court ruled in January 1999 that any confession made to the inspectors by NIB staff would not be used against them in any subsequent criminal trial. In response to the court's ruling, a number of NIB managers issued a statement through a solicitors' firm saying they had acted at all times to the direction of their employers and that they welcomed the court's finding which enabled them to co-operate fully with the inspectors' investigation.

This wasn't the only court battle for the inspectors. In March 1999 the High Court rejected a claim from NIB that the inspectors should not be allowed to investigate the bank's compliance with Deposit Income Retention Tax (DIRT), the tax that would cause much embarrassment for the entire banking sector during public hearings later that year. Those hearings would show that tax evasion was widespread in Ireland, largely ignored by the state and facilitated by the banks in the late 1980s and 90s. The next chapter of this book shows that NIB wasn't the only Irish bank to evade DIRT and assist customers in dodging their own tax liabilities.

The inspectors' investigations were still ongoing in 2003. In July of that year the High Court heard that the inspectors' work at NIB was being delayed by a lack of co-operation from people 'against whom adverse findings were likely to be made'. The inspectors handed over copies of an interim report to the bank. The following February the High Court expressed concern about the length of time the bank was taking to respond to the interim report. High Court judge Mr Justice Peter Kelly said he was anxious that a final report be produced by 31 July 2004.

While the inspectors were dealing with their court battles, the bank tried to control the damage caused by the scandal on its own terms.

In August 1998 it said it was repaying £131,166 plus interest to 370 customers arising from the improper charging of interest and fees on accounts. In May 1999 the bank said its own internal inquiry into the overcharging of fees and interest found no evidence that it had been orchestrated by senior managers in the bank's head office.

The final report on the inspectors' six-year investigation into NIB was handed to the High Court on 13 July 2004. When it was published at the end of that month, it found that RTÉ had been correct in its reports about the bank six years earlier. The inspectors' report was a damning condemnation of practices at NIB that dated back to the late 1980s. It was arguably the most critical and comprehensive report ever written about the affairs of an Irish bank. The inspectors had conducted 235 sworn interviews, including 142 with customers and 87 interviews with present or former bank staff. Once again the banking sector was rocked by their findings.

The investigation concluded that bogus non-resident accounts were opened and maintained by NIB and were widespread in the branch network between 1986 and 1998. The bank was improperly encouraging customers to evade tax owing not just on the money deposited in the bogus accounts but on the interest earned on the deposits. Fictitious and incorrectly named accounts were opened by NIB bankers and were widespread in the branch network until 1996, and customers were encouraged to use these accounts to evade tax. The inspectors concluded that CMI policies had been heavily promoted as a way for customers to hide hot money.

The inspectors concluded that taxes had been deducted from Special Savings Accounts (SSA) at a reduced rate. The Revenue attached stringent rules governing SSAs and if the customer abided by these rules, then they would be entitled to a reduced rate of DIRT. Customers had to fill out a detailed declaration and had to give 30 days' notice of a withdrawal.

An audit conducted by the bank in December 1994 found that declarations were either missing or incomplete in about 20 per cent of SSAs held by the bank and that notice was not provided in 79 per cent of withdrawals. The audit concluded that branches found it difficult to impose SSA notice requirements because they feared losing deposits and there was a lack of understanding about the procedures. NIB eventually made a tax settlement of €500,000 over these failures.

But perhaps worst of all among the inspectors' findings was their confirmation that the bank had loaded extra interest, fees and charges on unsuspecting NIB customers. The bank was effectively stealing money from its customers by forcing them to pay fees and charges they did not owe.

The inspectors also chose to name and shame the people responsible for the practices which began in 1986. They named and criticised 19 former senior NIB executives, including Jim Lacey and Beverley Flynn. NIB's external auditors, the accountancy giant KPMG, was also censured for failing to ask the management at the bank to quantify the potential liability for DIRT. The inspectors said that if KPMG had pointed out the significance of DIRT to NIB's senior management, they may not have ignored the issue. The inspectors also rapped the knuckles of the bank's own audit committee for not knowing more about the whole DIRT issue.

Many of those named by the inspectors were still working in financial services when the NIB report was published. Kevin Curran, NIB's former head of retail banking, worked on a consultancy basis with Irish Life and Permanent. Patrick Cooney, a former investment manager with NIB, was a private clients portfolio manager with Davy Stockbrokers. Philip Halpin, a former chief operating officer with NIB, was a management consultant with the Irish Management Institute.

The bank responded to the inspectors' report by revealing that it was paying for its past sins. The bank apologised again for the practices highlighted and announced that the whole affair had already cost the bank €64 million, including €30 million in compensation paid to the state and customers who had been overcharged or who had been advised to invest in CMI. NIB estimated that the total cost of the scandal to the bank would exceed €75 million.

The practice of fee and interest-loading at the bank was found by the inspectors to be random, unscientific and calculated at the whim of the bank official who was filling in the customer's charge sheet at that particular time. So how did NIB officials decide what was the right amount to charge its customers? 'It was a guesstimate,' one NIB official told the inspectors. 'Well, I would have sort of thought what sort of a nuisance has he [the customer] been over the previous period and come up with a figure,' said another. 'Truthfully, I would say there was a lot of guesswork done on troublesome accounts, put on a bit here and there,' said another. 'There was no basis really. It was really just how much trouble you had with that account during the previous charging period and it could have been as simple as just adding €10 or €5,' said one NIB official.

Thirty-seven current and former branch managers and staff admitted to the inspectors that the bank had no way of recording managing time or a system for charging customers for that time, so the fee had to be guessed. 'There wasn't a system; what was there was archaic. You were relying on memory for a good number of years,' said one NIB banker. In a memo dated 24 July 1992—and circulated throughout the bank—branch managers and staff were told by NIB's head of retail Dermott Boner to apply charges to accounts that were 'troublesome and time consuming'. Charging procedures were 'arbitrary', 'crude' and 'clumsy', the inspectors said.

They also found that NIB's FASD, where Beverley Flynn worked selling CMI investment products, told prospective investors that their investment would be kept hidden from the Revenue and that the money would pass to their beneficiaries after their death without the tax authorities finding out. Most CMI customers interviewed by the inspectors said that, prior to investing in the scheme, their money had been in bogus non-resident accounts or in fictitious accounts. According to the report, the CMI policies were sold by the bank to earn commissions, retain deposits and gain new deposits. The inspectors found that the NIB-CMI scheme was highly lucrative. A typical £100,000 investment in CMI would earn the bank £15,000 over a five-year period. At the time of the publication of the inspectors' report, the *Irish Independent* claimed that almost 15 per cent of NIB's total profits in the early 1990s came from charges and fees associated with hot money that the bank was hiding for CMI investors.

When the inspectors asked Flynn if she had been aware of the source of the money invested in CMI products, she made the same argument she had done at her libel trial against RTÉ. 'Not generally, but at times it did become apparent,' she said. '[The] source of funds wasn't an issue for me. I was an investment adviser.' Flynn, like the other FASD salespeople, was directed by branch staff to customers who were regarded as possible investors in a CMI product. According to the inspectors' report, from 1992 the head of NIB's FASD, Nigel D'Arcy, knew that money which had not been declared to the Revenue was being targeted by bank personnel for investment with CMI, but 'he failed to stop this practice'.

NIB made a DIRT settlement of €6.7 million with the Revenue in the aftermath of the DIRT inquiry. As revealed in the next chapter, the

Former Taoiseach Garret FitzGerald and former AIB deputy chief executive Paddy Dowling leave the Moriarty Tribunal after explaining how the bank had written off part of a loan taken out by FitzGerald. (Photocall Ireland)

John Rusnak, the rogue trader at AIB's US subsidiary Allfirst, pictured at his home in an upmarket suburb of Baltimore, shortly after the bank revealed that he had lost $691 million of its money gambling on foreign currency markets. (*Baltimore Sun*)

John Rusnak leaving the Federal Court in Baltimore after a judge sentenced him to seven years in prison for hiding $691 million losses in the fourth largest rogue trading scandal ever to be discovered. (Reuters)

Eugene Ludwig, former comptroller of the US currency under President Bill Clinton, was hired by AIB to investigate what went wrong in the Rusnak scandal. (Topfoto)

Dublin businessman Lochlann Quinn, chairman of AIB at the time of the Rusnak scandal, prepares to answer questions from the press on the affair. (Reuters)

AIB chief executive Michael Buckley and chairman Dermot Gleeson face the media after the overcharging scandal broke in May 2004. (*The Irish Times*)

AIB official Seamus Sheerin, head of the strategic development unit at the bank, leaves the High Court. Sheerin took a case against the bank to try and stop his dismissal. He claimed he was scapegoated over the overcharging scandal. (Garrett White/Collins)

Allfirst's head of treasury David Cronin. AIB sacked Cronin from his post at the Baltimore bank after the Rusnak affair in 2002. Cronin was named in 2004 as a beneficiary of the offshore Faldor scheme, which was established by the bank's investment management division. (*The Irish Times*)

Former AIB executive and later Irish Permanent chairman Roy Douglas, another beneficiary of the Faldor scheme. He eventually made a tax settlement of €53,259 over his investment in Faldor. (Photocall Ireland)

AIB chief executive Gerry Scanlan and chief executive designate Tom Mulcahy outside AIB Bankcentre in Dublin after publication of the bank's results in 1993. It emerged in 2004 that money was invested in Faldor on Scanlan's behalf, while Mulcahy had tax issues over an offshore account. (*The Irish Times*)

AIB's former director of strategy Diarmuid Moore discovered he had been linked to the Faldor scheme when he picked up a newspaper at Manchester airport in the summer of 2004, on his return from a sailing holiday in the Mediterranean. (Lensmen & Associates)

Former AIB deputy chief executive, the late Paddy Dowling. His family learned, after his death in the autumn of 2003, that AIB had been asking questions about an investment made on his behalf in Faldor. (*The Irish Times*)

DIRT inquiry discovered tens of thousands of bogus non-resident accounts, leaving most Irish banks with substantial DIRT liabilities. The inspectors confirmed what the DIRT inquiry had found in other banks—the use of bogus non-resident accounts at NIB was rife and bank officials rarely checked whether people were actually resident when they opened the accounts.

One NIB manager told the inspectors: 'As a manager I was delighted to see people coming in with over £100,000. I wouldn't be running around the streets to check if they were resident or otherwise.' Another manager said: 'If somebody came in to open an account and said they were non-resident and they signed the declaration, we accepted that. We didn't question them further.' The inspectors found that Lacey, NIB's former executive director Barry Seymour, and former chief operating officer Philip Halpin had failed to ensure that DIRT was deducted from interest paid or credited on all accounts. In other words, they had not done their jobs properly.

Given the explosive nature of the inspectors' report, the reaction to its publication was significant. Tánaiste Mary Harney, who had petitioned the court to have the inspectors appointed six years earlier, again spoke bluntly about the practices at NIB. 'The vast majority of people rely on the banking system to conduct their everyday affairs,' she said. 'When we give our money to the bank, the least we are entitled to is an assumption that it is safe and that it will be dealt with honestly. It is simply unacceptable that one of the country's leading financial institutions should breach that trust and behave in this manner. What went on in NIB was not some minor oversight. What I find most shocking is the culture which prevailed at the highest level in the organisation which allowed and even encouraged wrongdoing. Too many people, and indeed the bank itself, saw themselves as above the law and felt that they could simply get away with this.'

The Director of Corporate Enforcement Paul Appleby, the man in charge of policing corporate Ireland, was adamant that NIB would not get away with its practices. He described the inspectors' findings as 'deeply disturbing'. He launched disqualification proceedings against nine former NIB executives named in the inspectors' report—Lacey of Grove House Gardens, Blackrock, Co. Dublin; Seymour of Amersham, Bucks, England; D'Arcy; Brennan of Ardglass, Dundrum, Dublin; Boner of Chesterfield Avenue, Castleknock, Dublin; Curran of Avondale Court, Blackrock, Co. Dublin; former head of finance

Patrick Byrne of St Helen's Road, Booterstown, Co. Dublin; former general manager of banking Michael Keane of Corr Castle, Howth, Co. Dublin; and former regional manager Tom McMenamin of College Grove, Castleknock, Co. Dublin. In October 2005, D'Arcy agreed to be disqualified from being a director of a company for ten years over the affair.

At the start of 2006 the eight other former NIB executives were still contesting Appleby's disqualification proceedings. Appleby asked the High Court in late 2005 for access to documents from the inspectors that were not used in their final report to fight his case. However, two of the executives responded in December 2005, claiming in the High Court that Appleby was attempting to 'reopen' the NIB investigation and 'turn it into some sort of phase two inquisition'. Counsel for the inspectors said their clients did not want to hand over any papers to Appleby because they felt they should not be required to revisit their findings. The court refused to allow Appleby access to the inspectors' papers, saying that it would essentially involve the inspectors in a 'mammoth task' of revisiting their entire six-year investigation, would place an 'oppressive burden' on them and could lead to an 'endless obligation' on the inspectors to revisit their 'final' reports.

The bank and the executives were not the only ones paying for the scandal. The bank's customers who invested in the CMI scheme were also hit hard. By the end of 2005, 306 customers who had invested in NIB's CMI tax dodge had been forced to pay the Revenue a total of €56.9 million, including interest and penalties amounting to €28.5 million. Up to the beginning of March 2006, the largest published settlement was made by NIB customer Oliver Brennan, a company director with an address at Belvedere, Mullingar, who paid the taxman €1.3 million, including interest and penalties of €777,000 arising from the Revenue's investigation into NIB. Many CMI customers who had chosen to invest undeclared income with NIB in the early 1990s ultimately ended up losing their entire nest-egg and more to the Revenue. In some cases the invested money had already been spent and some customers had to take out loans or sell properties to pay for their tax settlements arising from the whole affair. Others lost their life savings. The financial impact was, for some, too traumatic, too hard to bear.

National Australia Bank's Irish subsidiary never really recovered from the scandal. The damage had been too great. NIB, once a promising, customer-focused alternative to the two dominant players in

Irish banking, AIB and Bank of Ireland, lost some of the ground it gained in the 1990s. The bank's market share had fallen below the 5 per cent mark around the time the inspectors' report was published. The bank was sold in December 2004 to the Danish bank, Danske.

With the sale, a line was drawn under the shocking litany of illegal practices at NIB. The publication of the NIB inspectors' report in the summer of 2004 came at a traumatic time for Irish banking on the back of overcharging at AIB (see Chapter 12) and alleged tax evasion by former senior AIB executives (see Chapter 13). Bank customers were shaken by the mounting scandals and their confidence was understandably rattled. The DIRT problem had been industry-wide in the banking sector (see Chapter 8), but RTÉ's reports on NIB in January and March 1998 specifically put one bank under the microscope. No other Irish bank was scrutinised more by the state than NIB.

NIB had desperately wanted to be one of the big boys of Irish banking but was overwhelmed by greed. As the use of bogus non-resident accounts dried up in the 1990s, NIB found a new way to beat the system. It believed it had a foolproof investment scheme in its CMI products, a surefire way to retain its 'hot' deposit base, an essential asset for the growing bank. But complacency sank NIB. Its staff did nothing to hide the nature of the CMI scheme. The scheme was shamelessly sold for what it was, a vehicle to hoard secret money anonymously in the bank's deposits, earning its crack team of salespeople sizeable commissions in the process.

Like later bank scandals, the NIB controversy was blamed on the culture within the bank. That culture involved the bank setting relentless targets to lower-ranking staff that forced them to adopt practices that would later jeopardise the bank's entire operation. But the culture was nurtured from above. By laying down these targets, NIB senior management was pitting branch managers against each other. The competition became so intense that staff were forced to take shortcuts over proper procedures and this ultimately cost the customer. Overcharging may have been carried out by junior staff, but the procedures at the bank had been weakened by a management structure that placed greater importance on making profits. Corners were cut and when mistakes were found, they were covered over and customers were none the wiser.

Using a simple anecdote, one former banker likened deliberate overcharging to theft. One banker suggests to another that they add extra interest and charges on to a customer's account because they have been difficult. The other banker dismisses the idea, saying: 'I tell you what, why don't we just break into his house tomorrow night while he's asleep and steal his television?'

The NIB scandal showed that systematic overcharging and bank-sponsored tax evasion had boosted profits and bankers' salaries. Proper management and ethical standards were pushed to one side by the go-get-'em, aggressive sales staff and branch managers whose only remit, it seems, was to boost income, commissions and the bank's market share.

The bank's *modus operandi* was all about making money, but at the expense of proper standards and legal procedures. Despite Flynn's claims that she didn't offer tax advice because she was just an invest-ment adviser, the inspectors found that questions were indeed asked about whether a customer had undeclared income sitting in the bank. This was the sole focus of the investment drive. Tax dodgers were the bank's clear target for this highly lucrative investment scheme.

To NIB, it didn't really matter who they were or where their money had come from, as long as they had the money. In the early 1990s there were plenty of seasoned and wealthy tax cheats around who needed to find a new outlet for their hidden money. To the bank, it was all about earnings over ethics. Tax evasion was actively encouraged as it improved the bank's bottom line. Overcharging had the same effect. The victims were chosen at random. The more difficult a customer you were, the greater the likelihood you would get ripped off.

Even when the overcharging was discovered by senior NIB manage-ment, the practice was quickly ended and quietly buried. The bank's law-abiding and taxpaying customers knew nothing about their stolen money. A short time later, the bank needed another way of making money and found it by offering its tax-evading customers a costly but advantageous service. Helping some customers to evade tax and overcharging others ultimately had the same benefit to the bank and its staff—it boosted profits and increased wages. The customers happily continued to evade tax until two journalists exposed the ugly practices at one of the country's fastest growing banks with crucial assistance from some NIB insiders who were more than willing to spill the beans.

Chapter 8

The DIRT Scandal: bogus non-resident accounts

N ever have so many known about a scandal for so long and done so little. There was no name more appropriate for it than the DIRT scandal. The whole affair left a stain on the Irish banking sector; no one emerged from it clean—not the banks, not its customers, not the tax collectors, not the politicians. The controversy revealed that in 1980s and 90s Ireland there existed a culture of state and bank-sponsored tax evasion.

The scandal initially centred on the evasion of Deposit Income Retention Tax (DIRT) by the banks, but it later emerged that tens of thousands of people had opened accounts with false names and addresses to hide large sums of money which had not been declared for tax. What made the controversy even more contentious was the fact that the bank's customers had not acted alone. Bankers, senior civil servants and tax inspectors were all accessories to the fraud. They simply turned a blind eye while the banks and their customers abused the system, depriving the country of tens of millions of pounds at a time when Ireland was in dire economic straits.

Civil servants had known for years that people living in Ireland had deposited money in accounts that purportedly belonged to people living overseas. Many of these non-resident accounts were a sham. They allowed depositors to evade tax. Official Ireland had long suspected that the non-resident accounts were being abused but did very little about it until the practice was publicly exposed in 1998. The subsequent parliamentary inquiry revealed how every bank in the country had systematically facilitated tax evasion by ignoring the obvious problem with non-resident accounts or by blatantly encouraging and helping customers to open these accounts and to break the country's tax laws. The Department of Finance and the Revenue Commissioners had known for some time that there was a problem with these accounts but chose to turn a blind eye to the whole charade, fearing that a crackdown might lead to economic meltdown.

The Fine Gael-Labour government thought the introduction of DIRT in 1986 would clean up this grey area of Irish banking. Until then, the onus was on Irish depositors to declare and pay any tax on the interest earned from deposit accounts. But officials in the Department of Finance believed that bank customers were flagrantly ignoring the rules by not declaring their deposits. This meant that the state was losing out on taxes worth millions of pounds. The new tax put the responsibility back on the financial institution—the bank would deduct a percentage of the interest and forward it to the Revenue on behalf of the customers.

The only depositors who didn't have to pay DIRT were non-residents. To declare their non-residency when opening an account, they had to fill out a bank document called Form F which included the name, address and country of residence of the depositor. The Revenue was not allowed to inspect Form F's, creating a simple loophole that could be used and abused to the benefit of customers. A depositor would put in a name and address, but not their own; they typically belonged to a relative living in London, Manchester, New York or Boston, somewhere where there were plenty of Irish people, so that if the taxman came searching there would appear to be nothing out of the ordinary. Many bogus accounts were opened in this way, but some bank officials—often in collusion with their customers—got a little more adventurous. They would not only write down a fictitious name but a fictitious address as well. It could be John O'Brien with a home address at 1 Main Street, New York, for example. There was no John O'Brien and of course there was no such address. With their new fake account, the customer avoided DIRT because the money supposedly belonged to a non-resident and the individual's identity would remain a secret in case a tax inspector came calling.

It was a straightforward way of evading tax. But it didn't stop there. Because the account was hidden from the Revenue, the money deposited in the account was usually hot too. Bank officials were happy to help customers break the law by opening an account for them. Some bank officials themselves suggested the bogus non-resident account to the customer as a way of depositing money in a savings account and not paying tax on the cash.

The bankers benefited from the arrangement—the more money on deposit in a branch, the higher the commission earned by the branch manager. The bank officials' justification was a simple one. It was well known that tax evasion was widespread in banking. The bankers, not wanting to be left out, thought, if everyone is doing it, why can't we? Even though it was illegal, banks felt that if they weren't involved, the customer would simply go down the road to a competitor and open a bogus account there. Such was the scale of the practice that some banks even advertised for non-resident deposits in the windows of their branches.

This simple mechanism, in operation throughout the banking sector, allowed customers to evade tax and tens of thousands of them availed of it to hide hot money from the Revenue. It was a cosy relationship which benefited the customers and the banks alike.

One former senior banker said bank managers were under huge pressure in the 1980s and 90s to meet massive targets and generate profits. Impossible sales objectives were part of the culture of the time, he said, and bankers were expected to go to extreme lengths to meet them. He said bogus accounts would have been opened because of the intense competition for deposits between the banks, including the state-owned ACC which offered favourable deals to customers.

The state knew there was a major problem with bogus non-resident accounts dating back to the early 1960s. The Revenue, the Department of Finance and the Central Bank all knew something was not right. However, not enough cases were discovered to prove how widespread the practice of tax evasion actually was. It was not until the DIRT inquiry in 1999 that the country's compliant taxpayers discovered a practice that had been ignored for more than a decade. They learned that there had been a two-tier tax system in operation in Ireland for many years—one for law-abiding taxpayers and another for those with lump sums, usually individuals who were involved in cash businesses who didn't want to part with their hard-earned money.

The DIRT inquiry, when it began in 1999, was the start of the cleansing of rogue Ireland, the beginning of an end to the wink-wink, say-nothing culture that had permeated Irish banking life. A subcommittee of the Dáil Public Accounts Committee (PAC) set out through televised hearings in August and September 1999 to get to the bottom of the scandal. It turned over many rocks and asked awkward questions of senior bankers, civil servants, tax inspectors, politicians and accountants. It shone a light into the dark corners of Irish financial life and highlighted some despicable practices that had been ignored for years. The subcommittee examined the period from 1986, when DIRT was introduced, up to 1998. One senior AIB official said of the 1999 DIRT inquiry: 'It was one decade casting a judgment on the practices of the previous decade.' Not only was the judgment damning for the Irish banking sector, but the punishment was severe.

Despite the official organs of the state being aware of the problem, little was done over the years to resolve it. The state feared that if the Central Bank and the Revenue started clamping down on non-resident accounts, it would force the holders of genuine accounts to close them and cause a flight of capital from the country. Civil servants and banking regulators believed this could threaten the state, which in the mid-1980s was on the verge of bankruptcy. The amount of money stored in non-resident accounts stood at £2.5 billion during the early 1980s, so the issue was a significant one. As was later discovered, capital had been flying out of Ireland throughout this period anyway; thousands of Irish individuals were evading tax on large sums of money in Ansbacher (Cayman) and offshore trusts and accounts.

Maurice Doyle, a former secretary at the Department of Finance and a former governor of the Central Bank, told the DIRT inquiry that the country was on its knees financially at this time. He used a simple example—in 1986 for every £6 that the state was collecting in tax, it was borrowing £1 and spending £7, but not repaying its loans. As a result, government debt had risen to 133 per cent of GNP. Ireland had a higher foreign debt per head of population than Poland and a higher national debt than Brazil, both of which were regarded as 'basket cases'. Doyle said these were the figures of a Third World country, and against this backdrop he said the state was expected to find an effective anti-evasion tax regime to ensure DIRT was paid.

However, Ireland was unwilling to lift the carpet and see the potential dirt underneath. Better to ignore it.

An attempt had been made by the Fine Gael-Labour coalition in the 1983 Finance Bill to introduce a measure that would have forced non-residents to swear an affidavit proving they were in fact not resident in Ireland, but the Central Bank opposed the idea, believing that more than 50 per cent of non-resident deposits would move abroad if more stringent proof of non-residence was required from customers. The idea of an affidavit was quietly dropped.

While some officials believed that the bogus non-resident issue was not a huge problem, the truth was that no one really knew how much money was being salted away into these accounts by bogus and genuine depositors. The difficulty was that to find out, the state would have to take a risk and introduce vigilant measures to prevent abuses of the system. But no one was willing to take that risk. This was a self-serving and not uniformly accepted argument put forward by the state at the time. The tax crackdown, which has targeted bogus non-resident accounts since 2000, did not precipitate a flood of capital from Ireland, although the economy was at this time among the richest in Europe.

Two former secretaries at the Department of Finance, one of them a former governor of the Central Bank, told the DIRT inquiry that 'a failure of political will' had created the problem. However, the inquiry team dismissed this theory as being groundless. It said that no proposals were ever made to successive ministers by senior civil servants to strengthen the law between 1986 and 1998. 'I realised that there was no point in recommending to ministers that Revenue should be given these powers and if I were to do it, I think I would be worried myself that they would cause the outflows [of capital],' Sean Cromien, secretary of the Department of Finance from 1987 to 1994, told the inquiry. 'I found it wasn't in the national interest to make proposals.'

Commentators criticised the stratospheric tax rates introduced by the successive governments as one of the main reasons for the growth in the number of bogus non-resident accounts. Punitively high taxes turned the country's citizens towards phoney accounts, and their bankers were only too happy to acquiesce.

The Central Bank was also unwilling to tackle the problem. Central Bank governor Maurice O'Connell claimed that the dire economic situation of the mid-1980s prevented the state from striking a proper balance between preventing the flight of capital and the creation of an effective tax regime for collecting DIRT. O'Connell, who also worked in the tax and exchange control sections of the Department of Finance, told the state watchdog, the Comptroller & Auditor General who investigated the non-resident accounts scandal in 1999: 'We did our best. We were not as efficient as we might be in terms of collecting tax. We were broadly aware of the fact that people were avoiding tax. Everybody agreed it was wrong.' But O'Connell said there was a fear that if the regime became more stringent, it would unhinge the economy. He said the culture at the time was, 'For God's sake, whatever you do, don't rock the boat, the boat being the exchange rate. That was the culture.'

The Revenue also turned a blind eye. An internal Revenue memo dated 24 July 1986, which became known as SIM 263, directed tax inspectors not to ask the banks for declaration forms on non-resident accounts pending 'further instructions'. (SIM stood for Superintending Inspector's Memorandum. A superintending inspector later became known as a chief inspector.) When the scandal came to light in 1998, further instructions arrived. The DIRT subcommittee never discovered who wrote the 1986 memo. No documentary evidence concerning the drafting of the memo was ever discovered and there were no papers found showing who wrote it, according to the Revenue.

Tax inspectors expressed regret at the DIRT inquiry that the Revenue did nothing about the problem. 'It would be difficult to challenge it, given the weight of the establishment above you. I'm sorry we never did it and I do regret it,' tax inspector Paddy Donnelly said. The Dáil subcommittee concluded that 'the existence of SIM 263 and the failure to countermand it adversely affected morale within the [Revenue] inspectorate. Furthermore, the situation, leading as it did to a scenario of taxes going uncollected, contributed to problems for governments as they grappled with a fiscal crisis and the restoration of order in the public finances.'

But even the Revenue passed the buck. It was not a case of just one arm of the state ignoring non-resident accounts; everyone ignored them. A senior Revenue official, Christopher Clayton, told the inquiry: 'We all knew you didn't have to be the Revenue Commissioners to know that the whole system as brought in was subject and liable to abuse. That was common knowledge. I think it was even knowledge the government knew and the Dáil knew; they were doing the best they could in the circumstances. What we didn't know was that there was a very large widespread problem. We weren't aware of the scale of it.' It was also suggested that given the paperwork involved, it would have required 'an army' for the Revenue to resolve the problem.

Even though the Revenue did not move against non-resident accounts, some officials recognised there was a problem. In 1991 tax inspector Sean Moriarty researched and wrote a paper examining the use of deposit accounts and other forms of investments to avoid paying tax. Even though Moriarty was ahead of his time, his research was regarded as speculative. Moriarty himself said he was 'plucking at scraps of information. What I was trying to build was a framework of perceptions of experienced investigators that was leading us in a certain direction,' Moriarty told the DIRT inquiry.

Moriarty's report may have been regarded as tenuous, but in 1992, the year after he presented his report to his superiors, the Revenue discovered a specific example of tax evasion using bogus non-resident accounts. It should have set alarm bells ringing within the Revenue. A special investigation by the Revenue's 'special inquiry branch' found that customers of the Bank of Ireland's branch in the small village of Milltown Malbay, Co. Clare, had been using bogus non-resident accounts to evade tax and that the bank was avoiding the payment of DIRT on these accounts. The bank's chief executive Pat Molloy described the Milltown Malbay case at the DIRT hearings as 'intensely embarrassing' and 'an appalling situation'. The discovery failed to trigger a wider investigation of the banking sector. Again, excuses were put forward by the Revenue: there was a lack of resources, it was claimed, and an investigation of non-resident accounts in all Irish banks would take years. The Revenue also complained that they were powerless to go into branches to investigate the banks.

The first person to highlight the true scale of the problem was a banker, Tony Spollen, group internal auditor within AIB. He was instrumental in breaking the DIRT scandal. His investigations and conclusions, which were revealed in the face of strong opposition from his employers, suggested that vast amounts of money were being hidden in non-resident accounts. Spollen's 1991 internal audit report sparked the controversy and the DIRT inquiry. He believed that the bank was sitting on a potentially massive liability arising from its non-resident accounts and it had not even recorded the problem in its books.

AIB officials first realised they had a major problem with Irish deposits in 1989. The bank also took deposits in its branches in Britain, which were subject to a tax called Composite Rate Tax (CRT), the British equivalent of DIRT. The bank offered CRT-free accounts to non-residents. However, in 1989 the tax authorities in Britain, the Inland Revenue, carried out audits on several AIB branches in Britain and found that some of the non-resident accounts were in fact held by British residents and so should have been taxed. The bank was forced to pay stg£3.7 million in CRT owing on these bogus non-resident accounts. This alarmed some staff at AIB back in Dublin— the bank might well have a similar problem on its hands with its Irish deposits.

A senior AIB executive, Henry O'Brien, head of the bank's Irish inspection unit, joined the dots between the British problem and a similar one in Ireland. He wrote a letter to Spollen in 1989. 'I feel decidedly uncomfortable about the position in the Rep. of Ireland. When DIRT was first introduced there was a move to clean up the position, but then word went round the branch system that Revenue would not exercise their rights to review the position at branches and progress more or less ceased . . . we carried out a 100 per cent sample at a number of branches and the outcome was disconcerting. In general there is not a major problem in Dublin or the east coast area, but from west Cork to Donegal the position is bad in a large number of branches.'

O'Brien acknowledged that the bank was 'acting improperly', but he said that resolving the non-resident accounts issue would lead to 'higher interest rates payable on resident accounts' and 'a probable loss of deposits'. 'I would like to see a gradual move towards putting our house in order,' O'Brien told Spollen, who forwarded the letter to the bank's finance director, John Keogh.

The bank decided to examine the matter further but didn't bother to tell AIB's chief executive Gerry Scanlan or the board of the bank. Little was done to get to the bottom of the matter in 1990, but early the following year Spollen sparked a crisis within AIB. He said the bank should have paid the Revenue £10 million for its DIRT liability for one six-month period, so the bank might be facing a massive tax bill for unpaid DIRT dating all the way back to 1986.

Around the time Spollen was warning AIB about its massive DIRT liability, the Revenue also started making noises about the issue. In early 1991 Tony McCarthy, a senior inspector in the Revenue's investigation branch, knew there was a major problem concerning the payment of DIRT and felt it was time to take action. For McCarthy, it was little more than a hunch, as there was not much evidence available. The issue had after all been ignored for so long. He had come across a few cases of DIRT evasion in AIB branches and in late 1990 he had been in touch with the bank about two cases in particular, so he decided to start with AIB. He set up a meeting with some senior staff at the bank in early February 1991. What transpired at the meeting remains a bone of contention within AIB to this day.

The bank claimed that at a meeting on 13 February 1991 in its head-quarters in Ballsbridge, Dublin, its representatives met four senior Revenue officials, including McCarthy, and that during the meeting the Revenue and the bank agreed a deal whereby the bank would clean up the non-resident accounts problem and the tax officials would not seek tax owing before April 1990. The bank claimed that an amnesty had been agreed at this meeting and confirmed this in follow-up phone conversations with McCarthy. This was vehemently denied by McCarthy and the Revenue. McCarthy later told the DIRT inquiry that 'a settlement wasn't even on the agenda or wasn't on my mind . . . settlements wouldn't have arisen at that stage' and that 'there was no question of reaching an agreement or an amnesty—an amnesty wasn't even within my remit'.

McCarthy said he could not have offered an amnesty without the approval of the board of the Revenue Commissioners. However, the bank claimed that McCarthy told its representatives that he was acting with the approval of the board. He said he would not have agreed an amnesty because he did not believe that the bank had examined all its non-resident accounts in full. The bank was of the belief, following the meetings and telephone conversations with the Revenue, that the tax authorities were prepared to 'look forward rather than backwards' and that the bank would redesignate bogus non-resident accounts and resolve the whole issue by 30 September 1991. The alleged 1991 'deal' became something of folklore within AIB. It was even suggested by Gerry Scanlan that the deal was done with McCarthy at a gaelic football match either in Cork or Croke Park. Scanlan later withdrew this suggestion and apologised to McCarthy when he objected. Senior AIB officials still claim that the bank negoti-ated a deal with the Revenue in 1991, even though the DIRT inquiry concluded that no deal was done.

Spollen was sceptical about the alleged deal and demanded that the bank seek a letter from the Revenue confirming it. He felt there was no way that the Revenue would agree to deal with the bank without knowing the full extent of the DIRT liability.

Another former AIB official said: 'There may have been an understanding between the bank and the Revenue after this meeting, but there was no amnesty or deal.' In February 1991 Spollen suggested that a deal would require legislation for it to become effective, but said this was 'not desirable for this type of issue'.

The bogus accounts problem was not going away for AIB. In 1991 an examination by AIB found that 53,000 of its 87,000 non-resident accounts were bogus and that they contained £600 million owned by depositors who claimed to be living outside the state. It was a huge sum and illustrated the size of the problem facing AIB.

Another matter relating to Spollen complicated the DIRT controversy for AIB. In January 1991 John Keogh, group finance director, told Spollen that Gerry Scanlan had decided to transfer him out of his job as group internal auditor. Spollen refused to move. The decision was made at a time when the DIRT issue was causing turmoil within AIB. The Dáil subcommittee said it created 'its own mini-inferno in the higher echelons of the bank'. Spollen refused to sign off on the DIRT liability until it was investigated in full and the Revenue deal was scrutinised. He was an old-school, by-the-book banker who stubbornly asked the simplest of questions if he didn't understand something, and continued asking them until he did.

At this stage the bank probably realised that it had an internal whistle blower on its hands. Spollen's proposed transfer was eventually dropped in early February, at which stage he had outlined to the bank that its 'Form F problem could run into hundreds of millions of pounds'. Spollen wrote to the head of internal audit Ireland, Don Walsh, asking him to put a figure on the amount of money in deposits. 'Please quantify immediately the amount of false Form F money on the books of the group. The estimate (£350m–£400m) which you have given me is frightening,' Spollen wrote to Walsh. In March, Spollen estimated that the bank's DIRT arrears could be an estimated £100 million, excluding interest and penalties.

Eight years later, at the DIRT inquiry, Scanlan and other AIB officials played down Spollen's estimate. Scanlan said he dismissed the figure when he saw it, describing it as 'infantile' and 'a back of beyond calculation'. The DIRT inquiry heard that Scanlan had no real contact 'in any formal sense' with his senior managers about the matter. It concluded that it was 'unusual' that Scanlan was kept fully informed of Spollen's transfer but 'extraordinary' that he was not told about the scale of the DIRT problem. In other words, the inquiry team didn't believe him.

Things got personal with Scanlan's 'infantile' reference at the DIRT hearings. Scanlan had turned on Spollen. The suggestion behind the issue of Spollen's transfer was that he might have been driven by a personal grudge against the bank. He was being painted as something of a conspiracy theorist with an axe to grind. This enraged Spollen. He returned to the DIRT inquiry the following day, evidently shaken by Scanlan's comments. Spollen raised the DIRT issue, not because he was pursuing some crusade, but because as group internal auditor of the bank he felt he had to question everything and was simply doing his job. He believed he had found a major problem in the bank which had to be dealt with. He rejected the claims that he had a gripe towards his employers, describing them as 'scurrilous'.

Some sources within AIB attributed the tension between Scanlan and Spollen to the fact that Spollen was a close friend of AIB chairman Peter Sutherland—the two became friends when they were 8 years old and attended Gonzaga College in Ranelagh, south Dublin. This may have discomfited Scanlan because as AIB chief executive he had to report to Sutherland. Also, Spollen had not initially told Scanlan about their friendship and the AIB chief executive became aware of it independently at a later date.

Spollen would later be vindicated by the DIRT report and AIB's DIRT settlement. The bank made a tax settlement of £90 million (€114 million) with the Revenue, the largest tax settlement ever to be made in the history of the state. However, Spollen had been put through the wringer during the inquiry. AIB sources recalled that the bank had agreed, before Scanlan gave his evidence at the DIRT hearing, that it would not attack Spollen. However, according to a former AIB executive in the bank at the time, Scanlan 'performed a solo run'.

The deteriorating relationship between Scanlan and Spollen not only threw light on the DIRT scandal but raised another controversy. The day after Scanlan criticised Spollen personally at the hearings, the former AIB auditor felt it was necessary to explain why they had fallen out—it had not been over the DIRT issue, but the bank's underwriting of a failed share issue in the oil exploration company, Dana Exploration, in 1988. Spollen referred to the fact that AIB had placed almost £250,000 worth of stock in the bank's pension fund accounts when the market failed to take up the total placing. He later claimed that he had been instructed by Scanlan to change an audit report. The bank later claimed that it had just asked Spollen to remove something that was potentially libellous. 'It went badly wrong,' Spollen said, 'and rather than face the music and admit it, the bank had been left with an underwriting stick—what happened was the shares were put into the widows and orphans' accounts [and] into the staff pension fund accounts . . . The stock exchange was never informed.' Spollen investigated the affair and said the bank's actions were 'civilly wrong and in breach of fiduciary duty'. A later report by AIB's finance director John Keogh found that although there was 'a clear breach of group standards and of good practice, no notifiable offence had occurred'. Keogh's report was passed on to the board in December 1989 and it accepted his findings. The bank felt this should have been the end of the matter.

But Spollen felt it was important to raise the issue again. He sent further details about the Dana affair to Scanlan, who returned the material back to him with a letter saying: 'In terms of my personal time management, it would be impossible for me to discharge my role in the group if executives generally decided to bypass the normal reporting arrangement.' Spollen later said this letter brought matters between the men to a head. 'It was either him or me,' said Spollen. In March 1991, as the DIRT controversy was causing headaches for senior staff at AIB, Spollen wrote a memo outlining his grave concerns about the Dana affair. A short time later Spollen and AIB agreed a severance deal and he left.

But Spollen's work on DIRT returned to haunt the bank. His controversial internal 1991 report outlining the scale of the bank's DIRT liabilities triggered the whole DIRT scandal. On 5 April 1998 journalist Liam Collins revealed the contents of Spollen's 1991 report in a story in the *Sunday Independent*. Six months later *Magill* magazine published more details about the extent of the tax owing arising from DIRT. The reports prompted the Comptroller & Auditor General to investigate the scale of the tax owed from bogus non-resident accounts across the financial sector. The comptroller's report led to the setting up of a subcommittee of the Dáil Public Accounts

Committee and the televised inquiry into the scandal that dredged the financial sector for more details. Large numbers of viewers tuned in to watch the daily DIRT proceedings live on the television channel TG4. Many elderly spectators showed up in person at the hearings in Kildare House across the road from Dáil Eireann in Dublin city centre. They came to watch the politicians pontificating before the television cameras, while the bankers squirmed under questioning.

The inquiry subsequently led to multimillion pound tax settlements by the banks and their customers. While it was later revealed that AIB, being the state's largest bank, had the lion's share of the bogus accounts and liabilities, nearly every other bank also had bogus accounts, in particular the state-owned ACC, which was established to manage the affairs of the country's farmers.

The subcommittee's findings on the DIRT inquiry made a mockery of the banking sector. It showed that banks had facilitated widespread tax evasion through the use of bogus non-resident accounts. Not only did the bank itself evade DIRT by setting up these accounts, but in some instances they actively encouraged customers to open these accounts.

The banks had to cough up huge amounts of back tax. After conducting a series of look-back audits between 1998 and 2000 the Revenue collected €225 million, including €133.5 million in interest and penalties, from 25 financial institutions. AIB's settlement made it far and away the worst offender in the whole affair.

Even the state-owned bank was involved and had to pay up in the scandal. ACC was forced to pay a DIRT liability of £17.9 million, even though the bank said at the DIRT hearings that it estimated its total DIRT liability at just £1.5 million. The PAC subcommittee concluded that successive finance ministers, as the owners of ACC, should have been alerted to the non-resident accounts problem in the bank. 'None of the ministers appear to have discharged their responsibility for the ACC in an appropriate manner,' the DIRT report said.

It emerged during evidence at the DIRT inquiry that the orders of the directors of the state bank had not been implemented, including one which would have solved the DIRT issue. The former chairman of ACC Bank Dan McGing explained that because the ethos at the bank was on agriculture, not on finance, and that many of the bank's branch managers were 'agricultural science graduates rather than business graduates . . . they were local people and they were prominent people locally… they were good footballers, they were hurlers.' Former senior

ACC executives said at the hearings that they had more important issues than tax evasion to deal with, staying in business being the main one. In 1992 the bank's auditor said ACC could owe £17 million in unpaid DIRT. At the time ACC had assets of just £20 million.

Other banks also put their hands up and made multimillion pound tax settlements. The Bank of Ireland settled its DIRT bill with a cheque for £30 million. The Ulster Bank paid over £4.2 million.

The money collected from the financial institutions was not the end of the affair for the Revenue. Tax inspectors knew from past experience that this was just the tip of the iceberg. The Revenue collected tax of £200,000 from Bank of Ireland over the tax evasion discovered at its branch in Milltown Malbay in Co. Clare in 1992. However, the bank's customers coughed up €2.5 million. The Revenue realised there could be tens of millions more untaxed money out there.

After it had dealt with the banks, the Revenue turned its attention on the customers who had hidden money in the bogus accounts. To identify the depositors, the Revenue needed names and addresses from the bank, even the false ones, if it was to get the real identities of the tax dodgers who still owed money. The pressure was on. Hundreds of thousands of compliant taxpayers had paid their taxes throughout the 1980s and 90s, yet one group of citizens had ignored their civic duty and stashed large sums of money away. The tax authorities were determined to get the names and addresses of the people who had cheated the system.

So the money wasn't the only thing that the banks handed over. The 1999 Finance Act gave the Revenue new powers to trawl bank records for the identities of the tax cheats. Before the act the Revenue was likened to a lone fisherman on a riverbank fishing with just a line in the water and no hook or bait. The new law gave the Revenue a large net to cast.

The Revenue obtained a series of High Court orders that forced the financial institutions to hand over details of the customers who held bogus non-resident accounts. In many instances the banks wrote to the customers in advance, telling them that they had been identified as having a bogus account and that their names and addresses were being handed over to the Revenue. For many, the letter was quite a shock. Some claimed they had not been aware that their accounts had been bogus. However, most people knew well that they had bogus accounts.

Before the Revenue started chasing the customers, they offered an olive branch. They were given a six-month window to November 2001 to come clean, declare any bogus accounts that they had ever held and pay the tax due. If they came forward, interest and penalties would be capped at 100 per cent of the tax due. This was enough of a draw for 3,675 people to make voluntary disclosures. They paid over a total of €227.2 million. The Revenue agreed not to publish the names of those who came forward. This was an attractive proposal to many people. Being named and shamed as a tax cheat in the 21st century no longer carried the badge of honour it once did. It was an embarrassment for a professional or business person, a black mark on their career.

The benefit of making a voluntary disclosure and remaining anonymous was not open to those who ignored the November 2001 deadline. Once the deadline passed the Revenue set about chasing down the remaining tax cheats. Working from the lists of names and addresses it had obtained from the banks, the Revenue sent threatening letters warning depositors who had bogus accounts to come forward. By the time the Revenue's campaign was drawing to a close at the start of 2006, it had collected €386 million from 8,500 people. The figures show that those who failed to come forward voluntarily and were later caught paid much higher interest and penalties. These totalled €262.5 million of the €386 million collected after November 2001, whereas interest and penalties made up €111 million of the €227.2 million collected before the deadline.

For some depositors, the amounts handed over to the Revenue were huge. As of the start of 2006, insurance broker Charles J. McCarthy of Glencorrin, Cork Road, Fermoy, Co. Cork, held the record for having made the largest settlement arising from a bogus account. He paid €6.4 million to the Revenue, including an astounding €3.9 million in interest and penalties, because he failed to pay tax of almost €2.5 million when it fell due. McCarthy, a shareholder and director of the McCarthy Insurance Group which had offices in Dublin and Cork, said the money had been left to him by his parents and it had been lodged to an account in AIB. He claimed that the bank 'blackguarded' him over it. 'I took advice from the bank and afterwards they hung me out to dry,' he said. The settlement must not have left McCarthy too strapped for cash, however; when contacted on his mobile telephone for comment in June 2004, he was attending the races at Royal Ascot in England.

Some remarkable and tragic stories surfaced during the Revenue's trawl of the bogus non-resident accounts. One story concerned an Irish woman living in England. Mary O'Neill, a retired woman living in Ilford, Essex, received a letter in early 2003 from ACC Bank telling her that details of the joint bank account she held with a Pascal O'Neill had been identified as a possible bogus account and were being passed to the Revenue Commissioners. At this stage the Revenue had written to all the banks and financial institutions in the country, asking them to write to customers who held bogus non-resident accounts in their branches to tell them that their accounts would soon be investigated by the Revenue. O'Neill was stunned. She had never opened an account, nor had she ever had dealings with ACC before. She said she had never even heard of ACC. She had been living in England for 50 years and visited her relatives in Ireland several times a year. What made the account even more mysterious was that Pascal O'Neill had been dead for more than 70 years. Pascal O'Neill was, in fact, her husband's older brother who had died in Strokestown, Co. Roscommon, in 1932 at the age of three months from bronchial pneumonia. She made some enquiries and discovered that £94,000 had passed through the account in the late 1980s and early 90s. The account was in her name and had her English address on it. She carried out an investigation of her own and found out that the account had been opened in a rural branch in Co. Cork. It turned out to be a bogus account, but not O'Neill's. It belonged to a relative.

'My husband has never got over it,' said O'Neill. 'More so because they used his baby brother's name. It was like grave robbing—I felt that if you took the name, you might as well take the bones. I could not believe that they could do something like that.'

O'Neill's story is one of the best examples of the lengths to which people went to conceal undeclared money in Ireland in the 1980s and 90s. By putting a false name on an account, money could be hidden from the taxman and the real account holder could pop down to their local branch as they pleased and withdraw the money that supposedly belonged to someone overseas.

For some, the price of being named as a tax defaulter for having a bogus non-resident account was too much. Just a few days before Christmas 2002, a man in a rural area of Munster committed suicide over the pressure of having a bogus account. His wife said her husband could not face the shame of being named as a tax defaulter.

The woman claimed that the couple didn't know that their account in the local AIB branch was a bogus non-resident account until they were told by the bank in March 2002. By then, the woman said, it was too late for him to settle his affairs without being named. The man owed just €15,000 in tax, slightly over the Revenue's then threshold of €12,700 for which names would be published as tax defaulters. She said her husband had planned to settle by 17 December, but there had been delays in finalising the matter. 'It might have saved his life, because the longer it dragged on, the more stressful it was,' his wife said. 'He was extremely troubled at the thought of being named and shamed publicly. No matter what happens, I am without a husband, my children without a dad.'

Other unusual cases emerged. One woman claimed to the Revenue that she had lived in relative poverty for years only to discover several years after her husband's death that he had hidden a sizeable sum of money from her in a bogus non-resident account.

A TD cropped up in the list of bogus non-resident account holders. Fianna Fáil TD Michael Collins, brother of the former foreign affairs minister Gerard Collins, was found to have squirrelled away money in a bogus account. In 2003 he made a tax settlement of €130,602. He was twice elected to the Dáil for Fianna Fáil but resigned from the parliamentary party over his bogus account. He has decided to retire from politics at the next general election.

In some cases people had to take out loans and sell assets to pay for the tax bills over their bogus accounts. It didn't matter if the hidden money had been spent; they still had to make a payment to the Revenue. For many the money was long gone. It had been spent on their children's education or homes for their sons and daughters. The Revenue had little discretion when it came to dealing with depositors who failed to come forward after the November 2001 voluntary disclosure deadline. Revenue officials argued that the customers should have known their money was being deposited in a bogus account which could lead to a tax settlement further down the line, and if they did not, then they should have at least asked. For many customers, it was a case of see no evil, hear no evil. They never asked the question. Better to ignore what was happening and blame the bank official if the Revenue found out.

Unfortunately for many depositors, they had no comeback when it came to making bank officials accountable. Many came forward to claim that they had no knowledge of having had a bogus account and had no involvement setting it up. A group was set up by a former AIB manager from Co. Cork, Conor O'Mahony, to represent those who claimed to have been duped into setting up bogus accounts by bank officials. O'Mahony's group was for many a comfort because it put bank customers in contact with others in a similar situation at a traumatic time. However, a legal action remained a difficulty for many bogus account holders, primarily because of a precedent set in a case taken by a Co. Tipperary farmer, Michael Gayson, in 2000. Gayson had claimed that bad advice from AIB had led to him paying a tax bill of £175,000. The judge said the bank was not only heavily involved with Gayson in hiding his money from the Revenue but actively advised and encouraged him about how it could be done. However, the judge said that Gayson's conversation with a bank official, who told him not to avail of the 1988 tax amnesty, was 'off the cuff' and the bank could not be liable to Gayson for any advice given by one of its staff. Gayson's tax bill would have been £84,000 if he had availed of the amnesty. The judge said he inferred AIB's failure to call its official as a witness was because the bank feared the evidence would be embarrassing.

The law also threw up an obstacle. Criminal cases could only be taken against bank officials who set up bogus accounts for customers if the customers themselves proved that the bankers had 'aided and abetted' them by getting them to sign a false income tax return. This meant proving that the banker had been at the shoulder of the customer assisting them and encouraging them to fill out the form falsely. This would have been highly unusual, given that the bankers would only have set up the accounts for the customers. This stopped many cases against bankers, despite the fact that the Revenue examined a number of cases and considered taking a prosecution. Steps have since been taken to change the law in this regard.

By March 2006, the Revenue had collected a total of €838 million from its investigations into the use of bogus non-resident accounts by Irish citizens and financial institutions. Everyone involved in the scandal was badly hit by the affair.

The back tax amounted to €331.2 million, while the total paid in interest and penalties far exceeded this figure—it came to €507 million. Some depositors had to pay up to five times the tax due in interest and penalties, in many cases wiping out the money hidden in the first place. It was a bitter pill for many customers to swallow, especially those who had been advised where to put their money by their bankers.

The Revenue's bogus non-resident accounts investigation began to wind down at the beginning of 2006. Thousands of bogus account holders were named in the Revenue's quarterly tax defaulters lists over the previous four years, in some cases with multimillion euro tax settlements beside their names.

The investigation triggered further inquiries by the Revenue into widescale tax evasion scams used by Irish people. During the investigation, the Revenue discovered that depositors had also used offshore assets and accounts, including those in subsidiaries of Irish banks in places such as the Isle of Man, Jersey and Guernsey. In some cases the Revenue found that some people had taken their money out of bogus accounts when they thought they were about to be discovered and invested it in overseas accounts, only for the Revenue to find these as well. Others had transferred their money from bogus accounts to single premium insurance products, lump sum investments made with life assurance companies. The bogus accounts investigation gave Revenue officials the scent of other trails involving major tax evasion by Irish citizens. The hunt would eventually lead to more tax settlements, amounting to hundreds of millions of euro.

The DIRT inquiry exposed a murky side to Irish banking. The financial institutions had acted as willing accomplices to facilitate tax evaders, recognising that the state was not willing to interfere in the process, all because of a perceived threat to its economic stability. After the inquiry published its conclusions, the state set about righting past wrongs and making amends for the decades when the tax affairs of tens of thousands of Irish citizens had been ignored and the banks flagrantly allowed its customers to breach the laws of the country. The introduction of DIRT turned bankers into tax collectors, but they had no intention of fulfilling this role. As a result, the state lost out on tens of millions of pounds in unpaid taxes at a time when public spending was curtailed, hospital waiting lists grew and income tax rates stayed at exorbitant levels.

In the early 2000s the state reaped massive tax windfalls from the investigations into the widespread tax evasion of the 1970s, 80s and 90s. The money collected, running to more than one billion euro, went to the state. It should have been collected many years earlier.

The DIRT scandal exposed an ugly face of Irish banking that existed for almost two decades. The exposure shocked the system and raised the bar on the standards of tax compliance, proving to people that tax evasion was no longer accepted, that tax dodgers would be pursued and that there was nowhere left to hide. It was an embarrassing lesson, not just for the Irish banking sector, but for the state and its people.

Chapter 9

Offshore Tax Evasion: nowhere left to hide hot money

In the mid-1990s some managers in Bank of Ireland were actively encouraging some of their wealthy customers who did not want to pay Deposit Income Retention Tax (DIRT) to put their money on deposit in the bank's trust company in Jersey in the Channel Islands. A long-established tax haven, Jersey was popular with customers because they could be guaranteed confidentiality.

Trusts are a legitimate and useful way of putting aside money for relatives or friends, as long as the sole control of the funds is handed over to a trustee and the money is declared for tax.

Frank, a businessman from the south of the country but living in Dublin, was one such customer. He said his bank manager put him in touch with an official from the Bank of Ireland Trust Company in Jersey in 1994 after the manager told him he would have to deduct DIRT on the interest earned on the money in his Irish bank account. Frank had a large, six-figure sum of money on deposit in Ireland and was not happy paying DIRT on his nest-egg. His bank manager realised this and told his customer that he was advising all of his 'large deposit customers' to move their money to the bank's 'special trust business' in Jersey.

Frank did as his bank manager advised him. He telephoned the official in the Bank of Ireland Trust Company in Jersey. 'The official suggested that I meet him in the car park of the Mill House in Stillorgan in Dublin. I thought it was unusual to meet there and I said it to him. But he explained he was very busy and he was driving around meeting a lot of people, and it was handier for him,' Frank said. The Mill House suited the Jersey-based official because it had a large car park and he could pull up in his car and conduct the business there and then. When they met, Frank handed him a bank draft for £750,000 in the car park. This is how he came to set up his Jersey trust.

Over the nine years that Frank held the trust he travelled to Jersey via London 'seven or eight times' to check on his money. He said that as soon as taxi drivers at the airport in Jersey heard his voice, they knew where to take him on the island. 'When they heard my accent, they asked me was I going to the bank. So I wasn't the only one,' said Frank.

John, a professional, has a similar story to Frank's. John had a large sum on deposit with Bank of Ireland in a branch in the midlands. He made the money from selling properties and said that his earnings had been declared for tax. He said his branch manager advised him in 1994 to put his money into an offshore trust with Bank of Ireland in Jersey. If he did, the manager said he would have no liability for DIRT and would be able to pass the money on to his children in a tax-efficient manner.

'I was given a number in Jersey where I spoke with a bank official,' said John. 'He was primarily interested in how much money I wanted to invest. I arranged to meet him in the car park of a well-known Dublin 4 hotel and he explained everything about the trust and gave me a brochure. We agreed on the sum that I would invest and arranged to meet in the same place the following week. He told me I should bring a draft payable to the Bank of Ireland Jersey. The sum involved was in excess of two million Irish pounds, which I handed to him at our next meeting.

'I told the official that I considered the entire transaction most unusual, but he explained that as the Jersey trust operation had no office in Dublin, it was necessary to conduct our business in this manner, particularly to reduce the involvement of other Bank of Ireland staff outside of the Jersey office. He told me that the trust business operated outside all other Bank of Ireland branches and had its own in-house computers,' said John.

'It was a very highly confidential operation, details of which would never be divulged to anyone by Bank of Ireland. The official explained that because almost all of the money going into the trusts was hot money, the Bank of Ireland was conscious of the need to impress upon its clients the strict secrecy and utmost confidentiality of the entire scheme. He explained that in the event that Bank of Ireland Jersey Trust Co. passed information to the Revenue, then the Bank of Ireland Trust Co. would indemnify all of its clients against any Revenue liability,' said John.

The bank later denied it gave any indemnity to trust customers in the event of them having to pay money to the Revenue. Asked in early May 2003 if Bank of Ireland provided banking services in other car parks, a spokeswoman for the bank described Frank's encounter with the official in the Mill House as 'bizarre'. She said that 'things have changed' but declined to comment further, saying that the bank did not discuss 'individual cases'.

To describe Bank of Ireland's car park-banking operation as 'unusual', as John did, is downplaying the whole episode. That the country's second largest bank was taking multimillion pound deposits in the car parks of Dublin pubs and hotels was highly peculiar. It reeked of a covert operation more at home in a gangster story than in Bank of Ireland.

Frank and John were among 400 customers who received letters from Bank of Ireland Trust Co. (Jersey) in April and May 2003 advising them to settle any outstanding tax debts arising from the money in their trusts before the Revenue Commissioners launched an investigation into the bank's Jersey operation. The Revenue had been tipped off by the British Inland Revenue, which had come across a case of tax evasion involving the Bank of Ireland's trust business in Jersey. The Revenue in Dublin immediately started sniffing around the bank.

The investigation into Bank of Ireland was the first in a new Revenue investigation that would reveal widespread tax evasion involving offshore subsidiary companies of Irish banks and thousands of Irish citizens. It did not only involve offshore assets such as trusts but also accounts and other investments. The Revenue had stumbled across yet another multimillion euro tax scam.

As in the bogus accounts investigation, the Revenue chose a softly, softly approach at first. It needed to smoke the tax defaulters out, but given the complexity of overseas banking operations, it could take

years if the banks and customers were unwilling to co-operate. The
Bank of Ireland Jersey investigation was the test case. The Revenue
decided to approach the bank first rather than investigate the customers. If it could convince the bank that it would eventually get the
names of the Irish trust holders, then maybe the customers might be
willing to put their hands up and admit they owed large amounts of
tax and pay up without the need for a costly and time-consuming
investigation. The bank agreed to the Revenue's demand.

The bank wrote to its customers, saying that it had come to an agreement with the Revenue to recommend that its customers make a voluntary settlement. The strategy worked. The warning letters prompted
254 trust customers of the Bank of Ireland in Jersey to pay €105 million
in back taxes, interest and penalties. About 80 per cent of the Irish
residents who held trusts in Jersey came forward, paying an average of
about €400,000 per person. One individual handed over €7.3 million,
while 27 people made settlements of between €1 million and €2 million.
The scale of the tax collected was higher than the money involved in the
bogus non-resident account inquiry. The Revenue had stumbled across
a major tax fiddle. If other financial institutions were at it as well, then
the exchequer could be set for a massive windfall.

When he received the Revenue's letter, Frank had €1.27 million on
deposit, having seen his initial £750,000 (€950,000) deposit grow in the
Jersey trust. He criticised Bank of Ireland for acting on behalf of the
Revenue in offering the customers a tax deal. 'It seems to be a betrayal
on the bank's part,' he said. 'It was supposed to be confidential. That is
how it was sold to me.'

The Revenue knew there were substantial sums of hot Irish money
on deposit in the overseas branches of Irish banks, particularly in the
well-known tax havens of Jersey and Guernsey in the Channel Islands
and the Isle of Man. However, the Revenue recognised that those
banks were also offering their services to Irish people living in the
North, Britain and other European countries, and that they had very
large sums of money owned by non-Irish customers. Buoyed by the
sizeable windfall from the Bank of Ireland Jersey investigation, the
Revenue started contacting other Irish financial institutions.

In June 2003, shortly after the Bank of Ireland customers made
their settlements, Anglo Irish Bank chief executive Sean FitzPatrick
said it had handed over general information to the Revenue on Irish
customers with money in the bank's Isle of Man branch. FitzPatrick

told *The Irish Times* that only 3 per cent (€30 million) of the bank's €1 billion on deposit in the Isle of Man belonged to Irish residents.

During that summer Permanent TSB also wrote to 3,000 customers warning them that the Revenue would launch 'a formal investigation' into the Irish customers of the bank's Isle of Man branch on 17 November 'to establish the identity of Irish residents who hold or have held accounts with Irish Permanent (IOM) [Isle of Man] Limited'. The letter was enough to scare some Permanent TSB customers into making tax settlements totalling €45 million.

The amount paid to the Revenue per individual in the offshore accounts was slightly higher than the bogus non-resident accounts investigation. It had been suspected for some time that vast amounts of hot money from the Republic had been hidden offshore in overseas Irish bank branches. A report by KPMG in 1999 found that there was the equivalent of almost €4 billion on deposit in Isle of Man subsidiaries of Irish financial institutions. The belief at the time was that at least some of this money must belong to Irish residents. If it did, why were Irish residents lodging large sums of money outside the state? The suggestion was that the money had not been declared for tax. Recognising the amount of money at stake, the chairman of the Revenue Commissioners, Frank Daly, met chief executives of Irish financial institutions to discuss offshore assets and accounts held by Irish residents.

Shortly after Daly's meeting with the financial chiefs in late 2004, all the other financial institutions with overseas branches sent 120,000 letters to their offshore Irish customers warning them that the Revenue was going to start looking for the names, addresses and bank account details of any customers who held accounts in their overseas branches. Bank of Ireland, AIB, Ulster Bank, National Irish Bank, Irish Permanent, ACC, ESB, Irish Nationwide, Anglo Irish and First Active all sent letters to these customers, advising them to sort out their tax affairs before 29 March when the Revenue was due to begin its investigation. The financial institutions warned the customers to come forward if they had any tax liabilities arising from the money hidden in the accounts.

The financial institutions were aware that the Revenue had been given new powers in the 1999 Finance Act to demand any information from them which could help them identify tax cheats. The Revenue had used these new powers successfully in its investigation into the bogus non-resident accounts by obtaining High Court orders forcing the banks to hand over information.

The financial institutions knew that the Revenue would come up against major obstacles if it tried to get information on Irish customers from their overseas branches, especially given the stringent secrecy laws in existence in many of the tax havens. However, clearing accounts in banks in the Republic had been used by the financial institutions to siphon money into offshore branches. The banks knew the Revenue could get hold of information on these accounts, so they felt it was better that their customers heard the bad news first from them, rather than from the taxman.

Incredibly, the same banks that had (in some cases) advised customers to set up offshore accounts in their overseas branches were now advising and encouraging the same customers to put their hands up and surrender to the Revenue. For many customers it was hard to stomach. A Reaction Group, set up by former AIB manager Conor O'Mahony to take some kind of action against the banks on behalf of customers whose bogus non-resident accounts had been exposed to the Revenue, decided to assist the customers who now had to pay up over the offshore accounts. Those people who had hidden hundreds of thousands in offshore accounts were now having to pay that much again—and in some instances more—to settle their tax affairs.

One tax official said: 'Most people knew what they were doing. Some of them didn't even care. They wanted to know how they could best protect what had been siphoned off, away from the Revenue, for years. Sure, some of the customers might have been advised by their bank managers to set up these accounts, but I don't think they needed a lot of persuading.'

While the Revenue waited to see how many people would respond to its voluntary disclosure deadline of 29 March 2004, it announced that from the following May it would use new powers, forcing tax dodgers to hand over details of offshore bank accounts held with Irish banks. The Revenue had lobbied the government to have the extra powers included in the 2004 Finance Bill to strengthen its powers in advance of its investigation into tax evasion through the use of offshore accounts. The new controls gave them the opportunity to get their hands on documents held by Irish financial institutions relating to their overseas branches.

By the end of March 2004, 15,000 people had contacted the

Revenue to say they had offshore accounts and wished to make a disclosure. Many of these people had no tax liabilities; and some declared bank accounts that they had opened in the North and Britain when they lived or studied there. However, many did have liabilities and the amounts involved were huge. By March 2005 the Revenue had collected €812.8 million from 13,730 people who held offshore accounts. The money collected from the offshore accounts investigation comprised €375.6 million in back tax and €437.3 million in interest and penalties. This went some way to cutting the borrowing that the exchequer had been expected to make that year and left a surplus for the exchequer.

The bogus and offshore accounts inquiries led the Revenue in turn to examine the use of single premium policies—lump sum investments sold by life assurance companies—to evade tax. These products were similar to the CMI investments that led to multimillion euro tax settlements from National Irish Bank customers, only in that case it was a bank that sold the products rather than the life assurance companies.

By March 2005 almost €400 million was collected from 5,000 people who had hidden hot money in single premium policies. In 2006 the Revenue also began looking at the use of offshore credit cards sold by overseas banks to Irish customers. The cards have proved to be an effective way to evade tax on large sums of money in other countries. A tax investigation in the United States found that individuals had been 'front-loading' credit cards bought from foreign companies by lodging large amounts to their accounts in advance and then spending openly on the cards. It appeared that the individuals were racking up huge debts, when in fact they were spending undeclared money. The amount of tax collected in the US turned out to be relatively small.

Aside from massive amounts of tax collected by the Revenue from its investigations into bogus accounts, offshore assets and single premium policies, the inquiries also had a psychological impact on taxpayers and tax compliance in Ireland. Widespread tax evasion had been detected and eradicated. It created an atmosphere in which tax evasion was no longer a socially acceptable practice. The thinking had changed. If you evaded tax, you were not only avoiding your civic duty, you were robbing your fellow citizens, compliant taxpayers, of money that would be used for everyone's benefit. 'Tax is what pays for state services,' Revenue chairman Frank Daly told the Dáil Public Accounts Committee. 'If you hide money we will come after you. The culture of compliance is improving. People realise that the tax authorities will not go away.'

The 1999 and 2004 Finance Acts opened the books of the banks to
official scrutiny. Previously, banks could run offshore schemes and
lure customers with mouth-watering guarantees that their accounts
would be kept hidden, while at the same time growing sizeably with
interest.

The backgrounds of the tax cheats linked to the different scandals
spoke volumes about how they became involved in the various
schemes. Ansbacher involved the big boys of Irish business. The
average amount paid in tax settlements by Ansbacher depositors was
roughly €521,000. This compared with an average settlement of
€185,000 in the NIB-CMI scam, €58,000 in the offshore assets investigation and €49,000 in the bogus accounts inquiry. These figures
show the sliding scale of tax evasion in the scandals and reflect the
participants' standing in society.

Ansbacher depositors were largely high fliers from Dublin and
Cork, the main centres of money in Ireland, with a notable number of
its customers living near Des Traynor, the architect of the scheme, on
the northside of Dublin. The NIB customers involved in the CMI
scheme were primarily living in the border counties of Donegal,
Cavan, Monaghan, Leitrim and Louth and slightly further south
towards north Meath where many NIB (formerly Northern Bank)
branches were located.

Offshore account holders tended to be centred around Dublin and
the surrounding counties, while bogus accounts were endemic in the
counties along the western seaboard from Cork to Donegal. Many
people, who had voluntarily declared offshore accounts to the Revenue
and paid back taxes, and who had accounts in the North, were from the
border counties. Many with offshore trusts and accounts most likely
had six-figure sums on deposit outside the country.

Bogus account holders were more likely to be living in areas of the
country where local people had close personal relationships with their
bank managers, which explains why so many of them later complained
that they had opened fictitious accounts on the suggestion of the bank
manager or with their assistance. The holders of bogus accounts
tended to access their money more frequently than participants in the
other scams, while the owners of offshore assets and accounts were
wealthy enough to leave their money sitting in an account outside the

state for years on end earning substantial sums of money in interest.

Leona Helmsley, the widow of a New York property heir who was dubbed the 'Queen of Mean' after a famous tax evasion case, once said that 'only the little people pay taxes'. The Ansbacher and National Irish Bank scandals revealed a gold club for influential, well-connected and cash-rich people. However, the DIRT inquiry and the bogus non-resident accounts investigation proved that the little people were at it as well. Tax evasion was rampant across the country, endorsed and supported by the country's banks. The follow-up offshore and single premium policies investigations not only showed that evaders had to pay tax but drastically reduced their options for hiding money. The climate had changed for good.

Even though many local bank managers and officials suggested that customers open offshore accounts or trusts and helped them deposit money in them, the customers had no comeback. They would not be able to recoup money from the bank in compensation for the tax paid.

Many bank officials and managers benefited from offshore accounts and trusts. Commissions and bonuses were based on the amount of money an official had on deposit in an account or trust under their supervision, so the more money they managed, the more they were paid. Some local bank managers and officials also benefited financially from referring customers on to offshore subsidiaries and opening accounts or setting up trusts with them. In some financial institutions, even though the money was offshore, it was regarded— for the purposes of assessing a branch manager's commission-based bonuses—as being on deposit in the customer's Irish branch, from where they had been referred to the overseas branch.

Unlike the DIRT inquiry, the country's banks emerged relatively unscathed from the offshore accounts episode. Instead, the customer was hit worst of all, having to pay hundreds of millions of euro in back taxes. Other than the embarrassment suffered from yet another scandal in the industry, the banks walked away scot-free.

Chapter 10

Politicians and the Banks: clearing debts for VIP customers

It was the story that everyone wanted to read but nobody could ever write. However, in early 1983 business journalist Des Crowley felt he had enough information to write it.

Questions had been asked for years about how the Fianna Fáil TD Charles Haughey, one of the most controversial figures in Irish politics, had become so wealthy. No one was really sure where his money came from. It was widely believed that Haughey had earned his fortune through a series of astute investments in the 1950s and 60s. This made him appealing to voters; they believed that if he could enrich himself, then as a public representative he could make the country rich too. Or so some thought.

Crowley was between jobs in January 1983 and writing the occasional story as a freelance for the *Irish Press* and *Evening Press* since leaving the *Sunday Tribune* the previous year. However, he was concerned that his work for the *Irish* and *Evening Press* might dry up. He felt that if he wrote an exclusive story, it would impress his editors enough and guarantee him more work in the future. One of the ideas he had in mind was the story about the source of Haughey's money.

The Dublin politician earned a modest salary as a TD, yet he was living a conspicuously lavish lifestyle with a large mansion in north Co. Dublin, an island off the coast of Kerry, bloodstock and a stud farm. There was a glaring incongruity between how much Haughey earned and how he lived. It just did not make sense. Nothing concrete had ever been written in the press about his money. Haughey had been Taoiseach for nine months in 1982, his second term in power as leader of Fianna Fáil, but by early 1983 he had lost power and was sitting on the opposition benches in Dáil Éireann.

Around this time a number of reliable sources told Crowley that Haughey owed the country's biggest bank, AIB, about £1 million— about €5 million in today's money. It was a staggering figure when you consider that at the time the price of a pint of Guinness was £1.08 (€1.37), the average annual industrial wage was £7,500 (€9,500) and the average house cost about £20,000 (€25,400). To have overdrawn your bank account by £1 million was unthinkable in the early 1980s, a time of relative financial penury in Ireland. This is what makes the story of Haughey's bank debts all the more unbelievable.

'I had been going in and out of AIB for a few years,' recalled Crowley. 'I knew a lot of people in there because they were always having social drinks. An awful lot of the guys in there would come up to me and tell me about this Haughey story. I remember asking them for documents to back it up. They all wanted me to do the story but they would not give me documentary support. Eventually I realised that five or six AIB people had given me the information, so I felt if I was running a story I would be able to attribute the information to sources close to the bank and could run the story without going to Bob Ryan [AIB's public relations man] for confirmation.'

Crowley wasn't the only journalist to get wind of Haughey's precarious finances. While editing the *Sunday Tribune*, Conor Brady, who later edited *The Irish Times*, said in his 2005 autobiography that in 1981 he received an anonymous package in the post that appeared to be Haughey's personal bank statements from AIB in Dame Street. They showed an overdraft of about £200,000. Brady decided not to publish the story. 'Wrongly, in light of subsequent revelations, I gave Haughey the benefit of the doubt', Brady wrote. He said that Crowley, who was business editor in the *Sunday Tribune* when Brady edited the paper, was unhappy that he had decided not to publish it.

Crowley, however, was happy to write the story while working for the *Irish Press*. He believed that it was correct because he had built up relationships with a number of reliable people within AIB and felt they were telling the truth. He filed the story to the *Irish Press*. His editor had a 'high opinion' of it, he said. On Friday, 28 January 1983, the *Evening Press* published the article under a 'Special Correspondent' byline. It was based on 'well-informed speculation'. Crowley's article read: 'It has been rumoured in discreet financial circles for years that Mr Haughey owed £1 million to a major bank and that the bank had held its hand because of his elevated position.' It continued: 'This correspondent can confirm that sources close to Allied Irish Banks (AIB) insist that he owed them around this sum last year.' Publishing the article was an audacious move because it confirmed what many had suspected of Haughey privately for years—that the money he was spending was not his own.

It caused a storm of controversy. A couple of days later Crowley was in the Ilac Library in Dublin city centre when he received a phone call. It was his editor who wanted to know if he had any documentary evidence to back up what he had written. He said he had nothing.

Three days after the article was published, on 31 January, AIB released a statement attacking the *Evening Press* for its article about the financial affairs of a 'well-known figure'. The bank disputed Crowley's claim that Haughey had owed the bank £1 million the previous year. 'This statement is so outlandishly inaccurate that Allied Irish Banks feel bound, as a special matter, to say so positively and authoritatively', said the bank. The statement was damaging to Crowley's reputation and credibility as a journalist. 'It stopped me getting a staff job as a journalist for two years,' he said.

What made the episode most bitter for Crowley was that his story was almost entirely correct, except for one crucial detail—Haughey had owed AIB £1.143 million, but the reference to 'last year' was wrong. Some £750,000 had been raised by a number of Haughey's benefactors and paid to the bank in January 1980, three years previously, and the bank accepted this as settlement of the entire debt. The bank simply wrote off the rest.

These facts would not come to light for another 14 years, and even then it would take a battalion of barristers and solicitors in the late 1990s a considerable amount of probing to reach the conclusion that Charles J. Haughey had indeed owed the bank over £1 million. What Crowley wrote, based on informal meetings with bank sources, took two government-appointed tribunals of inquiry and months of statements, letters, questioning and direct evidence to confirm.

In 1997 the government-appointed Moriarty Tribunal, which began investigating Haughey's finances and his relationship with AIB in great detail, proved that Crowley's article had been almost entirely accurate, contrary to AIB's statement. 'The statement showed how people behaved in those days when you upset them. They didn't just keep their head down. They expected you to insert a lie into the newspaper,' said Crowley. There were plenty more revelations to come behind the lies.

Any time Haughey was asked about where his money came from, his stock response was, 'Ask my bank manager.' In 1997, when he appeared before the tribunal, he tried to deflect this question again. This time it wasn't to his manager. He claimed that Des Traynor, his friend and one-time colleague at his accountancy firm Haughey Boland handled all issues relating to his money. Traynor, having died in 1994, was not around to defend himself against the accusation.

Even though Haughey admitted at the Moriarty Tribunal in 1997 that from 1960 he had handed over sole control of his financial affairs to Traynor, the tribunal discovered that Haughey had handled his own affairs and that he had numerous dealings and rows with AIB over his spiralling debts. Haughey had claimed that the late Traynor 'took over control of my financial affairs from about 1960 onwards. He saw it as his personal responsibility to ensure that I would be free to devote my time and ability to public life and that I would not be distracted from my political work by financial concerns. The late Mr Des Traynor had complete discretion to act on my behalf without reference to me.'

The tribunal eventually unearthed evidence which showed that Haughey's bank manager had endured a horrid time trying to deal with the Dublin politician and curb his spending throughout the 1970s. The tribunal eventually estimated that Haughey had received more than £8 million between 1979 and 1996. This money helped fund his magnificent lifestyle. The source of most of this money has never been identified and probably never will.

From the moment Haughey was elected to the Dáil in 1957, he perceived himself as the new crown prince of modern Ireland. He felt his lifestyle should match this status. His pay as a TD was modest and later, even as a minister and Taoiseach, the money he was earning was not

nearly enough to keep him in the lifestyle to which he had grown accustomed. His interests lay in horse breeding and farming, both expensive
pastimes, and after 1969 he had a Gandon mansion, Abbeville, and a
250-acre estate in Kinsealy, north Co. Dublin to maintain.

Haughey might have felt that the stately Abbeville was a perfect fit
for this up and coming politician, but the cost of the house's upkeep
was far beyond the financial means of a lowly Dáil deputy. As lord of
the manor he was obliged to pay for the maintenance of the mansion
but simply couldn't afford to. Any observer could see that his extravagant lifestyle was well beyond the earnings of a public representative,
and he had no obvious source of additional income. It would later
emerge that in the 1970s he relied heavily on overdrafts and drawings
on his AIB accounts to fund his expensive lifestyle.

To a prudent bank customer, relying on bank loans at a time of
high interest rates might appear a risky business, but Haughey had
no qualms about owing hundreds of thousands of pounds to the
country's largest bank. And this was at a time when interest rates ran
into double figures and bank debts could easily spiral if not addressed.
The health of Haughey's financial position seemed to ebb and flow
during the 1970s, depending on his political strength. When he was in
a position of power, money flowed into his coffers from a variety of
sources and when he was in opposition the stream of cash dried up.
During the 1970 Arms Trial, Haughey was acquitted of importing
weapons to be used to protect the Catholic communities in the North
during the early years of the Troubles. However, his ambitions for
high office were in the short term ruined by the affair and he found
himself in the political wilderness.

As soon as Haughey was thrown out of the cabinet in May 1970, he
found himself in dire straits from a financial perspective. The 1970s
turned out to be a difficult decade for him money-wise, and he leaned
heavily on AIB. His borrowings from the bank began to mount as he
tried to continue running his home and stud farm. In September 1971,
Haughey was earning just £7,000 a year from his parliamentary
career, but AIB allowed him to run up debts of £255,000—36 times
his salary. He had promised to sell off some land to reduce the debt.
He continued to make promise after promise to the bank, but no
payments were ever made and the debt rocketed.

In 1972 Haughey made some efforts to clear his debt at AIB, which
had reached £250,000. He lodged £100,000 to his account, reducing

his overdraft to £150,000. However, the money used to pay off some of the AIB debt was not his own. It came from other banks—he was borrowing money from Northern Bank Finance Corporation to repay AIB. Haughey later said he banked with Northern because he was reluctant to bank extensively with the Agricultural Credit Corporation (ACC), as a member of its board had affiliations with Fine Gael. Haughey did not mind that people in AIB knew he was heavily in debt, but if a political rival found out, he might well be rumbled and left in a precarious situation politically. By November Haughey's AIB overdraft had risen again—to £183,000.

In the early 1970s Haughey was spending about £12,000 a month. Even though he was massively in debt, he did nothing to curtail his spending. The money was coming largely from overdrawn AIB accounts. He had to pay his staff and fund the upkeep of his mansion, stud farm and yacht. He continued to live way beyond his means. He owned one of the Blasket Islands, Inishvickillane, off the Co. Kerry coast, and in the 1970s spent £150,000 bringing electricity to the house.

Haughey also had an expensive extra-marital affair to support. In January 1972 he had begun seeing fashion journalist Terry Keane. Their affair lasted 27 years and became another costly drain on his finances; he treated Keane to jewellery, travel, and meals at some of the most expensive restaurants in Dublin, London and Paris. He later spent thousands of pounds on handmade shirts from Charvet outfitters in the French capital.

By the end of 1972 Haughey's spending was causing major problems for AIB officials. In November of that year he agreed to clear his debts by the end of February 1973. He planned to do this by selling property in Co. Meath and land next to his home in Kinsealy. He eventually agreed to sell 17.5 acres of his land in north Co. Dublin for £140,000 to Cement Roadstone Holdings (CRH), where the man who handled his financial affairs, Des Traynor, was a director. CRH claimed in 1999 that Traynor had no involvement in the purchase of the land, on which CRH established a production plant. By the end of 1973 Haughey owed AIB £295,000. He borrowed another £160,000 from Northern Bank Finance and used it and the money from the CRH deal to reduce his debt at AIB to £129,000 in February 1974. It wasn't long, however, before his debts started to mushroom again.

Haughey's indebtedness was causing huge problems for AIB's staff at its branch in Dame Street and higher up the chain of command within the bank. An internal memo from the bank's regional manager for Leinster, J. J. McAuliffe, to the manager of the AIB branch on Dame Street in February 1974 outlined the 'difficulties, strain and embarrassment which had been suffered by the bank due to Mr Haughey's proclivity towards making arbitrary, unauthorised drawings on his accounts'. In a letter to the manager of AIB, Dame Street, dated June 1974, McAuliffe said: 'Quite frankly we are appalled, notwithstanding the clear and unequivocal understanding that these accounts would be operated strictly within the limits sanctioned by the board, your client should commence once again to draw excessively on his accounts.'

During this period Haughey tried to assure the bank that he had money due to him from an insurance claim and that he would sell land and bloodstock at Rath Stud, his stud farm. But his borrowings for the farm had infuriated the officials. McAuliffe said in an internal memo written in June 1974: 'While it is observed that in very particular circumstances you gave permission to draw £20,000 additional on the Rath Stud account as a very temporary facility, he had gone much further and the account now stands at overdrawn £31,486 in excess of the limits. Your client's attitude cannot be tolerated and we have no doubt that the board will take a most severe view of the situation.'

At a meeting with AIB officials in Dame Street the following month, Haughey said he found any restraint on his accounts unnecessary and galling. In a letter sent to the bank that month, he fobbed the bank off with the promise of money from the sale of horses and an outstanding insurance claim. He added that he was 'preoccupied with Dáil business' and would be 'much freer' to deal with these matters the following week.

Haughey was trying the bank's patience. However, AIB held the deeds for Inishvickillane and on a house and land in Sligo owned by Haughey, and yet did not feel it necessary to force the sale of both to reduce the TD's debts. In another internal bank memo in October 1974 McAuliffe said Haughey had 'abused our confidence and trust and we can no longer entertain hope that his accounts will be operated in a regular fashion. Accordingly, it is recommended that he be informed that debts will not be allowed exceed present figures.' The bank wanted Haughey's debt to be cleared by the end of February 1975.

But Haughey's spending continued unabated in 1975. During that year he spent £18,000 paying the salaries of a manageress and eight men working at Rath Stud. The outgoings for his stud operations amounted to £32,600 for the entire year. However, at the start of the year, he had reduced his debt to £120,000 and this seemed to boost his confidence. He went back to AIB seeking additional borrowings. At a meeting in the Dame Street branch he confirmed his income was 'negligible' compared with his spending. However, he still told the bank he was going to build his summer home on Inishvickillane. McAuliffe wrote in an internal memo that during a meeting with Haughey the politician was 'vague about the source of income' for the work on his planned holiday home. Haughey was warned that he would only provoke the bank if he asked for more money. The following month the bank took matters a step further and asked Haughey for his chequebooks. While Haughey conceded that he was 'at crisis point', he refused to hand over the chequebooks but said he would take 'immediate and resolute steps to satisfy the bank'.

Haughey's debts climbed even further in 1976. By April of that year he owed the bank £246,871. By June this had grown to £272,980; and by September it stood at £304,964. He also owed £220,000 to the Northern Bank Finance Corporation. On 13 September, when his AIB debt stood at £304,000, he made detailed proposals on how he would cut his borrowings, which had amounted to more than half a million pounds, a staggering amount for a man earning just £7,000 a year. On top of the outlay on his bloodstock operations at Rath Stud, his domestic staff at Abbeville were costing him £5,000 a year and he had other miscellaneous lifestyle expenses of more than £9,000 a year. Still, he continued to enjoy the high life, despite the fact that AIB was footing the bill. During 1976 he used a bank strike as an opportunity to write even more cheques than usual, again racking up further debt.

On 14 September 1976, Haughey met the then AIB chairman Mon O'Driscoll and two other senior bankers for lunch and suggested in a civilised manner that AIB freeze his debts at its current level. One of the managers recalled the meeting, saying that Haughey raised the issue of his debts and proposed that they 'be allowed stand indefinitely without any specific arrangement in respect of repayment'. Did Haughey believe that the bank, after its acrimonious dealings with him, would actually write off his debt? The request was politely turned down. Haughey left disappointed. The following month Haughey met AIB officials in his Dame Street branch. This meeting was considerably less civilised.

The bank officials said they adopted a 'very hard line' with Haughey at the meeting which had been arranged by the bank in an effort to talk some sense to him and to confiscate his chequebooks, but it had little effect. Haughey's bankers demanded that he hand over his chequebooks.

'At this point Mr Haughey became quite vicious,' said an AIB memo, 'and told [the bank official] that "he would not give up his chequebooks as he had to live" and that we were dealing with an adult and no banker could talk to him in this manner. Furthermore, he stated that if any drastic action were taken by the bank, he could be a very troublesome adversary.' Haughey, then an opposition TD, refused to bow to AIB's demands. After the meeting, the bank actually ended up agreeing to lend him more money over the following two years. He had promised to sell 150 acres of land at Kinsealy to repay the bank.

Haughey's assets at this time were valued at more than £1.2 million. Proposals to sell these assets had been put forward by the bank in an effort to reduce his debt. However, no assets were ever sold and the bank never legally forced him to sell any of his land. A bank memo about the October 1976 meeting said Haughey 'stressed the importance of his position, prestige, etc. and on no account would he consider outright the sale of Abbeyville (sic) now as it is in his constituency'. His threat that he could be 'a troublesome adversary' seemed to have worked. The bank backed down and Haughey happily continued spending AIB's money.

After September 1976 any interest accruing on Haughey's debts was siphoned off to another account and not added to the money he already owed. This was done without his knowledge.

Early the following year, Haughey owed AIB more than £400,000. In March 1977 at a meeting with Haughey, AIB threatened not to honour his cheques because he had breached a £350,000 overdraft limit set by the bank. But the bank's threats did not have any effect.

Since being cast out following the Arms Trial, Haughey had devoted considerable time and energy to visiting Fianna Fáil organisations all over the country and building up his support among the grass roots of the party. This later became known as his 'chicken and chips' circuit and it gave him a reservoir of support at all levels of the party which enabled him to resist later challenges to his leadership. After Jack Lynch's landslide election victory in June 1977, Haughey had garnered enough support to merit a recall to the cabinet table. Lynch appointed him Minister for Health and Social Welfare. The promotion went to his head; his debt to AIB rose at an even greater rate than before. The bank was no longer dealing with a conceited opposition TD but a resurrected politician and a cabinet member whose political star was once again in the ascendant.

In 1977 Haughey's debt increased by an average of £36,000 a month. By October he owed £456,000 and by June 1978 it stood at £580,000. He no longer visited the bank during his years as a minister in 1977 and 78. When his bankers wanted to speak to him, they had to visit him at his offices, reflecting his newly elevated position. He was no longer a humble TD. By the time he met his bank manager again, on 1 December 1978, he owed the bank more than £700,000. At the meeting Haughey admitted he had been using the stud farm account for living expenses, contradicting a previous statement he had made to the bank.

By July 1979 the debt had soared to £887,000, primarily because of the very high interest rates at the time. At this stage Haughey's embattled bank manager, Michael Phelan, was at the end of his tether, but now knew Haughey was in a much stronger political position and may well live up to his threat of being a 'troublesome adversary' if the bank moved against him. The bank was willing to offer an olive branch. In July during a meeting in Leinster House, Phelan suggested to Haughey that he pay £767,000 to settle his debts. Haughey, showing his usual brass neck, declined and offered cash of £400,000 instead. The offer was rejected by the bank.

In a quite bizarre move, Haughey told the bank in July 1979 that there was a chance he could secure a deposit of £10 million—the equivalent of about €35 million in today's money—from Rafidain Bank in Iraq at below-market interest rates. He later denied at the Moriarty Tribunal that he had tried to influence his own standing with AIB by promising Iraqi money that had been offered to the Irish state. However, this was clearly believed to be the intention.

Rafidain Bank, which was controlled by the then Iraqi president Saddam Hussein and his regime, was the financial institution that had handled the transactions at the centre of the 1991 Beef Tribunal. The tribunal investigated how the sale of vast amounts of beef to Hussein's regime in Iraq had been underwritten by the Irish taxpayer. Implicit in Haughey's proposal was that if Rafidain gave AIB a massive deposit, then AIB should do Haughey a favour and excuse some of his debt. The bank didn't buy it. When the Rafidain connection was revealed at the tribunal, questions were asked about how a senior Irish politician could have such close ties to a bank linked to a Middle East dictator.

Haughey's prominent position as minister was clearly having an impact on his long-held disregard for his perilous financial state. In the period between June 1977, when he was appointed minister, and August 1979 he wrote cheques totalling £179,000 and accrued interest of £100,000. By August 1979 he owed AIB £913,000 at a time when the bank was charging interest at a rate of 26 per cent.

Around this time AIB was giving serious consideration to a proposal from Haughey to reduce his debt. It involved the sale of land at his home in Kinsealy to the young property developer Patrick Gallagher, whose late father Matt had been a close friend of Haughey. The bank felt that the deal might generate some much needed cash to reduce his debt. The deal was discussed by the bank but nothing ever materialised. In 1979 the bank officials were more concerned than ever about Haughey's borrowings. An internal bank memo written around this time said: 'Mr Haughey fails to see the precarious position he is in and obviously feels that his political influence will outweigh any other consideration by the bank. As the point has now been reached where the account appears to be out of control, consideration must be given to the taking of a firm stand by the bank. If this is not done, it seems inevitable that drawings will continue at the present rate of £12,000 per month approximately in spite of several assurances which he has given that "drawings would now be minimal".'

AIB's relationship with Haughey changed dramatically on 11 December 1979 when he became leader of Fianna Fáil and Taoiseach of the country. Overnight the bank turned from foe to friend.

Haughey's bank manager Michael Phelan wrote a fawning letter to the politician at his Kinsealy home congratulating him on his election as Taoiseach. The letter gave the impression that Haughey and Phelan had experienced nothing but good times up to then. 'It gives me great pleasure to convey to you my warmest congratulations on your election to the high offices of leader of Fianna Fáil and Taoiseach and to offer you my sincere good wishes for success in both', wrote Phelan. 'To say the task you have taken on is daunting is an understatement but I have every faith in your ability to succeed in restoring confidence in this great little nation.'

Ten months earlier, Phelan had been speaking of Haughey less favourably. After trying to force him to reduce his bank debt at yet another meeting with the politician in the Department of Social Welfare in February 1979, Phelan wrote to a colleague about the man who at the end of the year would be leader of the country: 'All in all, it is my considered opinion that this client does not believe the bank will force a confrontation with him because of his position. I feel that until his view in this regard is changed no progress will be made.'

During one of several meetings with Haughey in February 1979, Haughey told Phelan that he could 'trim off' a portion of his land at Abbeville and sell it to raise £200,000 to pay off his debt. It was quite ambitious for him to think that some ten acres of land in north Co. Dublin in 1979 could realise so much money. When Haughey's bank manager visited him in September 1979 and was told that cheques for £31,776 had been drawn on his accounts between 16 July and 5 September, the manager said he 'seemed very surprised by the high figure on the drawings and implied Abbeville had gone mad buying unnecessarily'.

On taking over as leader of Fianna Fáil and the country, Haughey suddenly felt his financial affairs had become a pressing issue. He had to get his money problem fixed. Whatever about the financial implications of his vast borrowings, his acute political sense told him that exposure of his massive bank debt would make devastating ammunition for his political enemies. If his borrowings ever emerged in public, he could be ruined. If he was declared bankrupt he would have to give up his seat. This did not seem to bother him when he was a TD, but as Taoiseach there was too much at stake. He had fought so hard to become leader of Fianna Fáil and Taoiseach, and he was not going to lose all he had fought for politically for more than two decades over what he clearly regarded as a measly bank debt of one million pounds.

By the end of 1979 Haughey's debt to the bank had reached £1.143 million. On the day he became Taoiseach, 11 December, Traynor, Haughey's bagman and financial handler, opened a 'special purpose' account at Guinness & Mahon Bank where Traynor was a director and carried huge sway because of the amount of money his secret Cayman Islands bank was channelling through Ireland. Starting that day and continuing for several weeks, a series of lodgements totalling £785,682 were made to the account. Traynor passed the money on to AIB to reduce Haughey's massive debt to the bank. Property developer Patrick Gallagher contributed £300,000, following a personal request by Haughey to help him out of some difficulties during a meeting at the politician's home. The gift was dressed up as a land deal in which the Gallagher Group took an option over some of his property at Kinsealy.

This still left almost £400,000 owing to AIB, but the bank was no longer dealing with some small-time politician from the northside of Dublin. This was the leader of the country who still owed a six-figure sum to the country's largest bank. Six years earlier the bank might have paid little heed to his threat that he could cause the bank difficulties if they made an enemy of him. But it was a different matter now—the bank was dealing with a much more powerful individual.

For Haughey, it was crucial that the bank debt be settled quickly. In the autumn of 1979, just months before Jack Lynch resigned as Taoiseach, Haughey made it clear to AIB that he wanted to clean up his affairs. He contacted his bank manager and said he wanted to deal with 'this dangerous situation once and for all'. The stakes had become too high for him.

Traynor entered the fray to play hardball on Haughey's behalf in September 1979. The accountant told the AIB regional manager Michael Kennedy that Haughey was only willing to pay £600,000, a little over half of what he owed, to settle the entire debt with the bank. Initially AIB said it was only prepared to write off £200,000; any more would have attracted the attention of the bank's auditors. But Traynor stood firm. He told Kennedy that there were 'no rabbits to be pulled out of hats or blood to be got out of turnips'. AIB agreed to a payment of £750,000 from an account at Guinness & Mahon Bank and wrote off the rest of the debt. Haughey was off the hook thanks to an act of extraordinary munificence by AIB.

The bank felt it could not have won against the leader of the country. Kennedy told the tribunal that if the bank had found itself in a legal confrontation with the Taoiseach, then people throughout the country would have resented the bank because of Haughey's popularity. He said the bank could have lost customers if it had taken this route. Kennedy agreed that writing off Haughey's bank debt had everything to do with the fact that he was Taoiseach.

After the settlement was agreed with Traynor, a loan manager within Haughey's AIB Dame Street branch was asked to hand over to senior AIB managers all the files relating to the history of Haughey's account. The bank was terrified that news of Haughey's fractious relationship with AIB throughout the 1970s and his massive bank debt would leak out into the public domain. Kennedy told the tribunal that extreme confidentiality was needed because of Haughey's public profile. The less the loan manager knew the better, Kennedy said. AIB still clearly feared Haughey after his debt was written off.

At the Moriarty Tribunal the bank explained why it had handled Haughey with care. Gerry Scanlan, a senior AIB official in the early 1970s and later chief executive of the bank, told the tribunal in February 1999 that Haughey was regarded in the fashionable marketing and banking language of the time as a 'key business influencer' or KBI. It was the banking equivalent of a VIP. Scanlan said that because Haughey was a prominent politician, influential and had all the appearances of being affluent, any bank would have been happy to have a KBI like him. Scanlan agreed with Mr Justice Moriarty's interpretation of the odd way the bank dealt with Haughey. 'If you owe us £1,000, it's your problem; if you owe us £1 million, it's our problem,' said the judge. Scanlan said that instead of being a banker's dream, Haughey turned into a banker's nightmare.

However, even in Haughey's darkest political times, AIB recognised that he could become a powerful political force. In 1975 Haughey's AIB branch manager Michael Phelan told his bosses that despite the difficulties of dealing with the politician's account, Haughey should be granted further drawings. The bank said in an internal memo dated September 1975: 'Despite the unattractiveness of the proposition Mr Phelan recommends sanction bearing in mind the likelihood of Mr Haughey being a man of influence in the future.'

Haughey himself knew he was a man of some authority and did not hide the fact that he was someone who could help or hinder AIB, particularly when the bank pressed him to repay his debts. In 1976, while threatening the bank, Haughey also tried to persuade AIB to stop hassling him about his mammoth drawings. He criticised the bank for not making 'use of his influential position and he indicated that he would be in a position to assist the bank in directing new business'. He pointed out that he intended to be in politics for another ten years. In other words, Haughey was prepared to offer AIB some influence in return for the bank cutting him some slack on his debts.

Taoiseach Charlie Haughey could have been talking about his own personal finances when he went on RTÉ television on 9 January 1980 to tell the nation that the state was spending way beyond its means and was in a deep economic crisis. At the time of the broadcast,

Traynor was in the midst of discussions with AIB to settle Haughey's overdrawn account.

'We have been living at a rate which is simply not justifiable by the amount of goods and services we are producing,' Haughey told the Irish people in his televised speech. 'To make up the difference we have been borrowing enormous amounts of money, borrowing at a rate which just cannot continue.'

Here was a man who had been living well beyond his means for more than a decade, who had racked up more than a million pounds in bank borrowings and then relied on money from rich benefactors to bail him out, who had a debt of almost £400,000 written off, who was spending £12,000 a month when he was earning just over half this in a year, telling the Irish people that the country was spending more than it was earning. Looking back on it, and knowing what we know now about Haughey's bank debts, the speech was a breathtaking display of arrogance.

In the end it never emerged who in AIB sent out the bank's statement describing Crowley's *Evening Press* story as 'outlandishly inaccurate'. The bank's public relations manager Bob Ryan told the tribunal he didn't write it or release it, and said it was the only time he knew of an AIB press release originating from outside the bank's press and public relations office. The authorship of the famous press release became the subject of much rumour and conjecture in the bank. Crowley's article was published at a time when Haughey's leadership within Fianna Fáil was being questioned by other members of the party, and AIB's denial poured cold water on a report that could have contributed to his political instability. The bank's rubbishing of Crowley's story bolstered Haughey's position. An accurate story about his highly irregular finances could well have spelt the end of his political career. Ryan said he still didn't know who wrote the release or whether it was written by someone in the bank acting on Haughey's behalf.

It is interesting to note that Haughey's problems intensified when he was not in a position of power. When Crowley's article was published in January 1983, Haughey's political fortunes were at a low ebb and Fianna Fáil was in open revolt. Haughey had lost power to the Fine Gael-Labour coalition the previous month and had survived two leadership heaves against him within Fianna Fáil.

There was also a marked difference in the way AIB treated Haughey following his return to the cabinet after the 1977 general election.

Bank officials visited him in his ministerial offices instead of Haughey coming to them in the bank. He dealt with the bankers on his terms, once he had regained his political credentials. And when Haughey was elected Taoiseach, the bank performed a volte-face, heaping congratulations and praise on their once difficult customer. This ebb and flow of influence became a feature of Haughey's finances over his career.

Haughey was not the only KBI to benefit from an act of kindness by AIB. Dr Garret FitzGerald, who succeeded Haughey as Taoiseach in 1981 and 1982, also benefited from a bank write-off after he left office. FitzGerald departed politics when Haughey took over from him as Taoiseach in 1987. Soon afterwards, FitzGerald was invited by Maurice Foley of GPA, the aircraft leasing company based in Shannon, to join the board of the company. The company was planning a stock market flotation and FitzGerald, as a board member, was entitled to buy preferential shares at a discounted rate and convert them into many more ordinary shares. With these shares FitzGerald could net a considerable profit in the subsequent flotation, particularly because in the late 1980s the company was riding a wave. He decided to buy shares at this time. He borrowed $281,250 from AIB to buy 20,000 ordinary shares as confidence in the company increased. The thinking was that if GPA did well on the market, then the directors would enjoy a cash windfall from the sale of shares, the banks would be paid off and everyone would emerge a little richer from the whole venture. They decided to buy the shares at what they thought was a bargain price, given the company's prospects on the stock market. The plan was that when the share price rocketed, the shareholders would sell some or all of their shares and make a fortune.

But all did not go according to plan. In 1992 the GPA flotation collapsed as the share offer failed. The company's share price plummeted and FitzGerald was left nursing massive losses and a sizeable bank debt. He undertook a lecture tour in the US and Europe and some consultancy work to raise much-needed cash, but he was ultimately forced to sell his house on Palmerston Road in Rathmines, south Dublin, to his son Mark for £150,000. Dr FitzGerald moved into an apartment in the house. After clearing the mortgage and funding some renovations at the house, he was left with about £30,000. Former AIB deputy chief executive Paddy Dowling helped FitzGerald negotiate a settlement with AIB. After the GPA debacle his debt to the bank stood at £170,000. On 17 November 1993 an agreement was reached—FitzGerald would pay £40,000 to settle the £170,000 debt. The bank would write off the £130,000 owed to it and FitzGerald, another KBI, would walk away.

FitzGerald told the author that he encountered problems when in 1992 he tried to restructure two loans—taken out in 1988 and 89— into one loan to create one repayment. He had taken the loans to buy the GPA shares. Both the earlier loans were non-recourse, meaning that the bank had no comeback and had no security on their money if FitzGerald defaulted on his repayments. Many individuals who borrowed money to buy shares in GPA had taken out non-recourse loans.

But the situation changed for FitzGerald. When he renegotiated the loans in 1992 and combined them, he lost the non-recourse element of the earlier loans. So now, if he defaulted, the bank could seize his assets as security and sell them to recover its loans. FitzGerald said he would not have agreed to the conditions attached to the new loan in 1992 if he had known he was losing the non-recourse nature of the older loans. He said the bank acted improperly by not telling him about the consequences of this, but he admitted at the Moriarty Tribunal that he did not read the small print.

'In my case what was peculiar was that the second loan was a recourse loan whereas the first loan was a non-recourse. I didn't know about these things,' said FitzGerald. 'When I said I wanted to make one payment instead of two, they should have said that this means extinguishing the non-recourse element. They didn't tell me that. That was what I objected to. In not telling me that merging the two payments would extinguish the non-recourse element of the first, yes, that was improper. I would never have known about that had the Moriarty inquiry not discovered that. Certainly they should have told me.'

FitzGerald said AIB did not treat him with the same leniency that Haughey enjoyed. FitzGerald's borrowings were nowhere near the scale of his political rival. Haughey also got to keep his very valuable house—FitzGerald had to sell his, albeit to a family member—even though AIB could have sold Haughey's home to reduce his huge debts. Perhaps AIB regarded Haughey's threats more seriously or viewed him as a more important KBI. Eight years after FitzGerald helped save AIB from its near fatal investment in the Insurance Corporation of Ireland, the bank reciprocated the gesture. The bank may not have been returning an old favour—it was simply helping a KBI out of a sticky situation. It was clearly not in the bank's interest to alienate this important person.

Another politician handled compassionately by the banks was Fianna Fáil TD John Ellis. The Sligo deputy was on the verge of being declared bankrupt in 1989 following the collapse of his meat business, Stanlow Trading. National Irish Bank had issued bankruptcy proceedings against him for £263,000 (€334,000) on the basis of personal guarantees given by him for the debts of Stanlow. If declared a bankrupt, he would have to forfeit his Dáil seat. The bank's threat not only left Ellis in a precarious situation, but the loss of a seat posed problems for Fianna Fáil. Charles Haughey was leader of the party and Taoiseach at the time, and the party was in coalition with the Progressive Democrats. The two-party government had a bare majority and if Ellis was forced to resign, then the government would have fallen. Haughey was not willing to let this happen.

To stave off bankruptcy, Haughey gave Ellis cash to help him settle some of his debts. He paid the Sligo TD a total of £26,000 drawn by Haughey from the Fianna Fáil leader's allowance. The more significant act of kindness, however, came from National Irish Bank, which in January 1990 agreed to settle Ellis's six-figure debt for just £20,000. The revelations about the £243,000 write-off and the bank's toadying behaviour, which did not emerge in public until 1999, incensed farmers who were left nursing debts of €380,000 arising from the collapse of Stanlow. The outrage was so deafening that Ellis was eventually forced to settle with the farmers.

Ellis was linked to another banking scandal in 2000, this time involving a bank outside the state. He and his wife resigned as non-executive directors of a Pakistani bank called Indus Bank in August 2000, a month before the State Bank of Pakistan cancelled its licence for 'mismanagement of its affairs'. Ellis and his wife had been invited to join the bank by Khurshid Sohail, a business associate the Sligo politician met while doing business in Britain in 1993. Ellis said he never gained a penny from the bank and that he resigned because he did not 'have the time or energy' to continue. Sohail was later questioned by the authorities in Pakistan and taken to court over his handling of the affairs of Indus Bank.

Ellis had found himself embroiled in an overseas bank scandal, but his gentle treatment at the hands of NIB years earlier caused considerably more controversy. And like AIB's treatment of Haughey and

FitzGerald, the way NIB indulged Ellis proved an unspoken rule in Irish banking: treat KBIS—powerful and influential people—differently to your ordinary customers. No doubt if a small business was to find itself in trouble and could not afford to pay off a working loan, chances are a bank would pursue it through every court in the land to get its money back. Not so for the VIP customers of Irish banking. Better to gift them a present, and write off their loans.

Chapter 11

John Rusnak: AIB's rogue trader and the lost $691 million

In mid-January 2002 David Cronin returned to his post as treasurer of us bank Allfirst, a subsidiary of AIB, after spending a relaxing Christmas at home in Ireland. Within a fortnight he would find himself at the centre of the biggest scandal to hit an Irish bank and the fourth largest rogue trading fraud ever discovered. Cronin and several others were left with their careers in ruins, and AIB found itself at the centre of another controversy and the focus of news reports around the globe.

A native of Cork, Cronin had been working in the us bank since 1989 when it had been bought outright by AIB. Allfirst was the second largest bank in Maryland and one of the top 50 banks in the us. A respected banker, he was appointed to the senior management team as treasurer to monitor the running of the bank for his bosses in Dublin.

In late 2001 Cronin had been having difficulties reining in one of his staff, John Rusnak, a 37-year-old American. Rusnak worked in foreign currency trading and had been using the bank's money to trade in huge amounts. Shortly after returning from Ireland, Cronin spotted something worrying. Rusnak's turnover in foreign exchange proprietary trading (trading with the bank's money, not that of

customers) during December had reached a staggering $25 billion—
despite the fact that he had been ordered by Cronin to reduce his
currency trading to below $150 million. Cronin knew he had a major
problem. Allfirst was a regional bank in the US and had a very small
proprietary trading operation. But Rusnak was by no means a small
trader. Cronin had a rogue trader on his hands who was using huge
amounts of the bank's money to play the foreign exchange markets
without sanction or supervision. Drastic measures were needed to
bring Rusnak under control.

Other irregularities with Rusnak's trading emerged around this
time. In early December 2001 the supervisor of the back office visited
the office and noticed on the back office employee's desk two trade
tickets with no confirmations attached. The back office was a part of
the trading operation where all Rusnak's deals were independently
checked and confirmed. (Being the front line of the operation, the
trading desks were known as the front office.) Confirming trades is
standard practice in foreign exchange trading, so this was a critical
lapse in risk control.

When the supervisor asked to see the confirmations, the back office
employee said the trades did not require confirmations as they
cancelled each other out and had been agreed with counterparties
(banks) in Asia. That would have required the employee to work late
at night to contact them because of the difference in the time zones.
The supervisor said all trades required confirmations, regardless of
whether they offset each other and irrespective of where the counterparty was. The supervisor directed the employee to confirm those
trades and all future trades. The employee later claimed that the
supervisor asked him simply to 'look into' the possibility of confirming the trades. The employee failed to mention that many other trades
had not been confirmed.

Realising that Rusnak was trading in massive volumes, Cronin
decided to shut down his trading desk. At a staff meeting on Monday,
28 January 2002, Cronin said he was closing down Rusnak's desk. Bob
Ray, who directly supervised Rusnak and had defended the trader on
numerous occasions since hiring him in 1993, told Cronin that he
expected Rusnak to quit as a result of his decision. On Wednesday,
30 January, the back office supervisor heard Rusnak's positions were
being closed and checked with the back office employee to see if
Rusnak had been conducting any trades. The supervisor was shown

two deal tickets and again he noticed that the trades had not been confirmed independently. Once again the back office employee gave the same excuse—because the trades offset each other and involved Asian counterparties, they had not been confirmed. The supervisor ordered a review to be carried out. The employee found 12 unconfirmed trades.

When the supervisor ordered the employee to call the Asian counterparties to confirm the trades, they said they had no records of the deals on their books. On Thursday, 31 January, Rusnak was called to the office of the most senior back office manager to explain what was going on. Rusnak said he would get confirmations by the next morning.

By Friday morning Rusnak had left 12 written confirmations on the back office employee's desk. But the back office staff thought they looked bogus. They were right—Rusnak had designed them himself and created counterfeit logos for the counterparties. He had even stored the phoney dockets in a file on his computer called 'fake docs'. The senior back office manager wanted answers. In a meeting with Rusnak and Ray, he told Rusnak's supervisor that the trades would have to be confirmed by phone.

Ray said it was the back office's responsibility to track the trades down and that this was a back office problem. Rusnak became angry when confronted. He had a history of bullying and aggressive behaviour towards other staff, so this was nothing out of the ordinary. He complained that he was making money for the bank and that if the back office continued to question his every move, he would quit his job. Furious, he stormed out of the meeting.

After Rusnak left, Ray was shown the confirmations and he agreed that they did not look right. But he repeated Rusnak's assertion that further scrutiny of his activities would force their star trader to quit. Ray warned that if Rusnak left the bank, it would lose his profitable trading operation which would in turn lead to job cuts in the back office. Ten minutes later Rusnak returned to the office. He had calmed down. He apologised for having walked out earlier but repeated his threat to leave the bank. He said he would do what he could to confirm the trades. Given that it was daytime Friday in Baltimore and the Asian markets were closed, they would have to wait until Sunday night to make the phone calls to Asia to confirm the trades. Rusnak promised that he would call the back office employee in charge of confirming his trades on Sunday with the phone number of the broker in Asia who organised the trades.

The employee had not heard from Rusnak by Sunday at noon, so he telephoned him at home. Rusnak said he wanted to speak to the broker first to say the employee would be calling and promised he would give him the broker's number at 9 o'clock that evening. Rusnak never called. The back office employee, his supervisor and the senior manager stayed in the office until the early hours of Monday morning, trying unsuccessfully to contact Rusnak and confirm the trades with his counterparties in Asia.

When Rusnak failed to show up for work the next morning, Monday, 4 February, the senior back office manager and Ray told Cronin what was unfolding. It looked like the bank had a rogue trader on its hands. Given that Rusnak had been trading hundreds of millions of dollars of the bank's money, the losses could be colossal. However, no one really knew how much was at stake because their trader was missing. Cronin and Ray drove to Rusnak's home in the upmarket Baltimore suburb of Mount Washington to see if they could find him. It was a last ditch effort to get answers. Rusnak was not at home and could not be found. All Cronin had was a large number of fictitious trade confirmations amounting to hundreds of millions of dollars. He broke the news to senior management at Allfirst.

That Monday evening AIB chief executive Michael Buckley was sitting at home in south Dublin having a cup of tea with his wife when he received a call from Susan Keating, the chief executive of Allfirst. She explained that a rogue currency trader in their Baltimore headquarters had run up hundreds of millions of dollars in losses. 'It was a bit like hearing my brother had died in a car accident,' Buckley said later. 'I never thought it could happen in our bank.'

Buckley assembled a team of investigators to quantify the losses in Baltimore. Fifteen senior bankers from AIB's group audit and treasury operations led by AIB group treasurer Pat Ryan flew to Baltimore from Dublin the next morning to begin an investigation. Buckley knew he had to break the news to the market and the bank's customers. AIB embarked on an elaborate communications exercise, bringing in public relations adviser Jim Milton, who had worked on ICI in 1985. The following morning Buckley met AIB's chairman Lochlann Quinn in the offices of Glen Dimplex, the electrical appliance maker where Quinn was deputy chairman. 'It was like looking at a road accident happening in front of you in slow motion,' said Quinn on hearing about Rusnak's losses.

AIB's senior staff may have been in shock, but the bank needed to know how much had been lost, whether it would affect the bank in the long term, and if any other employees had been involved in the fraud. The bank suspended Cronin and three other Allfirst staff. The bank also contacted the FBI to inform them of the situation. Within days Ryan and his team came up with an initial figure on the losses; he told Buckley that Rusnak had gambled and lost about $750 million of the bank's money.

On Wednesday, 6 February, Buckley went on *Morning Ireland*, the flagship news programme on RTÉ, Ireland's national broadcaster, to tell the country that the bank was investigating losses of $750 million at its bank in Baltimore caused by a rogue trader. By breaking the news, the bank was taking firm control of the situation and leading how the news would be broken to the public, its customers and the market. Buckley reassured listeners that this incident was not similar to the Nick Leeson rogue trading scandal. Leeson had run up losses of stg£850 million trading on currencies in Singapore, bringing down Barings Investment Bank in 1995. Buckley said AIB would survive. Rusnak's losses would wipe almost €600 million off the bank's 2001 earnings after Rusnak's losses had been taken into account.

The news caused shock waves in the Irish banking sector and business community and the international markets. It was front-page news around the world. AIB's in-house public relations team had to work almost around the clock, dealing with the world's media and taking calls from reporters in Australia and New Zealand.

The tabloid papers drew inevitable comparisons between Rusnak and Leeson. One newspaper even ran a column by Leeson in which he complained about the slipshod financial checks put in place by AIB at Allfirst. 'I am shocked nothing has been learned from my case and the same thing has been allowed to happen', wrote Leeson. 'There has been chapter and verse written about my experience at Barings but all that counts for nothing.' Other papers focused on the fact that the fraud had been perpetrated by an individual who was described as Mr Middle America. (One tabloid described Rusnak as 'Mr Fiddle America'.) They painted a picture of Rusnak as a church-going father of two who sat on the board of his local school—a person least likely to defraud a bank of hundreds of millions of dollars.

Although rival banks in Dublin pushed the line publicly that this was 'bad news for corporate Ireland', they privately wanted to make sure that they were not—or could not at any stage in the future—end up in the same boat as AIB. Consequently the boards of some of AIB's competitor banks insisted that the people managing their treasury operations made presentations on the controls they had in place and explain how their checks were superior to those at AIB.

The Rusnak affair was the largest scandal to hit AIB, and the share price responded accordingly. The day the story broke, AIB shares fell to early lows and ended the day 16.5 per cent lower at €11.35 in Dublin and more than 17 per cent lower in London. Buckley's reassurances that the bank's underlying business and profitability had not been hit by this 'once-off blow' were clearly not enough for some investors. The bank recognised that it would have to deal with the problem quickly if it was to survive.

The bank followed the same strategy used during the 1985 ICI debacle—be decisive, assure the market and resolve the crisis swiftly. Quinn said: 'The most important thing was communicating to the marketplace the full extent of the problem, the losses and what you are going to do, and do it all in 48 hours. Feeding bad news to the market on a drip-drip basis is bad because your investors lose confidence and desert you. The only thing that worried me was that we would call the number right. When Michael first told me, we didn't know the full number. It was a lot lower when he told me. It got bigger that afternoon. It got bigger that evening. It got bigger again the next morning. We figured the number was $703 million, but we had to go to the stock exchange at that stage.'

The bank, however, initially told the public that the fraud had cost it $750 million, much higher than its final estimate. This was a clever strategy. Pairing down rather than pushing up the figure on the estimated losses was important because, if the bank had misjudged the amount at stake and it turned out to be higher, then confidence in the bank would have been critically undermined. By the end of the week AIB had a better handle on the full scale of Rusnak's fraud after the bank had begun its investigation. The bank discovered during its investigation that by 31 December 1999 Rusnak's cumulative losses stood at $89.8 million, rose to $300.8 million at the end of 2000 and $674 million at the end of the following year. AIB eventually concluded at the end of the first week of its investigation that Rusnak had lost the bank a total of $691.2 million, a figure that would take a huge chunk out of the bank's annual earnings.

Putting an exact figure on the losses, however, wasn't enough. The bank had to probe every aspect of its operations to find out how a fraud of this scale could have happened. It needed to reassure the public, its customers and shareholders that this could never happen again.

On Friday, 8 February 2002, the board of AIB asked Eugene Ludwig, a former comptroller of the US Currency and a friend of former US president Bill Clinton, to head an inquiry. The bank gave Ludwig 30 days to investigate the fraud and report his findings.

At a news conference in Baltimore on 6 February, Allfirst executives said Rusnak had perpetrated a sophisticated and well thought out fraud. However, when Ludwig's report was published on 14 March 2002, he contradicted this. He described the fraud as 'inelegant' and said Rusnak would have been rumbled long before, if simple checks had been carried out. His findings chronicled poor management and lack of controls dating back to 1997, when Rusnak started hiding his trading losses with bogus trades and fictitious assets. Worse still, during the five years he was losing Allfirst's money, he was earning a massive salary; he was paid $530,000 and bonuses of $328,543 over the five years. He was due to receive his largest bonus ever from the bank, $220,456, on 8 February 2002, four days after Allfirst discovered his trading fraud. The bonus was never paid.

Rusnak joined Allfirst in July 1993 from Chemical Bank in New York where he had traded currency options since 1989. Ray hired Rusnak on the recommendation of a friend who had worked with him at another bank, Fidelity, in the late 1980s. Before Rusnak's arrival, Allfirst had a basic foreign exchange trading operation, making simple currency bets. However, Rusnak proved an attractive proposition, saying he could make the bank more money from more complex trades. 'Cronin and Ray were intrigued by Rusnak's style of trading, as he claimed it would diversify the revenue stream arising from simple directional trading', said Ludwig in his report. Cronin had hoped to make Allfirst a 'niche' currency player and Rusnak's method of trading filled this gap. To Cronin, he was an important addition to the Allfirst team.

AIB managed its US bank with a light touch, giving Allfirst's management a large degree of autonomy. It allowed it to operate independently rather than as an integrated and controlled subsidiary of AIB. The controls that AIB had in its own trading operations were much stronger than those at Allfirst, paving the way for Rusnak's excesses. Ironically, just months before Rusnak's fraud was discovered, Buckley had decided that he would bring Allfirst under tighter control from Dublin.

AIB regarded Cronin as capable and experienced enough to manage Allfirst's treasury operation. He had worked as a currency trader in the past and had managed a trading operation within AIB consisting of 40–50 traders, including currency traders. The bank thought he was the right man to become treasurer of First Maryland, as Allfirst was known in 1989.

However, his arrival at the bank was not warmly received. He was regarded as a 'home-office spy' and was largely excluded from senior management meetings. The situation improved when Frank Bramble was appointed chief executive in 1994. However, Bramble and his successor Susan Keating found '[Cronin's] energy and commitment levels to be wanting, and his analysis of problems to be often academic and not practical'. This was where institutional problems arose—management structures were weakened, eventually allowing Rusnak to abuse procedures. Cronin was 'highly protective' of Ray whenever senior Allfirst management questioned his treasury operation. Bramble wanted Cronin to be better supervised or removed, and in 2000 Keating suggested that Cronin should report to a new chief financial officer who could monitor his activities more closely.

Ludwig found that while senior AIB officers recognised that 'the Allfirst treasurer's [Cronin's] levels of energy and commitment were lower than expected, they nevertheless continued to believe that he was the best person for the job, particularly given the limited experience that other senior Allfirst managers had in supervising complex treasury functions and given that his presence helped to maintain the flow of information from Baltimore to Dublin'. AIB felt Cronin should report directly to the Allfirst chief executive because it believed it was important for the chief executive to understand Cronin's treasury operation. Ludwig later found that treasury had 'less consistent and reliable supervision'.

The chain of command within treasury was weakened further in 1999 when Rusnak's trading manager left. To keep costs down, Ray decided not to hire a replacement but supervise Rusnak himself. Ray's knowledge of foreign exchange was limited. He never devoted much time to monitoring Rusnak's proprietary trading, and after the departure of the trading manager, he did not focus any more attention on Rusnak. Despite Cronin's own understanding of currency trading, the Allfirst treasurer relied heavily on Ray to supervise Rusnak and report back on his activities.

Just as Cronin defended Ray when questioned by Allfirst's senior managers, Ray was equally protective of Rusnak. He often defended Rusnak when the back office and risk assessment personnel queried his trading. He even tried to force the bank's risk assessors to raise any queries on Rusnak's trading with him instead of with Rusnak.

This created the impression that the trading desk was given special treatment. In this atmosphere, with superiors protecting him, Rusnak felt he could abuse the system and avoid detection. Ludwig found that because of management failures at Allfirst, controls failed and the bank was exposed to fraud by an intelligent trader who could override procedures.

Rusnak knew Cronin placed a huge level of trust in Ray and that Cronin and Ray tolerated incidents of 'serious friction' between Rusnak and the back office staff. Ludwig found that no other Allfirst staff had been involved in Rusnak's fraud, but he was critical of Cronin's relationship with the trader: 'It would have been so much easier if we had found complicity with someone involved higher up in the organisation. In a sense there was a human dynamic here that was unholy.' A senior AIB source said: 'Cronin just got too close to Rusnak.'

Cronin and Rusnak knew each other outside Allfirst. They lived in the same upper middle-class neighbourhood of Baltimore and they were both active in their local Catholic church, the Shrine of the Sacred Heart on Smith Avenue. They both served on their local school board and sometimes played golf together. But while some in Allfirst found Rusnak to be a strong and confident employee, a hard-working and good family man, others found him arrogant and abusive. On several occasions Ray reprimanded Rusnak for his treatment of the back office staff, but he ultimately tolerated Rusnak's frequent abusive and disruptive conduct and praised his teamwork and interpersonal skills in reports evaluating his performance.

One former senior Allfirst employee who knew Rusnak well said: 'Typically, John had a silly grin on his face and had his shirt tail hanging out. He was the only speculator in the entire company of 6,000. He was eccentric, arrogant, and flaky. It fit the image of a trader—no one thought he was odd because that's what traders are like.' Another former senior staff member said: 'Bob [Ray] was viewed as someone who was arrogant and who didn't share information quite effectively enough. David [Cronin] was a likeable guy but maybe a little naive.'

The make-up of the personalities supervising Rusnak and the weak management structure allowed Rusnak to find and exploit chinks in Allfirst's armour. Like most rogue traders Rusnak's losses began to mount as he continued to trade in the belief that he could win back money to recover his initial losses. It was a vicious cycle. Fake trades entered on the bank's computer system made it appear that Allfirst's profits were on the rise. This in turn allowed Rusnak to make even larger bets on currency transactions.

Rusnak started making substantial losses on his trades in 1997 and it was around this time that his fraud may have begun, according to Ludwig. Proprietary trading on foreign exchange markets was complex. Trading in foreign exchange effectively involved placing a bet on whether a currency would rise or fall. A spot trade involved the purchase of a certain amount of currency for cash 'on the spot', whereas a forward trade was an agreement to buy currency for a price in, say, a month's time. Trading in foreign exchange options was even more complex but reduced the risk for currency traders. An option enabled a trader to buy or sell an opportunity to enter into a forward trade in foreign exchange at a price agreed between the buyer and seller. The pre-agreed price was known as 'the strike price'. Money was exchanged and the buyer then had an option to buy the currency at the future date. However, if the currency fluctuated, the buyer would not have to go through with the purchase of the currency.

Rusnak told the bank he was trading on the foreign exchange markets by exploiting price differentials between foreign exchange options and the spot and forward markets, but he was actually laying simple bets on how exchange rates would move in the future. He claimed he could make more money for Allfirst by buying options on the cheap and selling them when they became more expensive. The idea was simple but the application was more complex. In or around 1997 Rusnak bet wrongly on the future movement of the Japanese yen, only to see the value of the yen and the forward position, on which he had gambled, fall. This left Rusnak and Allfirst down a large amount of money.

Rusnak found a way of hiding his losses by creating fictitious options. This created the impression that his real positions were counterchecked or hedged. To get these bogus options on to Allfirst's books, Rusnak exploited a flaw he had identified in the bank's checking system. He discovered that he could enter two bogus trades simultaneously into the system. He would claim he had sold what was called a 'deep-in-the-money' option on Japanese yen to a bank (counterparty) in Tokyo or Singapore, and had also bought another option offsetting this transaction from the same counterparty. He convinced the back office staff that it was not necessary to confirm these paired options because they offset each other and so there was no net transfer of cash between the bank and the counterparty. This suited the back office employees because it meant they did not have to work through the night to ring Tokyo or Singapore to confirm the trade.

There was one major problem with Rusnak's scheme. Even though the bogus options matched each other, one option—the one involving the receipt of the premium for the option—expired in one day, on the day it was written. No one in Allfirst's treasury noticed this glaring anomaly. The bank's system failed to identify one-day options, so the debt, which the money represented, would not appear on the books. The other bogus option would expire weeks later, typically a month later, so it would appear as an asset on the books of the bank. These bogus assets would then be used to conceal Rusnak's trading losses.

However, the trades made no sense. The expiration dates were different, so the premiums should have been different, but again no one in Allfirst noticed this. What appeared on Allfirst's books was supposedly an unexpired deep-in-the-money option for which the bank had paid a large premium. Allfirst's balance sheet showed that it was holding valuable assets, yet these were really masking Rusnak's losses from his spot and forward trades. Rusnak took advantage of the poor control environment. He kept the apparently valuable but fake asset on the books by repeatedly rolling over new bogus options as the original ones purportedly became due. As Rusnak lost more and more money, he wrote more and more bogus options. He had discovered a simple way to beat the system.

From 1999 on, Rusnak managed to convince his bosses to set up prime brokerage accounts with Bank of America and Merrill Lynch (and later Citibank). These accounts, although unusual for banks and not used by AIB's foreign exchange traders, allowed Rusnak to increase the size and scope of his real trading. It allowed him to deal in much larger volumes. Prime brokerage accounts allowed foreign exchange traders like Rusnak to roll all their transactions into one forward transaction and allow the trader and the broker to settle their accounts in cash on a fixed date each month.

However, not all the blue-chip brokers were happy to take Rusnak's business. After the scandal broke, the *Financial Times* reported that some foreign exchange traders had grown suspicious long before AIB realised what was actually going on at its US bank. The newspaper said Goldman Sachs was so concerned about Rusnak that it refused to do business with him. One New York-based foreign exchange trader at the investment bank told the newspaper: 'We just weren't comfortable with him.' Rusnak had been arousing suspicions in the foreign exchange markets long before his fraud was eventually detected in 2002, but AIB did not hear about any of the concerns circulating in the market.

As Rusnak's trading escalated with the use of the prime brokerage accounts, so too did his losses, his bogus options and his use of the Allfirst balance sheet. In 2001 Rusnak's activities drew attention from other sections of the bank. Following inquiries by Allfirst's audit and internal finance, Bob Ray directed Rusnak to reduce his use of the balance sheet. This left Rusnak needing a new source of funds to finance his massive trades.

In February 2001 Rusnak decided to sell genuine year-long deep-in-the-money options to fund his losses and to keep trading. He sold five of these options for a total of $300 million. However, these were effectively loans and they appeared as liabilities on Allfirst's books. To get them off the books, Rusnak again turned to bogus options. He pretended he had conducted deals done with counterparties to the original deep-in-the-money options. This gave the impression that the original options had been repurchased. This left Allfirst saddled with massive, unrecorded liabilities; the bank was completely unaware of them.

Rusnak did not hide the fact that he had problems and was seeking money from Bank of America and Citibank. He even told one bank in an email: 'I have come to you with a problem. We need to outsource our balance sheet funding.' Rusnak was back using the bank's balance sheet before long, however. In late 2001 Cronin ordered him to get the trading figure below $150 million by the end of the year.

Emails between Rusnak and employees at Citibank and Bank of America proved that he was trying to hide his trading. In one email to Bank of America he warned that Allfirst should not find out about his online trades. 'I understand I can download the info from website but . . . I don't want my back office to have access to the website or any of the trade details,' Rusnak wrote. In another email Rusnak warned Citibank employees to stop sending confirmation letters about his trades with them. 'These confirms have to stop,' he wrote. 'My back office manager is very unhappy', adding that the manager 'thinks these are fake trades or something unethical.'

By the end of 2000 Rusnak's losses of $300.8 million consisted entirely of fake assets on Allfirst's books. When the fraud was finally exposed, the final figure of $691.2 million consisted of $291.6 million in bogus assets, $397.3 million unrecognised liabilities and $2.3 million in genuine trading losses incurred in 2002.

Other irregularities concerning Rusnak's trading position should have set off alarm bells. The bank gave Rusnak a monthly stop loss limit of $200,000. This meant that if his losses reached $200,000 in a particular month, he had to stop trading. Rusnak abused this by manipulating the spreadsheet used to calculate his daily limit. He engaged in 'holdover transactions' which distorted the figure. Ludwig found that Rusnak's use of these holdover positions was 'pervasive'. 'The fraud was so inelegant that on some occasions, Mr Rusnak would leave the same holdover position running for three straight days,' said Ludwig in his report. Ludwig found that a combination of various irregular practices, rather than a single deficiency, facilitated the fraud.

The most critical, however, was the failure of the back office to secure confirmations for all Rusnak's trades. If the back office staff had done their job, they would have picked up the bogus trades with the counterparties in Asia. Ludwig also discovered that the treasury unit failed to check foreign exchange rates from independent sources. It relied on a system that allowed Rusnak to manipulate the rates being read by the middle and back offices. When a risk assessment analyst asked in 2000 why rates were not being obtained independently, she was told that Allfirst would not pay $10,000 for a data feed from Reuters. A relatively inexpensive product could have detected the fraud long before the losses had reached $691 million.

Rusnak's cover was almost blown in August 2000 when an internal audit of Allfirst's treasury operation sampled 25 transactions to see if they had been properly confirmed. Of those, only one was a foreign exchange option and it turned out to be genuine. Ludwig found that checking one more foreign exchange option would have increased the probability of finding a bogus one by about 75 per cent. He found other deficiencies in the areas of internal audit, treasury risk control and credit risk review. Inadequate staffing and a lack of experience were all to blame for Rusnak's escape from detection for so long. Rusnak often exceeded the credit limits established by AIB and Allfirst for foreign exchange trading. Ludwig found that Allfirst was fully aware that Rusnak had breached the $100 million foreign exchange credit line by $86 million. It did not act on the discrepancies because the trades had been settled by the time the breaches were discovered.

Ludwig also found that Allfirst and AIB missed several opportunities to detect Rusnak's fraud. If Rusnak's phone line had been tapped, and if his daily profit and loss figures had been reconciled against the bank's general ledger, the fraud could have been uncovered much earlier. The back office did not always confirm the end of day settlements with Rusnak's prime brokers, and the front office failed to scrutinise each of Rusnak's trades. In the spring of 1999 Rusnak's temper and bullying behaviour had been described as 'one of extraordinary contention within Allfirst treasury', said Ludwig. Rusnak was singled out by some employees for berating the back office staff and even threatening to have some of them fired. The head of the back office handed over details of Rusnak's aggressive actions, but Cronin took no significant action other than to call a meeting and ask the workers to treat each other respectfully.

Despite the fact that the back office often did not seek confirmations on trades, when it did bring an unconfirmed trade to Rusnak's attention, he would produce late confirmations and the treasury management would accept them without exploring the possibility that he had entered the trade only after the back office had brought it to his attention.

Ludwig found that the back office perceived a management bias to favour traders when back office issues arose—primarily because the traders were making money. This created the perception among back office staff that the confirmation process was a pointless formality.

Rusnak's heavy trading came to the attention of senior AIB management in 2000 and 2001. On the first occasion, in March 2000, AIB group treasurer in Dublin, Pat Ryan, was asked by Citibank if Allfirst could cover a debt settlement of more than $1 billion at the beginning of April. Ryan said the bank could, but also asked Allfirst risk assessment staff to make a 'discreet' enquiry about the matter. Ryan was told that Allfirst's $1 billion debt was more than offset by a larger amount owed to Allfirst by Citibank. No one at either bank thought to ask why the offsetting Citibank amounts were so large.

The scale of Rusnak's trading had also come up in Allfirst's 1999 and 2000 annual filings with the US Securities and Exchange Commission (SEC). They showed that the notional value of Allfirst's foreign exchange trading was in billions of dollars. Also, as far back as 1997 a manager in AIB, who reported to the bank's treasurer, pointed out the trading being conducted by Rusnak. He said in some AIB file notes that Allfirst's 'average FX [foreign exchange] option book is $1bn nominal' and that 'John Rusneck [*sic*], FX options dealer, was accountable for 95 per cent of [Allfirst's] FX risk'.

In late May 2001 news of Rusnak's huge trades reached the top brass at AIB. A market source told Buckley that Allfirst was engaged in heavy foreign exchange trading. The source did not name Rusnak or refer to specific trades. Buckley said it was his practice to call an executive in charge of a matter, so he telephoned Cronin who, after looking into the matter, assured him that there had been no unusual or extra large transactions in the last two weeks. Cronin told Buckley that Allfirst's daily average trading was $159 million. In reality the figure was at least three or four times this amount. Ludwig concluded that Cronin's written response was 'a forceful and categorical denial of any problem' and it satisfied AIB.

However, one senior Allfirst staff member who was familiar with the Baltimore bank's treasury operation questioned Buckley's judgment in trusting Cronin's response. 'Michael Buckley gets a call from someone. He doesn't call Pat Ryan or Eugene McErlean [AIB's group internal auditor in Dublin]. He calls David Cronin. He didn't even call Frank Bramble or Susan Keating. He gives David a heads up that something doesn't look right. David Cronin doesn't even involve the audit department or Susan or Frank, and he reports back that the situation is fine. Buckley doesn't share that information with anybody. The judgment that Buckley used was no better than the judgment that some of the people used in Allfirst.' A former senior AIB official, who also knew the bank's treasury operations well, said he was surprised by Buckley's decision to call Cronin and no one else. 'If Gerry Scanlan [a former chief executive of the bank] had received the same information, he would have had a team from audit out to Baltimore on a plane within 24 hours to check it out,' said the official.

Ludwig found that, perhaps because of Buckley's query, Cronin started to focus on Rusnak's activities. From mid-June 2001 he began to receive daily reports on the number and notional amounts of proprietary foreign exchange transactions. Cronin found that Rusnak's notional daily positions occasionally totalled billions of dollars. On some days the turnover reached almost $4 billion, more than 20 times the figure that Cronin had provided to Buckley. The scale of Rusnak's activities was effectively moving markets and registering on foreign exchange trading screens around the globe. Yet no one in Allfirst or AIB noticed anything to worry themselves about.

In February 2001, while financial reports for the 2000 year-end were being prepared, questions were raised within Allfirst and AIB about the extent to which Rusnak was using the balance sheet and the size of the cash flow generated by his activities. The concerns were dismissed because Rusnak's trading was regarded as relatively low risk.

In September or October 2001 finance officials at Allfirst focused on its foreign exchange trading after the SEC made an inquiry about the cash flow on its trading. In response, Allfirst found that the bank had large foreign exchange contracts but that the amounts appeared to be offset, meaning that the bank did not owe money. Again, in January 2002, AIB queried Allfirst about its open foreign exchange positions worth over $100 million. In response, Rusnak said the positions were incorrectly reported. A member of the financial reporting team said the value of the positions had been reported as of their trade date, not their year-end values. This seemed to satisfy AIB officials.

On 20 January 2002 Cronin decided to wind down Rusnak's trading desk and the back office supervisor asked for the unconfirmed trades to be checked. At this stage Rusnak had cost the bank hundreds of millions of dollars. His trading was spiralling out of control. Allfirst had even allowed him to continue trading at home and on his holidays. This robbed the bank of a crucial opportunity to scrutinise his trading. Normally, holidays create a break from routine which can reveal any problems. Rusnak had even been trading from the back of a cart during a round of golf, his lawyer said.

Rusnak seemed to enjoy the elevated role that came with his highly active trading desk. It was after all making some people lots of money.

To those doing business with him, he was a VIP. Rusnak was inebriated by the dizzy heights he had risen to. The lifestyle that accompanied an apparently successful trader suited his ego. He enjoyed the best corporate entertainment—he was invited to the US Open in California, the Superbowl in Florida and black-tie corporate events in New York. His brokers would pay for his entertainment at a local bar, Peter's Pour House on Water Street in downtown Baltimore. He was treated to expensive food and wine at some of Baltimore's top restaurants, a gambling trip to Las Vegas and was flown to Italy for a holiday with his wife Linda. The brokers in other banks were quick to treat Rusnak well because he was earning them huge commissions and bringing their employers plenty of business.

All this ended in February 2002 when Rusnak started assisting the FBI with its inquiries. After his fraud was discovered, AIB said that Rusnak had fled the city and was a fugitive. However, Rusnak's lawyer, David Beckham Irwin, was quick to dismiss this saying Rusnak was assisting the FBI and that he had stolen no money from his Irish employers. Buckley rounded on this, saying in a radio interview: 'His lawyers tried to give the impression of a learner driver whose car has got out of control. This was a fraud.'

The court indictment revealed the lengths to which Rusnak went to perpetrate the fraud. He had rented a mailbox in New York city in the name of David Russell, a fictitious name, to receive mail for the purposes of providing the bank's independent auditors with a false confirmation of a bogus option contract that Rusnak had entered into Allfirst's books. Rusnak claimed that 'Russell' had an address at Suite 162 on Broadway in Manhattan. In fact number 162 was one of hundreds of mailboxes in a postal shop between an optometrist's and a hair stylist's in New York. Only one letter arrived at 'Russell's suite' from the Allfirst's auditors who were checking a trade. It was forwarded automatically to Rusnak's home address and he replied to it, signing Russell's name.

In February 2002 Rusnak came clean. He admitted to his wife that he had been hiding trading losses with fictitious trades for the past five years. She told him that unless he admitted what he had done she would leave him. He decided to confess his wrongdoing. In January 2003 he was sentenced to seven and a half years for covering up $691 million in trading losses at AIB's US bank. Thomas DiBiaggio, who prosecuted the case for the US state, said it was one of the longest sentences ever handed down for white-collar crime.

In an interview with the author at his law practice in the Baltimore suburbs, Irwin, Rusnak's lawyer, said: 'John is a rugged individual. Putting shackles on him was very difficult. It was clear early on that Rusnak was greatly relieved at being caught. His life was in a downward spiral complicated by drugs and alcohol. He was distraught, contrite, ruined, resigned and humbled, and now I think he is all of those things but also punished and sad.' Irwin said that Rusnak turned into a Dr Jekyll and Mr Hyde character, living a double life—that of a church-going family man on one side and a heavy-drinking, reckless trader on the other.

In an interview with the *Baltimore Sun* newspaper in his prison in West Virginia in March 2005, Rusnak came across as relieved and penitent. It was his first interview since being sentenced. It 'makes me sick,' he said, recalling his time at Allfirst. He said he felt 20 years younger being away from the pressure. Responding to the criticism that he bullied and abused co-workers, Rusnak said: 'People being berated was standard practice in the trading room.' He declined to answer questions about the role of other officials when he was hiding his trading losses: 'I've had time to think about everything that happened, and it's best for me and best for my rehabilitation if I focus on what I did and not on the actions of others.' He said he was going to Bible studies, exercising and even teaching personal finance to fellow inmates. He gave the interview against the advice of his lawyer because he had 'an overwhelming desire to tell people what was in my mind and in my heart', he told the newspaper. He said he realised the magnitude of his crime, how it had affected people and how he felt guilty about the suspension of his Allfirst colleagues.

Rusnak wasn't the only casualty of the scandal. Cronin and Ray were fired, as were two managers in the back office of the Baltimore bank, Larry Smith and Jan Palmer, and two internal auditors at Allfirst, Michael Husich and Louis Slifker. Two Citibank traders were also sacked for the entertainment they provided for Rusnak. In April 2006 the US Federal Reserve barred Cronin and Ray from working in the US banking industry again as a result of the scandal. The Federal Reserve based the ban on 'alleged unsafe and unsound practices in connection with [their] supervision of a subordinate.' Allfirst chairman Frank Bramble retired, but chief executive Susan Keating was allowed to keep her job. Michael Buckley and Lochlann Quinn offered their resignations to AIB's board, but the offer was rejected. The board believed their departures would have been unsettling at a precarious time for the bank.

The scandal also paved the way for the sale of Allfirst to M & T, a bank based in Buffalo, New York. Allfirst had been performing poorly, but the Rusnak affair hastened the deal. In return, AIB took a 22.5 per cent stake in M & T. The merger led to 1,132 job losses at Allfirst— about 20 per cent of the bank's staff. Peter Kimos, the owner of Peter's Pour House where Rusnak drank, said the whole financial area in Baltimore suffered as a result of the affair.

Although Ludwig described Rusnak as 'unusually clever and devious' and 'a lone wolf', he laid the blame for the scandal squarely at the door of the bank. He said the systems to monitor Rusnak were inadequate, not properly enforced and easily sidestepped. The bank initially claimed that its controls at Allfirst stood up to the best inter-national standards, but as Ludwig showed, they did not. He said Rusnak had 'an extraordinary firm grasp of, and influence over, the bank's systems and procedures'. The failure of Allfirst's management to follow the stated rules of trading allowed a shrewd trader to gamble freely and recklessly with the bank's money.

Looking back at the fraud in late 2002, Lochlann Quinn said: 'It's like you're driving along in a car and you decide to take your hands off the wheel and let it drive itself. It was literally two or three people stopped doing their job. This sort of thing should never have happened. It is not a question of having inadequate controls. The fact of the matter is that the people who were supervising stopped func-tioning. You can have all the control systems in the world, but three or four people decided not to operate them. The controls were adequate to have picked this up. Sophisticated controls prevent a fraud taking place and/or pick it up within 48 hours, so they [the controls in place] were not very sophisticated. But they should have been picked up within weeks when the loss rate was at $5 million or $10 million. If the controls that were in place had been applied, it would have been caught a long, long time ago.'

However, a former senior Allfirst employee said that low-level pro-prietary foreign exchange trading with a single trader was a risky strategy. He said few people in AIB and Allfirst felt that Rusnak posed a risk because his trading limits were so low. Because of this there was a belief that there was no point buying sophisticated and expensive checks and balances. He said US regional banks of Allfirst's size rarely dealt in proprietary foreign exchange trading, so the Baltimore bank was in an unusual position.

'If we had a big trading desk for foreign exchange trading, the bank would have spent a lot more money on it,' he said. 'There is a danger that in getting into a high risk business like this in a small way, you are not going to spend as much making sure the risks are checked. You should be in this business in a big way or not at all, and if you aren't in it big, you won't spend the money to check the limits.'

The former Allfirst staffer said the experience of AIB staff and the culture within the bank may have been a contributory factor in leading to Rusnak's fraud. He said that many people in AIB never worked outside the Irish bank, so their experience was limited. 'One of AIB's problems is that it is kind of insular,' he said. 'In the US, it's typical for people to work for several banks in their career and pick up different management styles, so staff can work from their different experiences. This wasn't the case in AIB and because everyone worked in the same way, they didn't anticipate problems. Everyone has blinkers on. It was a myopic experience. This may have contributed to a poor ability to exercise judgment when entering a new business line or a new market.'

The former employee said he didn't believe that Ludwig carried out an independent investigation of Allfirst. For example, when Ludwig's team interviewed Allfirst staff, AIB staff were also present in the room. 'The lawyers were not the main ones doing the investigating,' said the former employee. 'AIB staff were. Ludwig was put out there as an independent investigator, but Ludwig was hired by AIB's board to investigate and then he was given AIB employees to do most of the work in the investigation. Because AIB people did the real investigation under Ludwig, any role AIB played was diminished in the findings of the investigation. It was less objective.'

AIB's top management should have asked some pertinent questions when reviewing the annual performance of Rusnak's unit long before his fraud was ever detected. Why was a faraway outpost of the bank dealing in such huge volumes of money and making so little money for AIB? Why was there such a high level of proprietary trading (i.e. gambling AIB's own money) on such a large scale in its US subsidiary against a backdrop where AIB's overall policy was to confine such trading to a small percentage of its total treasury operations? However, just as operational issues were not adequately addressed within Allfirst, these fundamental commercial issues were not clearly addressed either, and Rusnak's fraud went undetected by auditors, regulators and managers at numerous levels for several years.

In the aftermath of the Rusnak scandal other Irish banks who had inspected their own operations found that their treasury operations stood up where AIB's had not. They ensured that there was a clear separation of the dealing, confirmation and settlement functions so that a trader would not have control over providing evidence of their own deals. To minimise the risk of undetected collusion between back and front office staff, other banks also ensured that employees in the back office were rotated between functions and that deals were handled by random rather than by a trader choosing who would confirm a particular deal. The banks also ensured that back office staff were drawn partly from a pool of former traders who knew the tricks of the trade.

Since the Leeson-Barings Bank scandal, many Irish banks had increased the number of internal audits they conducted on a regular basis. AIB's rival banks also made it compulsory that their traders took at least two weeks' holiday a year and that their place on the trading desk was taken over by a member of staff from another office during this time. While most banks had no internal control system that could guarantee against fraud and large-scale collusion, they had learned from the Leeson affair and installed systems that reduced the risk of a fraud to the absolute minimum possibility. AIB's standards did not meet the same standards.

Rusnak's fraud wiped out 47 per cent of AIB's profits in 2001. The bank should have reported a 10 per cent increase in profits to €1.4 billion, but it was forced to write off half of this covering Rusnak's losses. The bank was left with earnings of €612 million for 2001.

However, the bank's share price bounced back after the publication of the Ludwig report. The bank's communication strategy had worked; AIB moved on and continued to make huge profits. The upsurge in the share price, however, was primarily due to a certain level of anticipation in the market of a possible bid for the bank; many observers believed that a predator was well placed to take over AIB, given the fact that credibility in AIB's management was at an all-time low.

AIB moved on from the affair and continued to record profits of hundreds of millions of euro in the following years. After selling Allfirst to M & T, Buckley admitted that AIB had been trying to offload the Baltimore bank since autumn 2001. Taking the M & T stake gave AIB a back-seat position in the US, one it was probably happy to take after Rusnak.

AIB is not the only Irish bank to suffer losses in the US. Bank of Ireland bought First New Hampshire Bank, the largest bank in New Hampshire, in 1988 but its timing was all wrong. The property market in the state had just peaked and fell off sharply shortly after the acquisition. Bank of Ireland pumped hundreds of millions of dollars into the bank to keep it afloat, but the venture turned into a disaster. It was one of the reasons why Bank of Ireland chief executive Mark Hely Hutchinson lost his job in 1991. In 1996 Bank of Ireland merged its US bank with Citizens Bank, the New England bank owned by Royal Bank of Scotland. Bank of Ireland eventually sold its minority stake in Citizens in 1998.

The Rusnak affair continued to haunt AIB for several years. In February 2002 a group of US shareholders took a class action against the bank for damages over the slump in the share price after the exposure of the $691 million fraud. They claimed AIB's financial reports failed to reflect the losses. In late 2005 AIB paid $2.5 million to the disgruntled shareholders, settling the action.

At this stage the bank's $500 million legal action against Bank of America and Citibank over its part in Rusnak's fraud was still ongoing. In February 2006 a New York judge allowed AIB to proceed with its case and rejected an application by Bank of America to dismiss the action. AIB claims that Citibank and Bank of America employees helped Rusnak hide the fraud so that the banks could earn tens of millions of dollars in trading with Rusnak. It could be some time before the high-profile case is eventually heard.

Rusnak will be in an American jail until at least 2009. AIB could be dealing with the fall-out from his fraud for as long as he is behind bars.

Chapter 12

AIB and Foreign Exchange Transactions: overcharging by the €16 billion bank

On Wednesday, 5 May 2004, an anonymous caller contacted the RTÉ newsroom with a deeply damaging secret about AIB. Some officials in the bank had known about the secret for at least two years and had kept it under wraps over that period of time. But that Wednesday they could not hide it any longer and RTÉ carried the story as its lead news item—AIB had systematically overcharged customers on foreign exchange transactions since 1996.

The same anonymous caller who tipped off RTÉ had two weeks earlier contacted the financial regulator, the Irish Financial Services Regulatory Authority (IFSRA), about the overcharging. These telephone calls cost AIB dearly. As a result of the tip-offs AIB was forced to reimburse €25.6 million to customers for foreign exchange transactions. But this wasn't all that was discovered. An investigation into foreign exchange overcharging revealed financial irregularities in some of the bank's other operations. All told, the scandal ended up costing the bank €50 million, which included €34 million in refunds. The remainder was made up of the investigation and administrative costs. The money was a pittance compared to what AIB was making in 2004—the refunds equalled just over a week's profits at the bank.

Repaying a multimillion euro sum for overcharging customers over an eight-year period was embarrassing enough for the bank, but more damaging were the subsequent revelations that emerged. They showed that foreign exchange overcharging had been discovered by some AIB staff as far back as 2002. Over the years there had been at least seven opportunities for the bank to come clean and admit the overcharging to the regulator. These opportunities were ignored. There was a cover-up within the ranks of AIB to hide the mistakes. Just before the game was up, the bank tried to rectify the problem and reduce the foreign exchange rate to the amount it should have been charging. But it was too late. This only created the perception that the bank was trying to conceal the issue. A whistle blower was about to bring the roof down.

The story begins in 1995 when AIB decided to input into its computers a 1 per cent margin for non-cash foreign exchange transactions of more than £500. The following year, the responsibility for the authorisation of bank charges was transferred from the Central Bank to the Office of the Director of Consumer Affairs. In its 1996 application to the director the bank incorrectly submitted an application for permission to charge a 0.5 per cent margin on non-cash foreign exchange transactions. It had set a rate of double this amount into its computers the year before. AIB could well have applied for a 1 per cent rate and told the regulator it was doing so; it was well within its power to do so. But it didn't. It would charge customers the higher rate for another eight years before the bank admitted the error to the regulator and its customers.

In 2002 the mistake was spotted. The Strategic Development Unit (SDU), a division within AIB's headquarters in Bankcentre in Ballsbridge, Dublin, noticed that the margin being charged was different from the rate notified to the Director of Consumer Affairs in 1996. For some reason the issue was seen within the unit as 'an administrative one' and none of the senior executives above the unit was notified, a senior AIB executive later claimed. The people concerned were 'not sufficiently aware' that the margin needed to be authorised, the bank admitted. In other words, according to the bank some middle managers made a decision not to inform their superiors because they did not think it was something they needed to tell them about. Instead, they chose to deal with the problem themselves. Incredibly, the margin was not changed and AIB continued to charge double the rate that had been notified in 1996.

Two years later, in March/April 2004, AIB's SDU was facing a much bigger problem. It wanted to apply for a new range of charges. But to do this it had to report the new charges to the regulator, the IFSRA, which had taken back responsibility for bank charges from the Director of Consumer Affairs in 2003. If the bank did this, it would have to admit to charging the wrong rate for the last eight years. The SDU had a major dilemma on its hands. In the middle of April the margin was reduced from 1 per cent to the correct margin, 0.5 per cent. Internally the bank began working on how it would break the embarrassing news to the regulator. It also had to calculate the amount of money that had been overcharged and find a way to square it within the bank. The unit decided to break the news to the bank's executive management and the regulator by compiling a file. On 20 April, before senior management at AIB were told about the problem, the whistle was blown when an anonymous caller contacted the regulator.

On Friday, 30 April, the IFSRA started making its own inquiries. During a scheduled meeting with the bank's compliance officers, IFSRA officials raised the subject of the overcharging. The compliance officers had no knowledge of the overcharging. The anonymous whistle blower's second call to RTÉ on 5 May cast the bank into the eye of a storm. RTÉ broke the story and the rest of the Irish media picked up the news of yet another scandal emerging at AIB. To any observer, it appeared that there was something intrinsically wrong with AIB.

The scandal could not have come at a worse time for the bank's chief executive, Michael Buckley. He and his senior management team were meeting investment institutions in London to explain AIB's plan for 'driving for growth' when the overcharging revelations filled the Irish newspapers on Friday, 7 May. Buckley was at this stage adept at handling scandals as they emerged at his bank. In February 2002 he had had to deal with the world's press and convince the bank's inter-national shareholders that it could withstand $691 million in losses incurred by its star currency trader John Rusnak in Baltimore, Maryland. Buckley dealt with that crisis effectively, reassuring share-holders and customers that it was a one-off incident and that the bank could weather the storm and take the financial hit of one of the largest trading frauds in banking history. It worked. The scandal had, in the long term, hardly any effect on the bank's share price.

Now, just two years after the Rusnak affair, Buckley and his senior AIB colleagues were facing another crisis. This scandal was different, however. There may have been a lot less money involved, but this scandal threatened to undermine the confidence of more than one million customers in Ireland who contributed so much every year to the bank's profits. This crisis was different for another reason—when news of Rusnak's losses emerged at Allfirst, the bank could take control of the situation before news broke publicly and call the shots in the damage limitation exercise. However, the overcharging revelations emerged from an anonymous source within AIB, so the bank could not control the information. Damage limitation would be much more difficult because the bank was playing catch-up, dealing blindly with the drip-feed of bad news that was emerging. The bank was in an awkward position.

AIB launched an internal investigation to get to the bottom of the overcharging. The regulator wanted answers too. In particular the IFSRA wanted to know how the issue came to light in 2002 and why it was not dealt with then. 'We need to understand how an issue like this would not come on to the radar screen as a regulatory issue,' said the IFSRA's consumer director Mary O'Dea in May 2004. The Tánaiste Mary Harney spoke out too. She told reporters that she was surprised that the overcharging had been discovered as far back as 2002 and nothing had been done. 'If it was undercharging, I am certain it would have come to light a lot sooner,' she said. If Rusnak had taught the bank a lesson, it was that if something suspicious was discovered lower down the AIB chain, it should be reported to the top as quickly as possible. Yet when the overcharging was discovered in 2002, shortly after the Rusnak scandal, a decision was made not to report it.

The day after news of the overcharging broke, while hundreds of concerned customers were calling the bank, Donal Forde, managing director of AIB Republic of Ireland, apologised for the overcharging. He tried to play down the issue, saying it was an honest administrative mistake. He said that in 2002 the unit responsible for foreign exchange charges had examined the inconsistency between the rate advised to the IFSRA and the rate programmed into the bank's computers. 'There was some analysis of that, at department level, and wrongly the conclusion was reached that the advice was simply an administrative error,' said Forde. 'The critical issue here is that it wasn't understood or appreciated that the advice was the basis of approval, essentially, from the regulators.' Around mid-May the general manager of AIB's SDU, Seamus Sheerin, left the bank on unpaid leave.

On 16 May 2004, AIB placed ads in the national newspapers inviting customers to seek refunds on their foreign exchange transactions. The ad also asked customers who had been overcharged by 0.16 per cent on international payment transactions since 7 January 1998 to come forward.

Foreign exchange transactions were not the only part of AIB affected by overcharging. Late in May 2004 the bank admitted that it had repaid €3.4 million to customers who were wrongly charged on trusts in the bank. The bank said it was refunding €1.7 million to the holders of 43 trusts and paying €1.7 million in compensation. It also said it expected to pay an additional €2 million in refunds to customers who had been overcharged on trusts.

Another revelation further muddied the waters. It was reported three weeks after the overcharging emerged that some AIB branches may have altered the rates on foreign exchange transactions to increase profits because they were not meeting their targets.

Around the same time AIB was rocked by another controversy. At the end of May 2004 it was revealed that AIB had invested money belonging to several former senior executives in an offshore company in the British Virgin Islands and that tax laws had been breached. The bank said that about €750,000 was invested in the company, Faldor, between 1989 and 1996. Even though the tax breaches had occurred in the early 1990s, the revelations shook the bank to its core. AIB had been hit by a double blow—overcharging and tax evasion involving former executives who had held positions at the highest levels of the bank.

Buckley was under serious pressure and determined to limit the damage to AIB's reputation. He sent an email to staff to rally them, saying: 'Whatever changes are needed in culture, people, organisation and practice will be made to ensure that we achieve this vital objective.' A change of direction was clearly needed.

AIB hired a former comptroller and auditor general, the state watchdog, Lauri McDonnell, and accountants from Deloitte to investigate the extent of the overcharging and how it had happened. To save face and try to shore up whatever trust customers had left in the bank, AIB lodged €25 million with the Central Bank to compensate affected customers.

In late July the IFSRA issued a progress report on its investigation into the overcharging. AIB used the opportunity to announce that on top of the €25.6 million in charges and interest it would be refunding customers for foreign exchange overcharging, it had also uncovered 24 other areas where 70,000 customers were overcharged €8.1 million. This brought the total bill facing the bank to more than €34.2 million when interest and compensation were added. Of the 24 areas, eight involved amounts of €75,000, including 4,200 mortgage customers who were not charged the proper interest rate discount. Customers were overcharged a total of €3.6 million on these transactions. Again, Buckley vociferously defended the bank, saying that only 4 per cent of its 1.5 million customers had been affected by the overcharging over an eight-year period and there was not 'a culture of overcharging' at the bank.

More damning for AIB was the news from the IFSRA in July that it was investigating whether there was a cover-up in the bank when the overcharging first emerged in 2002. Liam O'Reilly, chief executive of the IFSRA, said it was 'strange' that the bank could have charged an incorrect fee on foreign exchange transactions for eight years without the issue coming to light. O'Reilly told reporters at a press conference that the IFSRA would not be holding an investigation into AIB 'unless we had grounds to believe there was some sort of cover-up'.

The following month AIB began refunding money owed to customers. The amounts overcharged may have seemed quite large in total, but when they were paid individually to customers they did not amount to a whole lot. About a third of the repayments were under €10, two-thirds were under €20 and 96 per cent were under €250. All these amounts were repaid with interest. But there were some large amounts too. One commercial customer was overcharged by €40,000. In total the bank identified 1.1 million transactions and about 173,000 that were eligible for refunds as a result of the overcharging.

Politicians responded angrily to the overcharging. Fine Gael's finance spokesman Richard Bruton said the tone of AIB's response 'smacks of complacency and a failure to understand the level of public frustration that needs to be addressed. The AIB statement is 1,800 words long, but the word "regret" appears only once, in the final paragraph.'

Despite the cost of the overcharging and the public hammering endured by AIB, the bank posted a 10 per cent increase in pre-tax profits to €699 million for the first six months of 2004. Investors may have seemed unperturbed by the whole affair, but AIB was still finalising its own investigation and taking steps to discipline the employees involved.

In mid-September 2004, AIB said its inquiry into the overcharging had been completed and was being considered by a subcommittee of the bank's board of directors. The committee members were AIB head of finance Gary Kennedy and two of the bank's non-executive directors, the former US ambassador to Ireland Mike Sullivan and the chief executive of the Barretstown camp for terminally ill children, Jenny Winter. The following month, speaking before an Oireachtas joint committee on finance and the public service, AIB's recently appointed chairman Dermot Gleeson, one of the country's top senior counsels who represented the bank at the DIRT inquiry hearings in 1999, hinted that the bank was looking at a possible cover-up of the overcharging in 2002. He said: 'Our failure to resolve the issue then is a matter of serious concern.' A month later the seriousness of the situation emerged. In mid-November the bank said that up to ten senior executives could be facing disciplinary proceedings. The bank's subcommittee wrote to them detailing the findings of the internal investigation and seeking a response. Some of the executives retained solicitors.

The bank had obviously learned lessons from the affair. In mid-November it announced that it was restructuring its retail banking operations and streamlining its processes to reduce errors. Responsibility for product compliance and pricing was removed from the bank's SDU, which was previously responsible for notifying the regulator of the foreign exchange rate. This function was passed to a new management unit. These changes might have given the bank a veneer of reform, but AIB took another massive knock three weeks later when the IFSRA issued its report into the overcharging. The findings were seriously damaging.

The IFSRA found that some staff and management at AIB had deliberately hidden from the regulator the facts of the overcharging over an eight-year period. The regulator's chief executive Liam O'Reilly said that AIB had had at least seven opportunities to identify and disclose the overcharging but failed to do so. The IFSRA also reported that an internal AIB memo was prepared in 2002 which raised the issue of the potential cost of rectifying the overcharging problem. The memo also pointed out that the IFSRA needed to be informed.

The regulator's report, however, proved to be a damp squib. It did not name the people responsible for the overcharging. It refused to discuss who had prepared the memo and who had circulated it within AIB. The IFSRA's excuse was that it did not want to prejudice the internal disciplinary action that was under way in the bank.

The regulator also found that AIB had not dealt with the problem properly until as late as early 2004. The IFSRA found that between January and April 2004, AIB took 'deliberate measures' to reduce the foreign exchange rate being applied. By April the correct rate was being applied. However, the IFSRA was never told about the change. 'These matters are open to the interpretations that AIB then intended to notify the regulator subsequently of a proposed increase and to do this without ever drawing attention to the previous breach, which had persisted for almost eight years', said the IFSRA. This in effect confirmed that there had been a cover-up within the bank.

The regulator also concluded that there was 'inadequate documentary evidence' within the bank of decisions made about the foreign exchange charges. The bank's internal procedures, which allowed for problems to be raised 'up the line', were inadequate and contributed to the problem. 'The failures within AIB uncovered by the investigations are completely unacceptable,' said O'Reilly. 'We will not tolerate such practices within the financial services industry.'

Richard Bruton said it was 'disturbing' that at least seven opportunities arose for bank executives to blow the whistle on the overcharging, but they chose not to. 'Many people were aware but did nothing,' said Bruton. 'These individuals may indeed have substantial individual responsibility, but they worked within a bank which sustained an environment where such activity was at worst tolerated and at best not vigorously pursued.'

The IFSRA's findings were a shocking indictment for Ireland's biggest bank. Buckley again responded forcefully, denying any knowledge of the 2002 memo on overcharging, saying it was never circulated to senior management. He refused to elaborate on the memo's contents or say who circulated it. He used the same excuse as the IFSRA did. If he named names, it might prejudice the disciplinary process within the bank. The IFSRA report focused attention again on how the bank was going to reprimand those responsible for the overcharging and the cover-up.

AIB was by no means alone when it came to overcharging customers. In December 2004 the state's biggest mortgage lender, Permanent TSB, began repaying a total of €600,000—€400 each to 1,500 customers—after an internal audit found they had been overcharged interest.

Four months later Bank of Ireland admitted it had mistakenly overcharged 65,000 of its customers on payment protection insurance since 1989 and could be facing a bill of up to €15 million to refund customers. The bank identified the error during an industry-wide investigation by the IFSRA into the sale of payment protection policies by financial institutions. Customers take out payment protection to cover repayment on a personal loan in case they suffer from illness or are made redundant. However, the policies only cover the first 12 months of the loan. The overcharging error arose when customers, who had taken out the insurance to cover the loan, paid it off before the agreed term was complete. Payment protection premiums and the loan repayments were made as one payment, so when the customer paid off the balance of the loan early, they paid for insurance premiums for the remainder of the loans. This should not have happened. The bank should have informed the customers and refunded them the extra premium payments. The revelations prompted an industry-wide examination of whether other financial institutions were charging on payment protection insurance as well.

As more and more stories appeared in the media about overcharging by financial institutions, customers started scrutinising their bank statements more closely every month and questioned why some charges were being made. This threw up more and more cases of overcharging by the banks. The AIB overcharging scandal spawned a general suspicion among the public that they could not trust their bankers. People were becoming increasingly financially savvy and Irish banks found themselves facing some awkward questions from customers. The financial regulator announced in late 2005 that since May 2003 it had uncovered 250 cases of overcharging worth €100 million and that €70 million of this had been refunded, so customers were right to be watching their accounts closely.

Foreign exchange overcharging was really only the tip of the iceberg. Overcharging in general by financial institutions created a cottage industry for consultants, usually forensic accountants and former bankers, who would examine a customer's account and assess whether they had been hit with any illegal charges, and approach the bank for reimbursement on behalf of the customer. They would then take a cut of the money refunded.

Eddie Fitzpatrick, a director of one such consultancy, Bankcheck in Co. Down, said that between 2002 and 2006 his company had recovered €3 million from banks on behalf of overcharged customers and in February 2006 was in the process of recovering another €3 million from between 100 and 120 cases. 'It is happening to so many people in so many branches in so many banks that it is not possible to simply quantify how much banks are overcharging across the board,' said Fitzpatrick. He estimated that Irish banks were making between €100 million and €200 million a year by way of errors and unnecessary charges on customer accounts. He said that in one day of meetings with a bank in February 2006, his customers were refunded €250,000. He said that overcharging often occurs when the wrong interest rate is charged on overdraft or loan accounts, particularly when an overdraft limit or loan expires. 'While it is not a scandal in the same sense as some other scandals we have seen in recent years, the practice of overcharging throughout Irish banking is scandalous,' said Fitzpatrick.

One customer affected by overcharging was Denis Murphy, a shop owner from West Beach, Cobh, Co. Cork. In July 2004 Murphy took on AIB and won. He sued the bank in Cork Circuit Court, which awarded him just under €20,000 including €9,687 he had been overcharged by the bank. AIB tried to pay Murphy not to take the case; they offered him €35,000 to drop his action on the morning the case was due to be heard. Murphy dealt heavily in cash in his business and the bank reneged on an agreement to charge him 17p for every £100 lodged in cash, instead forcing him to pay 45p per £100 cash lodgement. The bank also overcharged him interest when his account was overdrawn, all of which occurred between May 1999 and August 2001.

'They reneged on the original agreement I had with them and tried to take advantage of me because I was a small businessman,' said Murphy. He said that during the two years he was overcharged he had to deal with three managers in the bank at West Beach. He said he had been 'pushed from pillar to post' and claimed that one manager told him there would be no refund. Murphy said he brought the case because he was appalled at the way he had been treated. 'I'm delighted with the outcome and hope this is a wake-up call to AIB in general.' He said he declined the bank's settlement offer because he 'wanted the situation aired not only from the point of view of getting what was justly mine but for people in general. It shows that a small business person or anyone can take on a big company like AIB and come out as winners.'

The judge in the case, James O'Donoghue, criticised the bank for its 'arrogant and high-handed manner'. Part of the award comprised punitive damages of €5,000 because the judge said he wanted to 'discourage further incidents of this sort in the future. . . . In light of the recent overcharging scandal by AIB, it is timely for the court to show its disapproval. It is regrettable that matters could not have been resolved at the very moment he registered his complaints—in those circumstances, I find that he was wronged,' said the judge.

Minister for Finance Brian Cowen said in 2004 that overcharging could damage the entire financial services industry. 'I am happy to champion the cause of Ireland as a centre for financial services. I am happy to promote our industry as a provider of services internationally. But I will never be an apologist for bad service to customers, or for practices that put at risk the reputation not just of individual institutions, but of the Irish financial services industry at large.'

Despite being dogged with scandal and being forced to pay a €50 million bill for overcharging, in February 2005 AIB said it had increased its pre-tax profits by 40 per cent to €1.4 billion for 2004. This was the equivalent of almost €4 million a day, a record for the bank.

The overcharging scandal took an unusual turn in March 2005 when Sheerin, the 41-year-old head of AIB's SDU, went to the High Court to stop the bank firing him. He was the first banker to lose his job over the scandal, but he wasn't happy at the bank's treatment of him. He had left the bank on unpaid leave the previous May when the scandal broke, but on 9 March 2005 the bank moved to fire him. AIB sent him a letter recommending that he be dismissed. Sheerin reacted angrily. AIB gave him an opportunity to appeal, but he felt he had to take the matter beyond the bank to the High Court.

His court application was the first opportunity to hear how the bank had dealt internally with the overcharging. It brought the whole affair on to the front pages of the newspapers again. Here was AIB heading into an embarrassing legal battle with one of its own executives and this was no junior employee. Sheerin was a senior manager earning €10,000 a month after tax.

The timing could not have been worse for AIB. The previous day the bank had revealed its new chief executive, Eugene Sheehy, a career banker with AIB who would replace Buckley. The appointment of Sheehy was widely seen as heralding a new era in AIB. It was felt that he would draw a line under the Rusnak, Faldor (see Chapter 13) and overcharging scandals. However, Sheerin's actions took some of the gloss off Sheehy's appointment and forced AIB into a very public fight.

Sheerin claimed in court that he was being scapegoated for the overcharging and 'excluded from employment in order to facilitate others'. He claimed he first became aware of foreign exchange overcharging in September 2002, that he had simply 'inherited' the problem and had 'endeavoured to manage it' with other employees. He said in court documents that it was 'utterly perverse' that he be subjected to any sanction.

Sheerin claimed that the overcharging problem had been widely known within the bank at various levels. He said senior managers had steered clear of it. 'For example, the only area of revenue generation which was not increased since 1996 was the level of charges on foreign exchange transactions,' Sheerin said in an affidavit to the court. He said that he told 'a superior' in September 2002 that the issue had been brought to his attention.

While trying to protect his job at the bank, Sheerin dropped a few bombshells and drew Buckley directly into the controversy. He said that, according to Deloitte's investigation into the overcharging, one official, John O'Donovan, a senior executive of corporate and commercial treasury, believed Buckley was 'aware of this issue' when the chief executive was managing director of the bank's capital markets division.

Sheerin also said that O'Donovan told the Deloitte investigators that he believed Forde, AIB's Republic of Ireland managing director, was also aware of the overcharging. Forde was the man who announced shortly after the overcharging emerged in May 2004 that it had all been an honest administrative mistake at department level. Sheerin said he himself had told Forde about the overcharging in September 2002, 20 months before the error was revealed in public.

Sheerin also pointed a finger at Aidan McKeon, AIB's UK managing director. He said McKeon had 'unresolved issues' and was 'one of the original architects' of the overcharging and so should not have been the person to investigate Sheerin's own conduct in the affair. However, Sheerin's barrister later admitted in court that his client had participated in the investigation and had not objected to McKeon conducting it. It also emerged in court that Sheerin had been unhappy about references in the media linking him to news that a senior bank official had been suspended as a result of the overcharging scandal. He said he was concerned that AIB had failed to correct the stories about him in the media. He believed he was not responsible for the problem, so why wasn't the bank correcting the media's reports?

Sheerin's explosive revelations drew a robust defence from AIB. Forde said he was 'outraged' and denied ever being told by Sheerin about the overcharging. The bank came out to defend Forde and Buckley, saying they had no knowledge of the overcharging prior to May 2004. McKeon rejected Sheerin's claim that he was 'directly implicated' in the overcharging. He said he had been based in Britain since January 1996 before the obligation to notify foreign exchange charges under the 1995 Consumer Credit Act came into force. The only mention of McKeon in Deloitte's report on its investigation was that he was someone who had been interviewed during the course of its inquiry.

During the case, the bank denied that Sheerin was the only person being singled out to be disciplined by the bank. AIB said others were being disciplined. In court it emerged that another senior banker had his sizeable bonus frozen for two years because of the overcharging.

Events took an interesting turn at the beginning of April 2005 when an assistant manager in the SDU, Edward Mulhall, came forward to back up some of Sheerin's claims. Mulhall said McKeon was in charge of the unit responsible for the foreign exchange increase in 1995 before his transfer to Britain. He said McKeon addressed employees at a meeting in late 1995/early 1996 and made reference to the extra money being made from the increase in foreign exchange charges in the autumn of 1995. Mulhall said in a court affidavit that at the meeting he told McKeon that 'it was my understanding that those charges had not been implemented in a manner which was transparent to the bank network'.

'Indeed the manner in which the charges were applied was novel at that time and I had not seen it done before,' said Mulhall. 'In any event, Aidan McKeon did not appear to have much regard for what I had said to him at that time. I was simply concerned about the absence of transparency in the way in which the charges were being calculated for those transactions and I was concerned at the motivation behind this lack of transparency.' Mulhall said he told the Deloitte investigators about his conversation with McKeon in 2004, but Deloitte said McKeon had denied the conversation had ever taken place.

In a second affidavit Mulhall pointed out that the bank had actually been compensating people for overcharging on foreign exchange transactions from 31 August 1995. Mulhall said McKeon had been responsible for making sure bank charges and, specifically, foreign exchange transactions complied with Central Bank requirements from 1990 until January 1996. McKeon stated in his affidavit that until August 1996 it was retail bank management's responsibility to determine the foreign exchange charges. Mulhall replied, saying that this 'completely ignores' the fact that a bank official who reported to McKeon determined the foreign exchange price changes to be brought forward to the retail bank management. Mulhall said that was the direct responsibility of the official and 'in turn a direct responsibility of Mr McKeon up until January 1996 when he went to the United Kingdom'. McKeon vehemently denied Mulhall's claims.

AIB rejected all of Sheerin's allegations, claiming that they were without foundation. Sheerin and the bank eventually settled their differences. He was allowed to resign from the bank and was not fired. Being a banker, this difference was important. If he had been dismissed, the IFSRA could well have barred him from working in financial services again. By resigning he could now find another job in the sector. The end result though was that Sheerin's allegations had been made and remained on the public record, even though the bank released a final statement on the matter saying the case had been settled and that every single one of Sheerin's allegations had been rebutted by the board of the bank.

Just before the settlement, however, in another affidavit Sheerin tried to distance himself from the overcharging and put others in the frame. He said he took control of the SDU in April 2002, yet the overcharging had been going on since 31 August 1995. He said the IFSRA report stated that from 1996 onwards 'certain staff and management within certain areas of AIB appear to have been aware of the fact that AIB were charging over the amount notified to the regulator'. He said he was not identified in the IFSRA report until September 2002 and had been an area manager in Cork between 1994 and 1999. This raises the question of just who was responsible before Sheerin came on the scene in 2002.

In his last affidavit Sheerin named seven people in the bank whom he believed the IFSRA was referring to. 'The only people with an interest in burying the issue were those who were attempting to deny they had any knowledge or responsibility for it; in other words, the people who knew of the issues since 1995 but took no steps to deal with it,' said Sheerin.

Incredibly, while Sheerin was battling with the bank in a high-profile court case, AIB announced that it had increased the basic salaries of its four executive directors by 20 per cent in 2004, a year when the bank had set aside €50 million for an overcharging scandal. Buckley, as chief executive, received the most money in 2004—he was paid a total package of €1.445 million, comprising a basic salary of €775,000, a pension contribution of €210,000 as well as a bonus of €360,000. Aidan McKeon, the head of AIB's UK operations who was named by Sheerin in his case against the bank, received a basic salary of €356,000, an increase of 31 per cent on his previous year's salary, as well as a bonus of €242,000.

One group, however, chose not to make any more money out of AIB. The Irish rock band, the Walls, asked AIB to stop using one of its songs, 'To The Bright and Shining Sun', in the bank's advertising campaign and declined a lucrative licensing deal because of the scandal. Joe Wall, a member of the band, told the *Sunday Tribune* in August 2005 that the group did not want one of their songs, which was popular at the time of the scandal, to be remembered as a 'jingle' for a bank that was associated with overcharging its customers. 'We thought it would be wrong to turn a blind eye to the scandal and continue on as if nothing was up,' said Wall. The band had been offered 'a substantial sum' by the bank to renew the contract and use the song in its ads for another year, but they declined.

By the summer of 2005 the clean-up at AIB was not yet complete. During its internal investigations AIB discovered more instances of overcharging that dated back long before 1995. In August the *Sunday Business Post* reported that AIB was, in conjunction with the Financial Regulator (the IFSRA's new name), investigating new allegations that the bank had for more than 15 years deliberately and repeatedly altered foreign exchange rates on a daily basis to boost profits.

A spokeswoman for the bank explained that AIB had launched a new process known as 'speak up' to encourage AIB staff to raise 'any issue in any area of the business, past and present'. It was reported that the new overcharging allegations emerged after a staff member took advantage of the 'speak up' facility to disclose the claims. The spokeswoman for the bank said AIB had been investigating any potential issues that had come up, but that 'nothing approaching the magnitude of the foreign exchange charging issue of 2004 has been identified'.

Some staff, however, expressed concern to the newspaper that they would be scapegoated in this new investigation, claiming that this happened during the previous inquiry. 'There's no question of anyone being scapegoated,' said the spokeswoman for the bank.

According to the *Sunday Business Post* report, AIB compliance officers had interviewed staff at Bankcentre in Ballsbridge, Dublin, in July and August. Some members of staff were shown pieces of paper on which names were written. They were asked if those named were responsible for the overcharging in question. Employees were also told by the bank that any future tribunal of inquiry could use the evidence gathered during their questioning. Staff said they were sworn to silence following questioning by the bank's compliance officers and were not offered union representation at the meeting. The bank's spokeswoman told *The Irish Times*: 'In all circumstances anything that is investigated is investigated thoroughly and fairly.' It was reported that it would be difficult to trace the customers affected by this latest incident of overcharging because it dated back so far.

In December 2005 the *Sunday Business Post* published another report saying that AIB would have to reimburse customers for a second case of overcharging. The bank claimed that only ten branches were involved in the overcharging to boost profits. In its report the newspaper cited a senior current staff member who said it was 'a routine practice for staff to alter foreign exchange rates to the advantage of branches'. 'It would be accurate to say that almost all AIB staff knew this was widespread,' said another senior staff member, who added that many staff in AIB were 'surprised' by the bank's insistence that the overcharging cases were limited to a small number of branches. The newspaper quoted a former AIB auditor who said overcharging was 'endemic'. The auditor said: 'You were not going to get just ten branches out of a network of more than 300 branches. It was money for old rope.'

Also that month, RTÉ's *Prime Time* programme revealed new evidence of overcharging at AIB and the bank's business customers inundated its branches querying their bank statements. The *Sunday Business Post* followed up on the *Prime Time* programme with another story by its business editor, Eamon Quinn. Based on leaked documents, it said that senior AIB staff at its headquarters in Dublin were deeply unhappy with the way the bank had handled the overcharging affair. More than 200 staff made cutting comments in internal bank surveys carried out at the time of the overcharging investigation. 'The sense that recent scandals are a head office problem is ignoring other practices that went on locally,' said one member of staff. Other employees were angry at what they perceived was the 'scapegoating' of Sheerin over the whole affair, again a claim that was denied by AIB. 'One man is left to take the heat for what many people had a hand in,' said one employee in the surveys. Another staff member said: 'Unfortunately many of the media comments in relation to our culture and climate are all too true. We do whatever we can get away with.' Another said: 'We are not honest in our dealings. If we can avoid responsibility by hiding behind a technicality, we will do just that. We do not value our customers or our staff.' Another employee who was questioned about the bank's ethics said: 'The Pentagon has more credibility in its propaganda.'

The overcharging scandal spawned similar inquiries in other institutions. When the Financial Regulator revealed in December 2005 that it had uncovered €100 million worth of overcharging since May 2003, it confirmed the scale of overcharging in the industry.

The findings raised serious questions about who was responsible and why there were inadequate checks in the financial sectors to protect customers. The most serious question concerned the level of trust: can customers trust banks to follow correct procedures? The AIB scandal proved that the customers of Ireland's wealthiest bank, a €16 billion euro business and in the top three richest companies on the Irish Stock Exchange, could not.

Buckley had survived another scandal. He had offered his resignation during the Rusnak affair, but the board of AIB felt it was not necessary. During 2004 the bank did announce, however, that he would be retiring. He had been expected to retire in 2005, but the process of recruiting a replacement for the Cork banker was brought forward several months. This was widely thought to be as a result of the continuous scandals hitting the bank.

The pressure on Buckley did appear to motivate him to make a dramatic proposal in the autumn of 2004, when the bank was taking serious flak over the mounting controversies. It later emerged that he took the remarkable step of proposing to the board of the bank that

AIB be sold to the US bank M&T. AIB had taken a 22.5 per cent stake in M&T following the 2003 merger of the Irish bank's US subsidiary Allfirst with M&T. The non-executive directors rejected Buckley's suggestion.

Instead, the bank decided to get its house in order. While always at pains to say there was no culture of overcharging, the bank undertook some soul-searching. AIB had questions to answer, particularly after the Rusnak affair had taught it severe lessons about the strengths of its internal controls. The overcharging affair brought home the fact that changes were still needed at AIB.

The description of the overcharging as merely 'an administrative error' might be partly correct. However, it was an administrative error that was spotted early on and ignored, or worse, covered up. 'It was a classic case of cover-up,' said a former senior AIB executive. 'That was what surprised me. If there was a mistake made, the people concerned should have stood up and been counted.' Another ex-AIB executive said: 'To see what emerged was unpalatable and disappointing. It was not endemic in the bank, but it did happen and it was unacceptable.' A source who was intimately familiar with the overcharging scandal said: 'When we heard there may have been a concerted cover-up, it was a serious issue for the organisation. They say in an earthquake when the ground starts moving you have no reference point. That's what it felt like here. When systematic overcharging is discovered, you have to turn the place upside down and that's what the bank has done.' The source said the mistake of not informing the regulator about the proper rate was a sin, but covering it up was a mortal sin.

The overcharging has been described in general terms as a reporting failure compounded by poor communications. But more fundamental problems within AIB caused the problem. The bank discovered that there was a general fear within parts of AIB about making complaints or raising problems with superiors. 'The bank looked at the culture and found that there was a huge amount of local reliance within sections of the organisation. Managers felt they shouldn't push their problems up the chain because this was regarded as a black mark on their careers,' said a source close to AIB.

The fact that overcharging came to light through a whistle blower proved this point. The person clearly felt unable to report the issue within the organisation, so had to go anonymously outside the organisation to the regulator and the media. AIB still does not know the identity of the whistle blower. A spokeswoman for AIB said the bank could not launch an investigation into who the whistle blower might be because, if this person was targeted, it would send out a message to the bank's employees that it was wrong to come forward and admit mistakes.

Buckley himself conceded that the strengths of AIB's staff might have created problems. He spoke of the 'can-do' attitude of those working in the bank and their self-dependency. He said: 'There is too much self-censorship in the bank. We need to have more honest communication flowing up and down the organisation.' He said that despite AIB employees' positive outlook on their work, an emphasis on learning from mistakes was needed. 'If you don't, it can lead to a situation where people are reluctant to admit mistakes.' (Buckley and AIB's chief executive Eugene Sheehy declined to be interviewed for this book.)

Larry Broderick, general secretary of the Irish Bank Officials Association (IBOA), said bank employees worked in a 'culture of fear' and were afraid to speak out on any issues in case it would damage their career prospects. He said bankers felt less secure in their jobs because of the switch in the late 1980s and early 90s to performance-related pay. In 2005 bankers were joining banks at lower salaries than in the past and boosting their pay by earning commissions once they reached particular sales targets. Broderick said this change had fostered a culture of greed at the expense of good practice.

'There were dramatic changes with the switch to performance-related pay,' said Broderick. 'This linked a banker's status to maximising profit and minimising cost. It created an environment that was very much focused on sales rather than on the needs of staff. So, in these circumstances, who in the bank was going to speak out and say that something was wrong? Instead, the most important thing was to focus on making money.' Broderick said the emergence of whistle blowers showed 'very clearly the fear that exists in Irish banking'.

For the banks, profits came first, then customers and finally staff, according to Broderick. However, he said the banks had to shuffle their priorities and make performance based not just on sales, but on how the banks dealt with compliance, their staff and their customers. 'The scandals of the 1990s and more recent years were generated by the maximising of profits when there was a culture where people were afraid to speak up,' he said.

One anonymous AIB employee surveyed by the bank in the after-math of the overcharging scandal repeated the point made by

Broderick. 'The culture within AIB was always one of honest relationships with customers. The short-term focus on selling and immediate
profits has eroded this traditional strength of AIB.' Another staff
member said: 'We do not value our customers or our staff. Everything
is subservient to the short-term profit goal. Unfortunately, both
customers and staff can see this as it is often horribly transparent.'
Another employee said: 'I do not believe there is a culture where one
can be confident in speaking one's mind, especially if it goes against
the thinking of management.' Many of the comments made during
the bank's internal survey revealed a culture of fear and, to some
extent, loathing within AIB.

In interviews in the second half of 2004 Buckley encouraged AIB
staff to come forward if they had an issue with any part of the organisation. In an interview in June 2005 Buckley said the lesson he
learned from the overcharging scandal was 'that you can't have
enough ways of allowing your people to raise issues that concern
them'. The IFSRA said in its report that it was an 'unhealthy situation
if an institution has to work on the basis of whistle blowers'. It said the
bank needed to overhaul its culture so that problems can be identified
by staff without any fear of recrimination or punishment.

Responding to the IFSRA's progress report on the overcharging in
July 2004, Buckley said: 'If you boil the whole culture thing down . . .
it's doing what we can to make people know it is safe to speak your
mind and if you don't speak your mind on something that is concerning you, that is a bad thing.'

The overcharging scandal raised many doubts among bank
customers and Irish taxpayers. Most of all, it raised the question—if
you can't trust your bank with your money, then who can you trust?

Chapter 13

AIB and the Faldor Scandal: former bank executives in hot water

Just when it looked as if things could not get any worse for AIB, they did. At the end of May 2004, while the bank was still dealing with the fall-out from the overcharging fiasco that surfaced at the start of the month, another scandal broke. This time it involved senior managers from the 1980s and 90s, tax evasion, and some highly ir-regular practices within the bank's investment arm, AIB Investment Managers.

In the latest scandal it was the bank, and not a whistle blower, that released the bad news. The bank had clearly learned a lesson—better to break the news itself and control the release of information on its own terms. On 27 May 2004, in a detailed statement, AIB revealed that five former senior executives, some of them very senior former managers, had benefited from an offshore investment company, Faldor, which was based in the British Virgin Islands, the Caribbean tax haven. By investing in Faldor the former executives had broken Irish tax laws.

The following day, the media had the names of the former top AIB executives. Faldor's beneficiaries were the bank's former chief exec-utive Gerard Scanlan who had headed up the bank at the time of the

Insurance Corporation of Ireland debacle; the former chairman of Irish Life & Permanent Roy Douglas, a former group general manager for AIB in Britain; the bank's former deputy chief executive, the late Patrick Dowling; its former director of corporate strategy Diarmuid Moore; and the former head of its US treasury operations David Cronin. A total of €750,000 was invested in Faldor between 1989 and 1996, according to the bank.

Moore was sailing in the Mediterranean when AIB released its statement. On his way back to Dublin he stopped at Manchester Airport for a while. While enjoying a smoke at the airport he picked up *The Irish Times* and was stunned to read that he had been linked to the offshore Faldor scheme. Moore 'nearly fell on the floor,' said one of his friends; he was furious.

In its statement, AIB said Faldor had been managed by the bank's investment arm, AIB Investment Managers (AIBIM). The bank added that another five executives—three of whom still worked in AIB—had hidden money from the taxman in schemes unrelated to Faldor and that they too had 'tax issues', the euphemism often used when people do not pay their taxes.

The scandal was the most serious for AIB, as it involved tax evasion at the highest levels of the bank. What made the controversy all the more remarkable was the fact that Scanlan was the same AIB executive who had told the DIRT hearings six years earlier that he had no idea the bank had bogus non-resident accounts, which were being used to evade tax. Now, these former senior staff found themselves involved in a dodgy investment of their own, hidden from the Revenue Commissioners.

On the same day that AIB released its statement, the former chief executive of the bank, Tom Mulcahy, received a phone call from the bank's press office. It was bad news. The bank, his erstwhile employer of 29 years, told him it was about to release a statement revealing details of an internal investigation into the tax affairs of former and current senior AIB managers. While Mulcahy had no connection to Faldor, he was one of the two former AIB executives who had 'tax issues' arising from an offshore account. The bank did not name Mulcahy or any of the other individuals in its statement, but as with the other five executives, Mulcahy's name emerged later that day. The next day the Faldor scheme and the 'tax issues' of the former executives hit the headlines and led the news bulletins on television and radio. That weekend, after his name was linked to the emerging tax evasion scandal at AIB, Mulcahy resigned as chairman of the state airline Aer Lingus.

As more details emerged, one of the participants said the Faldor scheme was essentially an investment reserved exclusively for AIB's top employees, a gold card club for the bank's highest achievers. As the executives rose to the top, he said they were invited to invest their money and watch it grow, away from the eyes of the tax authorities. However, the executives thought their money was being held in a legitimate, professionally managed investment scheme that fell fully within the rules of the Irish taxation system. This was not the case. Faldor was being administered by AIBIM as an offshore scheme. It appears that the whole investment scheme came to light in 2003 when one of the beneficiaries, Roy Douglas, decided to disclose a tax debt on money invested in Faldor. AIBIM's offshore tax dodge club had been rumbled and its beneficiaries were left facing awkward questions from the bank and the taxman. They were unable to provide many answers because the executives had not known that their money had gone into Faldor.

The controversy did not end with the executives. AIB also found some dodgy practices within its investment division. By coming clean about his tax debt and tipping AIB off about Faldor, Douglas had inadvertently opened a can of worms. While investigating Faldor, AIB discovered 'unacceptable' practices in the bank's investment arm, AIBIM.

Like all fund managers, AIBIM looks after money for clients and invests it on their behalf, hoping to make them a return on their investment. By pooling their assets fund managers can trade in stocks on a much larger scale, and any profits are returned to the funds by a process known as deal allocation. It was here that AIB discovered serious irregularities.

In its statement, AIB said it had uncovered 'unacceptable deal alloca- tion practices' in nine transactions between 1991 and 1993 involving clients of AIBIM. As a result of this the bank said it was paying €330,000 to two clients—both specialist investment trusts—which the bank estimated should have been allocated profits worth €174,000 by AIBIM. The bank also agreed to pay the clients a further €156,000 in interest to compensate them for their losses. The bank said in its statement: 'Faldor appears to have been favoured to the extent of €48,000 at the expense of AIBIM in-house accounts and inappropriate deal allocation practices.' In other words, money belonging to two customers, one a senior executive of AIB and the other an outside investor, is invested in a fund and the fund is then used to buy shares which increase in value over a period of time. When the shares are sold, the guy on the inside—the AIB executive—is given more of the money from the pooled fund and the outside customer loses out.

The details in the statement were sketchy at best. The bank refused to elaborate on why it was underwriting a tax settlement of €800,000 which included tax, interest and penalties. It later admitted that the settlement involved a corporate liability arising from the whole affair and that it was not connected to Faldor. As the executives linked to Faldor made public statements in subsequent days, a clearer picture emerged as to how they came to invest in the scheme, how it had been managed by AIBIM, and how the executives had been treated to a company perk.

AIB first got wind of Faldor in late August 2003 when Douglas contacted the Revenue to clear up the debt which arose from a trust he had in AIB in Jersey. He had invested money in AIBIM which was later credited to the Jersey trust. He approached AIBIM while gathering information to make his tax disclosure and told them that he had also contacted the Revenue. As a result of his contact with AIBIM, the head of the investment arm, Eileen Fitzpatrick, became aware of Faldor and passed the information on to the board of the bank. AIB in turn informed the banking regulator, the Irish Financial Services Regulatory Authority (IFSRA), telling them it was launching an investigation into Faldor. The Revenue Commissioners were also informed about Faldor.

Three days after AIB released its statement, Douglas issued his, revealing his involvement in Faldor, his tax debts and how he had paid them. The bank may have landed the executives in an embarrassing and difficult situation, but Douglas's statement pointed the finger back at the bank.

Douglas made it clear that he had nothing to do with establishing or running Faldor—AIBIM bore all the responsibility. He said he had simply been invited to take part in an investment opportunity when he was appointed to a senior position in the bank—group general manager in Britain—in April 1989. 'I was invited to join an investment fund that was professionally managed by AIBIM on behalf of senior executives of AIB Group,' said Douglas. 'I regarded this opportunity as a benefit attaching to my position as group general manager and it was my understanding that it had been in existence for some time.' *Irish Times* columnist Sheila O'Flanagan later described the bank's scheme as the 'because I'm worth it' remuneration package. Not only were these executives being paid substantial six-figure annual sums, but they had the bank's professional fund managers at their service to grow their investments. It turned out, however, that the managers grew some of the investment at the expense of other client funds.

One former senior AIB official said he didn't believe it was a perk because, as another sweetener to senior executives, the bank's tax department filled out and filed their personal tax returns on their behalf every year. He said that any executive perks were recorded in the returns, so the Faldor investment should have been included too, if it was offered by the bank. The source also added that if it had been a perk, then other senior executives would have availed of it.

In 1989 Douglas transferred £33,000 from an AIB account to AIBIM. His money found its way into Faldor. The money grew nicely in the offshore scheme. When Douglas left the scheme, his Faldor funds had grown to £81,769 since 1989. In December 1995 this money was credited to his trust. (In 1991 Douglas left AIB to join the board of Irish Permanent Building Society.)

In his statement Douglas said the management of his money and the use of the offshore Faldor scheme was at 'the sole discretion of AIBIM. Consequently I had no knowledge of the investment practices being pursued, including the improper use of AIBIM in-house accounts and deal allocation practices.' He said he had assumed the fund had been managed 'in a proper and professional manner as would be expected from a leading fund management company'. He said he was 'shocked and dismayed to learn that AIBIM is suggesting that it was engaging in unacceptable practices in regard to the investment which it was managing on my behalf'. In the end Douglas sorted out his tax affairs and reached a settlement with the Revenue in October 2003.

Around the same time, Scanlan, who had served as chief executive of AIB from 1985 to 1993, was contacted by AIB and told about the existence of Faldor, which Douglas had brought to its attention. Like Douglas, Scanlan blamed AIBIM for the mess which he found himself in.

Scanlan, a non-executive director of fruit importer Fyffes and a former chairman of the Irish Stock Exchange, had featured prominently in previous AIB scandals. In 1985, his first year as chief executive, he led the damage limitation exercise that extracted the bank from its disastrous investment in the Insurance Corporation of Ireland (ICI). In 1999 Scanlan appeared before the Dáil Public Accounts Committee inquiry into tax evasion through the use of bogus non-resident accounts. The bank had played an active role in setting up these accounts for customers. Scanlan, however, said he had no knowledge of AIB's potential liability on DIRT arising from the accounts. The bank later made the largest tax settlement in the history of the state when it handed over £90 million (€114 million) to the Revenue arising from its DIRT liability.

In a statement released on 31 May 2004, Scanlan said that in 1985 his wife invested funds with AIB's investment arm in Dublin. AIBIM had 'sole and total investment discretion' over the funds, he said. By 1989 the funds amounted to £74,000 and were transferred by AIBIM without the couple's knowledge. In March 1990, a further £40,000 was placed either by Scanlan or his wife with AIBIM. The money was added to Faldor, he said, without his knowledge.

Scanlan said he and his wife were 'indirect and unknowing beneficiaries of the Faldor structure, which resulted in the generation of an unexpected tax liability'. He said they had never heard of Faldor until they were contacted by AIB's compliance staff in October 2003. He said their money had been placed with AIBIM 'in good faith to be managed in a proper and lawful manner in a taxed fund'. Shortly after the bank contacted Scanlan, the couple got in touch with the Revenue and made a disclosure settling the tax debt on the money invested in Faldor. Scanlan concluded that although he and his wife might have had 'a cause of action against AIBIM' over the tax liability, he decided not to pursue a claim, given his long-standing relationship with the bank.

Scanlan's statement, like Douglas's, turned the focus back on the bank. Scanlan's telling of the events behind his investment painted a bizarre picture of the practices in AIB—a member of staff within the bank's investment arm decided in 1989 to transfer money belonging to AIB's chief executive offshore into a scheme that broke Irish tax laws. It seemed remarkable that one of Scanlan's underlings would carry out such a bold transaction without informing the man who owned the money—the head of AIB.

The scandal and the responses from Douglas and Scanlan left some people, in particular a number of politicians, bewildered. Socialist TD Joe Higgins told the Dáil that the 'tax evasion in the banking system' and the 'air of injured innocence of the most senior people involved might have come from a Monty Python script. A chief executive who had £40,000 invested for him with magnificently generous returns is giving the impression that the closest he ever came to hearing a word like "Faldor" might be in a Dubliners' song containing the words "with me right fal-di-de-o". The same chief executive claims he is an unknowing beneficiary of this structure, resulting in "the generation of an unexpected tax liability", while another senior executive had £33,000 invested in 1989 and, inexplicably, a few short years later it has grown to a massive £81,000, at which he professes amazement. This must be the banking sector's own phenomenon of immaculate conception— amazing things happen but nobody knows quite how,' said Higgins.

Tánaiste Mary Harney didn't mince her words when asked by an RTÉ reporter for her opinion on the latest AIB controversy. 'It is really shocking that this could have gone on at that level in the institution after all we have gone through in recent years in relation to bogus non-resident accounts,' she said. 'I think that in many ways this is far more serious than some of the other matters that have come to our attention. Some of them have been genuine errors, but this was no error. I therefore regard it as far more serious. The consequences of it could be far more draconian than anything that has come to light to date, mainly because we hear that they were very senior management involved in this. Therefore, I believe that that says a lot about the culture that operated in Ireland and I believe that people are getting fed up of all these revelations coming into the public domain.' Taoiseach Bertie Ahern told the Dáil that he could not understand how people at the top in AIB could be involved without knowing anything about it. 'I do not understand that and I find it hard to believe,' said Ahern. Central Bank governor John Hurley described the episode as 'serious and deeply disappointing'.

Diarmuid Moore, AIB's former head of corporate strategy, retired in 1993. He found himself mixed up in Faldor because he handed over £30,000 to AIBIM to invest on his behalf in 1989. After the death of his mother, Moore sold her house, netting the five-figure sum. He decided he wanted to save and grow the money, so he went to the bank's in-house investment division, Allied Irish Investment Managers (AIIM), which later became AIBIM. One of Moore's friends filled in the detail about how the former AIB executive became involved in Faldor and how he found himself in difficulty with the Revenue.

When he made the investment in 1989 Moore told a senior AIIM official, a close personal friend of his, that he wanted the £30,000 invested to make a capital gain. He wanted it returned to him at a later date net of tax. He told the AIIM executive that he did not want his money invested in 'Bolivian tin mines'—Moore's way of saying that he did not want his investment ending up in some 'hot' product that would cause him tax difficulties. Unfortunately for Moore the AIIM official ignored his instructions. Moore was told by the AIIM official that the money would be invested in a tax-free fund based in Guernsey in the Channel Islands and the money would be used to invest in gilts of various currencies. The senior AIIM/AIBIM executive who handled Moore's money died in the mid-1990s. Moore's friend declined to name the late bank executive. However, two senior AIB sources said they believed the AIIM executive was Joe Soden, a director of AIIM who died in the mid-1990s, as Moore and Soden were close friends. Soden was a cousin of Michael Soden, the former chief executive of Bank of Ireland.

While Moore was sailing in the Mediterranean in May 2004, browsing the internet on his laptop he spotted a business article on the BBC website saying that Tom Mulcahy had resigned as chief executive of Aer Lingus. He was surprised at the news but thought nothing more of it. He was stunned when on his way back to Dublin he saw his own name in the news.

The first time Moore heard of Faldor was when he was contacted by the bank in the second half of 2003. He met an AIB compliance officer who asked him if he had ever heard of Faldor. He said he had not. Moore told the compliance officer that he thought his £30,000 had been invested in a legitimate fund in Guernsey, as he had been told by the AIIM executive. When Moore's name appeared connecting him to an offshore tax dodge and 'inappropriate deal allocations' at AIBIM, he was furious that he had been linked to something he knew nothing about.

Moore felt AIB should have consulted him about Faldor before making its statement, given that he had spent 37 years working for the bank. He was furious that his good name and reputation had been sullied. He could hardly believe that any of this was true. He had had no hand, act or part in the setting up or running of Faldor and he was furious that the bank had linked him to it and landed him in this very difficult situation, his friend said.

On his return from the Mediterranean, Moore found out that AIB had telephoned him at home at 2.40 p.m. on 27 May to say it was releasing a statement about Faldor. He later discovered that the bank had released its statement 20 minutes after its telephone call. He was outraged that the bank had given him such short notice about something that would feature in every major newspaper and lead to some difficult questions.

Prior to his name appearing in public, Moore had discussed the Faldor situation with Revenue officials. During these discussions he was told that his money had been sent to Guernsey for just a few days in 1989 and came back to Ireland after a few days in London. This appears to have been a method similar to that used in the NIB-CMI tax evasion scheme, in which money was sent offshore and then returned to the branch from where it originated and from where it could be accessed by the customer. It appears that although Faldor was linked to the British Virgin Islands, Moore's money only went overseas for a short time and was later returned to Ireland where it remained. He was never told about the transfer and had always believed his money had been invested in Guernsey until he was told otherwise by the Revenue and the bank.

The bank told Moore that his money had ended up in a bogus non-resident account. The Revenue upheld this view. Moore said that if he had a bogus account, he had been 'totally unaware of its existence', and that it had been set up without his knowledge or permission by AIIM. Moore's friend said the former executive was 'amazed that the money found its way into Faldor'. He said Moore had heard stories of bank customers claiming that bank officials had set up bogus accounts without their knowledge and he never really believed them. Now Moore, a former senior AIB executive, was pleading the same case as many others and was in the same predicament as them.

Moore's friend said he believed the late AIIM executive who handled his investment (Joe Soden) may have established the Faldor scheme. Moore's friend bases the theory on the fact that the AIIM executive (Soden) was an avid golfer and may have named the scheme after British golfer Nick Faldo who won the US Masters at Augusta in 1989, the year Faldor was set up. Moore had travelled to the US Masters in Georgia that year to watch the tournament. Trusts and investment schemes were not unusual in 1989; thousands were being set up at this time for Irish investors.

As in Scanlan's case, it was incredible that Moore, a senior executive at AIB, had not been told by his AIIM colleague that his money had been invested in a bogus non-resident account. Moore withdrew his money from Faldor in 1996 and paid tax on the settlement. Despite this, he was still dealing with the Revenue at the end of 2005 trying to settle his taxes over his links to Faldor.

When the affair hit the newspapers, as a result of being named, Moore lost a substantial amount of income from consultancy work, from which he had to resign, including one contract with an American company. 'If you work for over 30 years in AIB, you will leave with a reasonable reputation and find consultancy work. But then if your reputation is shot to pieces, you will undoubtedly lose that work,' said Moore's friend. He might have a good case against the bank if he considered taking his former employer to court, but he is not keen on suing. His friend said he is not the type to sue City Hall—in other words, he is not the kind of person who would take on the establishment.

Moore's friend said the ex-AIB man likened his case to the quandary faced by the fictional US soldier Robert 'Prew' Prewitt in the 1951 James Jones novel *From Here To Eternity*. Prew loves the army but is not sure whether it is the right place for him. Another character in the book quotes the Dutch philosopher Spinoza to Prew to advise him in his predicament: 'Because a man loves God he must not expect God to love him in return.' Moore feels the same way about AIB, according to his friend—even though he loved AIB, the institution, he should not have expected the bank to love him back. He felt that this was proven in the Faldor scandal. He felt angry over the bank's handling of the Faldor crisis after the years of service he gave AIB.

As in Moore's case, the Dowling family were only told about the bank's statement shortly before it was released. They were unaware of the involvement in Faldor of their late husband and father, Paddy, a former deputy chief executive of AIB. Within 24 hours of the statement being released, Dowling's name was in the public domain. 'It was a poor reward for Paddy's 42 years with the bank,' said a friend who worked closely with Dowling at AIB. Another of Dowling's close associates in AIB said: 'Everyone at the bank who knew him was shocked when Dowling was linked to Faldor because he was a very tax compliant and very upright person.'

The Dowlings are still livid at the bank's handling of the affair. Paddy Dowling was seriously ill when AIB, the Revenue and the IFSRA began looking into Faldor in August 2003. He died later that autumn. The bank decided not to contact Dowling about Faldor because of his illness. However, after his death his family were told by some of his former AIB colleagues that the bank had been asking questions about his links to Faldor. The family were furious that the bank had not contacted them first, and chose to ask others about Dowling without telling them.

Dowling's children, Stephen and Fiona, were eventually contacted by the bank in January 2004 and told that a report concerning their father's involvement in Faldor had been passed to the regulator. They saw excerpts from the report showing how their father's money had ended up in Faldor but did not understand how the investment had worked due to the complexity of the scheme. They discovered that very little money had been invested in Faldor by AIBIM on Dowling's behalf and the money had only been invested for a very short time.

The Dowlings were told that the tax file concerning their late father's affairs had gone missing within the bank. Like most senior executives at the bank, Dowling's tax returns were handled by AIB's own taxation department. Stephen and Fiona Dowling were also told that their father's tax returns for the years in question were also missing within the Revenue.

Despite the absence of this vital information, the family decided to begin talks with the Revenue to settle Dowling's tax affairs. They felt it was better to finalise his tax situation rather than challenge the assessment, leaving the matter to be dragged out for many years. Even though they found it difficult to obtain accurate information about Dowling's tax affairs given the fact that his tax returns were missing for the years in question, the family decided a tax settlement was the best worst-case scenario. This was especially so given that Dowling's name had already appeared in the media and that the names of some of the other former AIB executives involved in the Faldor scheme were going to have tax settlements published as well. They were furious that Dowling's name had emerged, particularly because he was no longer around to defend himself. They felt that because of this, his name should never have come out. They claimed that their father was compliant to the point of obsessiveness throughout his life and would in no way have allowed himself to become involved in any dealings with an illegal investment scheme like Faldor.

David Cronin was said to be 'surprised' at his name being linked to Faldor, according to a source close to him. The source said Cronin had never heard about Faldor before, but that it did not create any tax problems for him because he had been living in the United States since 1989.

AIB declined to comment on the Faldor scandal for the purposes of this book, beyond what the bank had already stated in public statements on the affair.

Three official investigations had been launched by state agencies to find out what had gone on in AIB over the Faldor scheme and the unusual practices at AIBIM. The Revenue launched a full inquiry involving its investigation and prosecutions division and officers from its large cases division, which examines the richest companies and people in the country. The Revenue said its inquiry would not be restricted to Faldor and the other five executives with 'tax issues' but would involve a full examination of AIBIM's books and records.

In March 2006 the Revenue revealed that four former top AIB managers linked to Faldor made tax settlements totalling €323,313 over their involvement in the scheme. Scanlan paid €206,010, comprising €103,120 in underdeclared income tax and capital gains tax and €102,890 in interest and penalties. Douglas paid €53,259, including underdeclared income tax of €17,380 and interest and penalties of €35,879. Moore paid the Revenue a settlement of €51,044, which included underdeclared income tax of €17,363 and €33,681 in interest and penalties. The settlement made by Dowling's family on his behalf was €13,000, including €3,267 in underdeclared income tax and €9,733 in interest and penalties. This amount was only slightly over the publication threshold of €12,700, which made the appearance of his name in a list of tax defaulters hard for the family to stomach.

The Director of Corporate Enforcement Paul Appleby, the man who had assisted in the investigation of the Ansbacher deposits when he worked in the Department of Enterprise, Trade and Employment, also started investigating AIBIM to see if there had been any breaches of company law. The banking regulator, the IFSRA, was already looking into Faldor following the tip-off from AIB in August 2003.

Just a week before the scandal broke it was announced that Douglas would be retiring as chairman of Irish Life & Permanent when he turned 60 on 3 June. On Saturday, 29 May, Tom Mulcahy resigned as chairman of Aer Lingus, a post he had held since 2001. His resignation came after the then Minister for Transport Seamus Brennan pressed Mulcahy for further clarification of his tax affairs following the press reports about Faldor. Brennan thought Mulcahy did not adequately explain his 'tax issues', and when asked for more details, Mulcahy resigned.

In his resignation letter Mulcahy said: 'This whole issue draws adverse publicity on Aer Lingus and a state company by association. In light of this, and in order to enjoy privacy for myself and my family in my retiring years, I resign my position as chairman of Aer Lingus.' In a statement to the media Mulcahy said: 'I have no prior knowledge or involvement in the investment scheme outlined in AIB group's statement of 27 May. I am fully tax compliant.' A short time later Mulcahy also resigned from the board of Kingspan, the publicly quoted building materials firm.

The following week AIB wrote to 152 clients who were owed money over the 'unacceptable deal allocation practices' that had favoured Faldor. These were clients of AIBIM in the two specialist investment trusts and were repaid €174,000 plus €156,000 in interest.

It was December 2004 before the IFSRA reported on the findings. Its report confirmed the explosive nature of what had dripped out in the media over the previous months. AIBIM had moved money from its own funds to a number of clients and dressed the transactions up as artificial deals to improve the appearance of the accounts of clients whom the company wanted to impress. The IFSRA found that Faldor was one of the beneficiaries of these transactions, so because Douglas, Scanlan, Dowling, Moore and Cronin benefited from Faldor, they also stood to gain from the dodgy practices within AIBIM, even though they knew nothing about them. The IFSRA found that Faldor benefited by €48,000 as a result of these practices during this time.

The regulator also identified inappropriate deal allocation practices on eight transactions between 1991 and 1993, in which some clients received preferential treatment and the two specialist unit funds lost out. As in the overcharging scandal, the IFSRA found that AIB had discovered unusual practices many years earlier but did nothing to rectify the situation and compensate customers. The IFSRA concluded that although internal auditors within the bank had identified inappropriate deal allocation practices in 1991 and 1993, no disciplinary action was taken against the people responsible. Nor was there any compensation paid to the unit trusts affected. The IFSRA did not find any evidence that the Faldor scheme was identified in these audits.

The regulator concluded its report saying that 'in certain parts of AIB, there were ineffective standards of governance and a culture that led to unacceptable behaviour and practices in the late 1980s and 1990s'. The reference to 'certain parts of AIB' suited the bank because it again played to AIB's tune—only a small part of AIB was affected by the scandal. AIB chief executive Michael Buckley, at this stage a veteran scandal handler at AIB, said issues found at AIBIM affected only a small number of clients. 'It was not something that was endemic,' he said. But this was too little, too late—the bank's reputation had been tarnished by yet another controversy. In the aftermath of the IFSRA report, AIB took disciplinary proceedings against some of its staff over the irregular practices and paid €470,000 to compensate customers.

In the days after the publication of the IFSRA's report, it was reported that damaging paperwork still existed within AIB showing that the bank's own trading funds had been used to boost the performance of some clients' portfolios at the expense of others. The *Sunday Independent* reported that 'deal dockets' were issued in some cases, despite there being no underlying assets. The newspaper claimed that the dockets recorded artificial contracts in currencies, ordinary shares and bonds which allowed money to be transferred from one account or client to another under the guise of fictitious trades. It was reported that the documents, including the fake deal dockets, were being handed over to corporate enforcer Paul Appleby to assist his inquiry.

AIB's *annus horribilis* drew to a close and Buckley, the Houdini of Irish banking, had survived another scandal-filled year at AIB. Customers had been overcharged, in some cases deliberately to boost the profits of bank branches; investment clients had been given preferential treatment to the disadvantage of others; and senior executives of the group had been unwittingly treated to offshore banking, supposedly as a perk of their jobs.

While all this was emerging, another bank chief executive, Michael Soden of Bank of Ireland, resigned two days after the Faldor scandal broke. The reasons behind his resignation were more tawdry than the news emanating from AIB—Soden had used his office computer to access a website of an adult nature which breached the bank's internet policies. He had visited a website purportedly connected to a Las Vegas escort service.

The weekend of 29–30 May 2004 was an eventful one for Irish banking. On the front pages of the Sunday newspapers were articles about the resignations of two high-profile businessmen linked to banking—Mulcahy's resignation as chairman of Aer Lingus over 'tax issues' arising from his time as AIB chief executive, and Michael Soden's departure from Bank of Ireland for viewing adult websites. Soden's parting must have been eased somewhat by his severance payment of up to €3 million. He remarked sometime afterwards that many people felt that 'the punishment was not commensurate with the crime'. Analysts, commentators and brokers, however, seemed to react positively to Soden's departure from the bank.

The Faldor scandal reared its head again in September 2005 when Mulcahy decided to speak out about how he had been treated by the bank. He told *The Irish Times* that he had made a voluntary disclosure to the Revenue in 2003 about an offshore account containing 'several hundred thousand' arising from the time he worked for AIB in Britain. 'I am not saying that I was always compliant. I made a voluntary disclosure and paid what I thought was due which is the right open to all citizens.' He said he knew nothing about the Faldor investment scheme used by the other former AIB executives; his 'tax issues' arose from an offshore account unconnected to Faldor, he said. He complained that AIB gave him no advance warning before it issued its 27 May statement, and that he had not been given an opportunity to explain his tax situation to the bank before the statement was released.

'Why did nobody ask me about my tax affairs before releasing that statement?' Mulcahy asked. 'It's a reasonable question. It is very odd in the sense that I was there 29 years and a press release emerged at two minutes' notice. Then the next day, my name emerges as one of the people with tax issues. One has to assume that was not a happy accident.' He said 'a significantly different story' might have come out if the bank had asked him about his tax affairs before issuing its press release. Mulcahy, who was chief executive of AIB from 1994 to 2001, told journalist John McManus that he resigned from Aer Lingus because he knew he 'could not prove that I was absolutely tax compliant in a time frame that was relevant. It was a state company and it had a lot of problems without my adding to it.'

Mulcahy subsequently told the author that he had no knowledge of Faldor. He said the Revenue told him that he was tax compliant. Asked by the author how his account managed to be linked to Faldor in the media shortly after AIB released its statement, Mulcahy said: 'Make up your own mind about that.'

The fact that the names of the AIB executives emerged publicly just a few weeks after the overcharging scandal deflected some adverse attention away from the bank. Faldor focused the media's attention on past misdemeanours that affected former senior AIB managers. The timing of the release and the reasons why those individuals in particular were named has never been fully explained. The affair was an embarrassing episode not just for the executives named but for the bank itself, coming so soon after the Rusnak affair and at the same time as the overcharging debacle.

Even Eugene Ludwig, whose 2002 report cleared AIB directors of responsibility for the breakdown in controls that led to the $691 million Rusnak rogue trading scandal, came out and criticised the bank for setting up Faldor to benefit its former executives. Speaking to the *Sunday Business Post* in June 2004, Ludwig said the bank had an entrenched 'legacy culture that needed purging'. He said: 'Our review showed clearly that a part of the problem at AIB, as with so many banks today, is the remnants of an old legacy culture that make it slow to identify and act on problems. It's a very large institution and it's going to take time to modify its legacy culture.' He said it was important to have 'complete openness with the media and the public, and to be very vigorous about punishing those folks at fault—but with measure.'

The Faldor and overcharging controversies came to light when individuals raised concerns about practices within the bank. In the first instance, an anonymous AIB employee blew the whistle; in the second, it appeared to be a former senior executive sorting out his tax affairs. The bank's defence following the overcharging scandal was that there was not a culture of non-compliance within the bank. This was severely weakened when, just three weeks later, it was revealed that the bank's investment arm had been involved in some very suspect practices which benefited senior executives in the bank (without their knowledge).

What is even more extraordinary is that the bank has weathered these storms. At the end of 2004, one of the toughest years for AIB, its share price was stronger than ever. The controversies might have shaken AIB's customers, but its investors were hardly bothered by the scandals—they continued to invest and make money from AIB shares. Indeed, this occurred after most of the scandals at AIB. The bank's share price might have taken a dip after a controversy, but it always recovered in the medium term. Despite the scandals, everything went on as before.

Incredibly, AIB was never fined by the banking regulator over the overcharging or Faldor controversies, and this certainly was not because the bank could not afford a fine—AIB clocked record profits of €1.7 billion in 2005. AIB's chief executive and many of its senior executives walked away with million euro pay packages for a job well done during those 12 months. The faith of its customers might have been rocked, but the confidence of the AIB board in its executives remained undiminished.

If AIB was to learn anything from the scandals that hit it between 2002 and 2005, it should be that banking is not just about profits. There are the concerns of staff, including anonymous ones who are willing to question irregular practices that contribute to profits and benefit executives.

And then there are the customers, the source of so much of the bank's profits. Buckley might have been right. There may not have been a widespread culture of corruption within AIB, but the scandals showed that some practices within the bank could be, and were, easily corrupted.